## PRAISE FOR FRANCIS J. GREENBURGER

"Francis Greenburger, perhaps most recognized as a business contrarian and distinguished for his understanding of real estate trends in a uniquely personal way, has a similar flair in the arts. Francis has been a consistent voice in the literary world from a very early age, and has evolved into a renowned art collector, offering his support and patronage to carefully hand-selected talent. He awards annual prizes to artists not yet recognized for their endeavors, much in the same way that he pursues undervalued properties. I have enormous respect for Francis's willingness to stand alone, confident in his assessments and keen to withstand the pressures of consensus-driven inclinations. His autobiography inspires us to do the same."

**—Bob Wilmers, chairman of the board and chief executive officer, M&T Bank**

"Francis is one of the most decisive people I know. He made a commitment to invest in our first venture capital fund in a five minute cab we shared to work one morning."

**—Fred Wilson, cofounder, Union Square Ventures, venture capitalist and blogger**

"Francis Greenburger's story is an inspiration to all. Anyone who cares about social justice and is motivated to turn words into action should look at the example Francis has set through his commitment to changing the world for the better. Everyone can learn something from Francis' experience and I am glad to call him a friend."

**—Congressman Jerry Nadler**

"Watching the development of Art Omi must be like watching Francis develop a real estate project. Great independent vision, attention to detail, and love of all forms of discovery. It just works."
**—Alan Fishman, chairman, Ladder Capital**
**and Brooklyn Academy of Music**

"For Francis, buildings are not just real estate; through his diligence and determination, they are a chance to accomplish something truly important."
**—Helmut Jahn, architect, 50 West Street**

"Francis Greenburger is truly a 21$^{st}$ century renaissance man—a highly successful real estate entrepreneur and developer, a literary agent and scout, an art patron and supporter, and an advocate for social and criminal justice, especially with respect to the rights of the incarcerated mentally ill. Greenburger's life story—and his life's passions—are at once fascinating and highly motivational."
**—Mitchel Wallerstein, president, Baruch College**

"Francis Greenburger is deeply committed to civic engagement, but his passion for advancing badly needed reforms of America's broken criminal justice system sets him apart. The work he has so passionately dedicated to this cause has helped move change forward in innumerable ways."
**—Senator Cory Booker**

"Francis Greenburger's range of interests and influence is vast, touching the worlds of real estate, literature, art, and the international exchange of art and ideas. Francis is an almost instinctual developer of new things: he develops buildings, cultural institutions, and vehicles for progressive social change . . . with elegance—and all without ever wasting a single word—which makes his opinions and guidance on arts ventures such as Art Omi and MASS MoCA exceedingly valuable."

**—Joseph Thompson, director, MASS MoCA**

"Francis Greenburger is a good friend, an innovative thinker, and a great partner. I don't admire him; I envy him."

**—Charles Benenson, real estate developer and investor and Time Equities Inc. Strategic Partner, The Benenson Capital Company**

"I and my family have been investors with Francis since the mid-1970s and our investments with him are the bedrock of our investment portfolio. The returns from our investments with him have supported three generations of my family through thick and thin. He is a person of exceptional integrity and insight."

**—Debra Chwast, investor**

"With the guidance of Francis Greenburger and his team, we have created eight cutting-edge residential condominium towers and a luxury hotel in the King West area of Toronto. I am proud to be a strategic partner with TEI and I look forward to years of investing and building together. Francis is thoughtful, decisive, and fearless."

**—Peter Freed, Time Equities Inc. Strategic Partner, Freed Developments**

"What I most enjoyed about [*Risk Game*] is that it didn't read like an autobiography or a biography. There were so many vivid scenes and wonderful dialogue that it was very much novelistic."

**—Luke Rhinehart, author of *The Dice Man***

# RISK
# GAME

RISK
GAME

# RISK GAME

· · · · ·

SELF PORTRAIT

*of an*

ENTREPRENEUR

· · · · ·

## FRANCIS J. GREENBURGER

*with* REBECCA PALEY

BenBella Books, Inc.
Dallas, TX

*Risk Game* copyright © 2016 by Francis J. Greenburger
First paperback edition 2020

BenBella Books, Inc.
10440 N. Central Expressway
Suite 800
Dallas, TX 75231
www.benbellabooks.com
Send feedback to feedback@benbellabooks.com
*BenBella* is a federally registered trademark.

Printed in the United States of America
10 9 8 7 6 5 4 3

Library of Congress has cataloged the hardcover edition as follow:

Names: Greenburger, Francis, 1949- author. | Paley, Rebecca, author.
Title: Risk game : self portrait of an entrepreneur / Francis J. Greenburger,
    with Rebecca Paley.
Description: Dallas, TX : BenBella Books, Inc., [2016] | Includes
    bibliographical references and index.
Identifiers: LCCN 2016012285 (print) | LCCN 2016019515 (ebook) | ISBN
    9781942952534 (trade cloth : alk. paper) | ISBN 9781942952527 (electronic)
Subjects: LCSH: Greenburger, Francis, 1949- | Businessmen—United
    States—Biography. | Real estate developers—New York (State)—-Biography.
    | Real estate business—New York (State)
Classification: LCC HC102.5.G7184 A3 2016 (print) | LCC HC102.5.G7184 (ebook)
    | DDC 333.33092 [B] —dc23
LC record available at https://lccn.loc.gov/2016012285
ISBN 9781950665778 (trade paper)

Editing by Vy Tran
Copyediting by Stacia Seaman
Photo editing by Donna Cohen
Proofreading by Michael Fedison and Cape Cod Compositors, Inc.
Cover Portrait of Francis J. Greenburger by Ricardo Clement
Cover design by Pete Garceau
Text design by Aaron Edmiston
Text composition by PerfecType, Nashville, TN

*For all of my children, Alexander, Morgan, Noah, Julia, and Claire—and for their mothers, Judy and Isabelle. I hope you know how much I love each of you.*

*And for all my very special friends, colleagues, and people who have enriched my life in such important ways. Whether you are named in this narrative or not, I think you know who you are and how much I appreciate, care about, and value each of you.*

# CONTENTS

*Prologue*

# EXPECT THE
# UNEXPECTED

· · · · · ·

Apart from the caissons jutting out from the ground, the site was completely blank and silent. The enormous metal pipes that dove fifty feet down into the earth at the tip of Manhattan were exposed and useless with nothing to anchor them to the solid bedrock below. Around the empty construction site a locked fence signaled the end of progress.

This was 50 West—my legacy project as a real estate entrepreneur, a sixty-four-story tower of glass and steel that was going to alter the city skyline. It was supposed to embody my career in real estate that began with leasing office space as a sixteen-year-old high school dropout; meandered through close calls, generous mentors, terrible disappointments, and moments of great luck; and arrived at success beyond any expectation. Only, 50 West had become a $500 million mud puddle.

I had seen my share of wild swings over the course of my fifty years in the business, but the radical shift from the abundance of money during the housing bubble to the global debt crisis set off by losses in the US subprime mortgage market was, to put it mildly, unexpected and unprecedented. As a seasoned developer and investor, I knew all too well that markets can turn on a dime. And I had spent my career always looking over my shoulder for signs of trouble and keeping an ear to the ground for the sounds of crumbling economic conditions. Even so, I completely missed the signs of this disaster that I experienced through the very expensive prism of 50 West.

When, in January of 2008, we began demolishing the three buildings on the site that sat across the street from Manhattan's Battery Park area, I was full of optimism. And why shouldn't I have been? Arranging the financing for the project had been a given. Despite the size of the project, which cost more than $6 million in architectural plans alone, it was only a question of which bank we would allow to give us the money. That's how flush the times were. As the starchitects we solicited to join a competition to design the property unveiled their plans before me, I felt the amazing sensation of being at the start of something great. And when my wife Isabelle and I saw the Helmut Jahn entry, I was overcome with a sense of possibility as soaring as the tower itself: We *were* going to do something great.

Six months later, construction workers were driving the caissons into the ground. Later that summer, truckloads of earth were dragged out of the ground and carted away as we started excavating the site for the foundation of the skyscraper.

Then on September 15, Lehman Brothers filed for Chapter 11 in the largest bankruptcy in US history, and the world got really strange really quickly. That autumn, when many investment banks fell as fast as the leaves on the trees, I made the decision to shutter everything at 50 West. As high as I had felt when I was surveying the plans for the skyscraper was as low as I'd sunk while putting a stop to its building.

There remained $15 million undrawn and available on the pre-development loan I had on the property to design and build the foundation (the plan had been to phase into a full construction loan to go straight up once the foundation was complete). I had to pull everyone off the site and begin the painful process of unwinding the long list of contracts we had with engineers, architects, and construction companies,

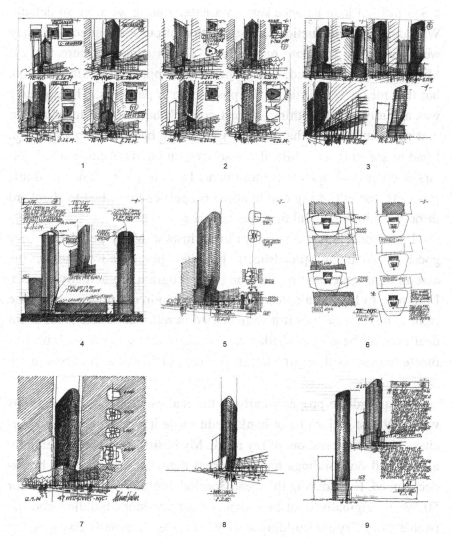

Early sketches of 50 West by Helmut Jahn

because the last thing any developer wants is to have a half-built building when the money runs out.

I was acting prudently (a few virtues were all I seemed to have left), but as soon as I halted construction, the bank with whom we had a $55 million loan balance sent us a letter stating we were in default. With ongoing construction as a stipulation of our loan agreement, they were entitled to foreclose on the land. The blindness of bureaucracy! My options were limited. The property was appraised at $150 million, but that meant very little in the post-Lehman paralysis. The property was actually worth nothing, since I couldn't have sold it to myself in that moment. Money that once flowed freely had dried up overnight. I had to sort this out while also resolving hundreds of millions of dollars of other development commitments I was trying to undo—and this was only one out of my two hundred properties that I had to shepherd through an international financial collapse.

I can conceptualize numbers in an instant. Many people are very good at producing spreadsheets, but they never know whether the assumptions generated by the computer program are actually correct. I am able to look at a spreadsheet with a hundred numbers and home right in on a mistake as if it were circled in red. Real estate is all about deal making based on whether the numbers make sense, so I am fortunate to possess this gift. But the problem of 50 West was about more than numbers.

I acquired the property early in the real estate boom of the 1980s when my first major line of bank credit made it possible for me to purchase properties once out of my reach. My business grew exponentially as I closed on buildings and converted them into co-ops at a breakneck speed. Even during this heady period, the $2 million I offered for 50 West (originally a lot that included a three-story building and the twelve-story Crystal Building at 47 West Street, internally connected to the eight-story building at 74 Washington Street) represented the biggest deal of my career up to that point.

The challenge of making such a big acquisition, however, was the least dramatic aspect of the property's tumultuous journey.

The first, and worst, chapter came immediately after the terrible events of 9/11. What began with me watching the unimaginable—the second plane hitting the World Trade Center moments after I dropped my small children at their school downtown—ended with the reordering of my priorities and responsibilities in a way I hadn't ever done before. I had to reach deep inside myself to create stability among chaos and some sense of safety in a suddenly terrifying world. People all over the city—and the country—were doing the same. In my case, however, that included monitoring all of our buildings downtown with only limited access because the army had sealed off the area.

Only two blocks away from where the World Trade Center had stood, the Crystal Building was located in the very last section of the city to be reopened. It was so close that debris from the towers had landed on its roof. So for six months, no one could get anywhere near the building where I had begun to convert some of the vacant units into living lofts. Understandably, nearly everyone moved out.

I had fallen off financial precipices before and survived them (battered and bruised but intact). This one, though, was different. The emotional toll was greater than even I realized at the time. As I fought daily to find solutions to an endless list of financial demands and crises, almost imperceptibly I slipped into a depression. Unlike in the past, I now had an expanded world of responsibilities that included not only an entire staff, as well as children, friends, and relatives who relied upon me, but also a range of charitable organizations for which I was the major lifeline. Even though it wasn't going to alter the fate of a billion-dollar real estate company, I busily set about cutting personal expenses.

It took nearly four years before I was ready to move ahead with the original plan and renovate the Crystal Building for a full residential condo conversion, which was what I was set to do when someone who worked for me suggested another plan: Demolish all the buildings on the lot and make one very, very tall building. Now, I had just spent years digging out of a financial and emotional hole (more like an abyss). Did I really want to do something as big and bold as, literally, aiming for the sky?

I listened carefully to the argument for building a skyscraper on the site (I always listen to other people's ideas because that is how you happen upon good ones)—and the argument was persuasive. The zoning of the lot itself allowed for a forty-story building. However, it sat right next to the Battery Park Tunnel, which possessed an astounding 2 million feet of air rights. The way air rights work in New York City is that every piece of land has the right to build a certain-size building on it. If any of those rights aren't used, they can be transferred to an adjacent property owner. The tunnel's large entrance and lack of buildings accounted for its huge number of air rights; if we could buy 150,000 of them, it would translate into a tower that would be among the tallest residential buildings in the city.

Although it wasn't the most conservative decision in the world, and I was just off a huge economic crisis, I wanted to do it. Make a skyscraper. Perhaps I was thirsting for optimism after such a dark time (and really, what's more optimistic than a skyscraper?), but in the end I made a deeply personal decision to pursue the project—more for a sense of personal accomplishment than for financial gain.

The first step was getting those air rights. The Manhattan Transit Authority (MTA)—the public-benefit corporation run by a board recommended by various elected officials—controlled them (or so we thought), even though the MTA was barely aware they had them when we presented the idea. Because the MTA needed the money, and the city was fully in support of any developer interested in rebuilding Lower Manhattan, things moved forward quickly and smoothly.

That is, until the MTA inexplicably reversed itself out of the blue. When I asked the person from the organization who called why the deal was off, he said they were worried the MTA might need the rights one day to use them in some other way. With 1,850,000 feet of rights left, the fear seemed ludicrous. They could have built the Tower of Babel if they wanted to. I tried to argue the point, but logic is no match for bureaucracy.

It looked like we were going to have to resign ourselves to an alternate, shorter version of the tower that didn't utilize the adjacent air rights until I met an architect who had a connection to the chairman of the MTA, Peter Kalikow. Through him I got an appointment with Kalikow, who was also president of one of New York's biggest real estate firms. After I made my presentation on 50 West, he looked at the plan and his staff, then said, "What's wrong with this?"

The yes that had turned into a no was back to yes. After working out a few more glitches (like the small one when the MTA discovered it was actually the city that owned the air rights and the MTA just had the ability to use them), in a process that took years, we finally made it to the last stop: a vote by the city council. Not surprisingly, the council started renegotiating the price of the air rights (one rule of real estate is that everyone renegotiates). More surprising was how wildly aggressive they were. The result was more months of long nights spent going back and forth. Often in real estate negotiations where the other party feels they have the upper hand, they aren't satisfied until they see you bleed. With these air rights, however, I was beginning to hemorrhage. Even after we came to another agreement, the bloodletting wasn't quite over.

Two days before the deadline for tax incentives we were counting on in building the tower, a city councilman appeared out of nowhere with another demand for community benefits before passing the deal. So we negotiated up until the very last minute; the council voted in favor of our assuming rights at ten o'clock the last day before we would become ineligible for a special real estate tax program the city was offering in Lower Manhattan.

There were many times I thought it wouldn't happen and many more that I wanted to give up out of sheer frustration, but three years after the initial idea to build a tower, we got approval to start construction on the $500 million building. And then six months later, before the foundation was completed, the economy collapsed. Left with a pile of debt instead of a building, I faced a major dilemma. Should I throw more money onto the pile or cut my losses there and then?

One of the dangers of the real estate business is that often you are competing against people who have money but are not that knowledgeable. It's a counterintuitive idea. Yet those with money (the only barrier to entry into the real estate market) but no experience in the buying and selling of property drive up prices because they want to get in on "the action"—and their power lies in their checkbook. If you pay a certain amount simply because the guy next door has paid it, you will not survive this ruthless industry that has created far more bankruptcies than it has billionaires. Saying no is the most important judgment you make. On the other hand, nothing happens until you say yes. Risk is an undeniable fact of real estate, mitigated only by having your own view of the market and believing in your instinct.

I have made my fortune from seeing value where others never thought to look. I pioneered the New York co-op market by taking apartments that no one dreamed anyone would ever buy, such as walk-up tenements in the West Village and housing complexes in middle-class black neighborhoods, and turning them into lucrative investments. In the process, I not only earned the title of King of Co-ops but also helped transform the city's landscape from neglected rentals to prized homes.

It's my life's work to find value where others don't. The unknown authors and agents that I enlisted to build up my father's literary agency after his death; the unrecognized talents who have turned Omi, my artists' colony upstate, into an internationally prominent cultural center; and those discarded in prisons or the political underdogs I have championed: All have brought an unparalleled richness to my existence.

I don't give up easily—not on people or properties—and I wasn't ready to give up on 50 West, not even after a global financial crisis made the land practically worthless. I struck a deal with the lender even though they were initially calling for me to either turn over the property or pay the $55 million I owed them, which I didn't have. Instead, I convinced the bank to sign a new agreement that turned the short-term line of credit for the foundation into a regular land loan. I offered up $10 million in good-faith pay-downs and a personal guarantee of $22 million to secure the loan, and I agreed to pay a higher interest rate.

Everyone told me I was crazy. Why would I pay $3 million a year in interest alone, in addition to property taxes and insurance that totaled another $2 million annually, for a piece of land with no income on it? Why take the risk when I could be done with the whole mess by giving it back?

Because that land was my chance to fulfill a dream of building an iconic skyscraper. Plus, I thought, one day it was going to be worth a hell of a lot more.

## Chapter 1

# EARLY REMEMBRANCES
# OF THINGS PAST

· · · · ·

**M**y father accompanied the writer out of his office.

"Sandy, this book is going to be a big, big best seller," the writer said to my father. "*Big*. Not just in Europe but here in America too. I'm going to make us lots of money. You'll see."

"Yes, yes, Lazi," my father said with a slight note of skepticism.

The Hungarian writer Ladislas Faragó had made his name as a foreign correspondent in 1935 covering the Ethiopian-Italian War, an assignment he turned into a historically important and wildly popular book, *Abyssinia on the Eve*. But he was as much an old friend of my father's as a valued client of Sanford J. Greenburger, my father's literary agency. So Dad took special care in showing him to the door, walking past my desk, where I was busy balancing the agency's checkbook, and my mother, who was tending to her usual administrative work. Faragó kissed her hand in the old-fashioned style before he was hustled out the door by my father—just as Leo was entering.

"What brought the Hungarian schemer?" Leo, lighting a cigarette, asked once my father returned.

1

It was true; Faragó, who had written many best-selling books on military history and espionage (including, later on, *Patton: Ordeal and Triumph*), had picked up a trick or two from his reporting. An expert on propaganda and other methods of using the mind as a weapon, he was assigned during World War II to a unit engaged in psychological warfare against the Japanese. When it came to his own business affairs, he was no less stealthy. Once, he sneaked into my father's office and helped himself to the company checkbook, writing a check to himself and forging my father's signature. Although the sum was not large, my father was perpetually broke, so even small amounts were a problem.

"Ah, Lazi's okay," my father said.

"You know, one can be a good writer and still not be a good person," Leo said.

Leo Frischauer did not mince words. In fact, offering up his opinion, solicited or otherwise, was about all Leo ever did. Each day he arrived like clockwork to my father's small office on 42nd Street that was half literary agency and half café for a variety of European intelligentsia, even though technically he didn't work there. In the context of the parade of writers and publishers who created a constant flow of smoke, gossip, and eccentricity, it wasn't odd that Leo had a desk but no title or work responsibilities. Efficiency was never a priority at the agency.

I watched my father and Leo smoke and talk as if this were new and exciting territory and not how they had spent every day of their lives for the last twenty years. I never asked my father how he felt about Leo; he was kind of just a given.

Like most everything else in the office, Leo's story was mythic, unconventional, and not at all clear. My hazy understanding was that Leo—who came from a family of wunderkind that included Paul, a well-known novelist, and Eddie, a champion bridge player who helped Austria bring home the 1937 world title—had made a huge sum of money as a very young lawyer in Vienna. He wanted to celebrate his windfall by taking his girlfriend on a trip around the world, but his mother disapproved. His girlfriend then committed suicide, which, although something of a Viennese habit during that period, gave Leo such a virulent hatred of money that he gave all of his away. Over five o'clock tumblers of whiskey, there were tales of Leo leaving the equivalent of a $100,000 tip for his favorite waitress at his regular café in Vienna. Once the money was gone, Leo decided he didn't want to work anymore. *Ever again.*

When Leo first came to New York, he went to see my father, who knew his brother Paul. He walked into the office, introduced himself, and then asked my father whether he could come the next morning to read the newspaper.

"Sure," my father said.

He came the following day and every day for the next fifty-odd years to read the newspaper. Leo not only read the newspaper, he read each edition of *every* newspaper. One of his early jobs in Vienna had been working at a daily, reading the competition to see whether there were any stories they had missed. Leo had loved this job and acted for the rest of his life as if he still had it. He even had an arrangement with the newspaper delivery trucks that came to the office building so that he didn't need to wait until the paper arrived at the newsstand. The truck driver was instructed to hand the latest edition to Leo waiting for it in front of the building.

I loved Leo, who spent his days smoking relentlessly, refusing to use an ashtray, preferring instead to let the ash on his cigarette dangle perilously until it ultimately fell onto his chest, which he patted into his suit—and he'd been wearing the same suit for as long as I'd known him, which was my entire life. His indulgent style extended to me, for which I, the son of a cautious father who was sometimes hard to communicate with, was grateful. One of Leo's and my favorite hobbies was throwing paper planes out the window of the thirtieth floor when the agency was located on 42nd Street. Watching our planes drift into the New York Public Library never got old with us.

Leo Frischauer at the literary agency

As Leo and my father continued their debate on Faragó's merits beyond writing, I returned to my bookkeeping. I had already entered the precious few checks we had received that day, paid the office's electric bill and a lawyer's fee, and prepared statements for a few authors. It was rudimentary work that I could have done in my sleep. Numbers, to me, were simple; unlike my father's clients, they either added up or they didn't.

My father assigned value in ways that rarely made a profit. Indeed, his decisions usually translated into disaster for my ledger. It hadn't started that way. His agency, which began in 1932, received a remarkable stroke of luck with the advent of World War II. While devastating for most of Europe, the war provided my father with an incredible opportunity. Because authors from the Axis powers couldn't receive royalties from sales of their books in the United States, German, French, and Italian publishing houses needed someone to hold the money until the war ended.

Because of my father's many European friends, he and a man named Marcel Aubry serendipitously found themselves approached by some of the continent's biggest and most venerable publishers to hold their copyrights until their countries were no longer enemy territory and subject to the US alien property withholding regulations. Gallimard in France hired Aubry and my father to represent them in the United States, and almost overnight the greatest minds of the twentieth century, such as Albert Camus, Simone de Beauvoir, Jean-Paul Sartre, and Antoine de Saint-Exupéry, were among my father's first clients. He also represented the estates of Franz Kafka and Alfred Adler.

My father's salon sensibility made him a perfect American counterpart to European publishers. After the war, he maintained his transatlantic affairs, not only continuing to represent their authors but also pioneering the editorial scouting business by advising European publishing houses on the best American writers to translate and publish for their markets. But if he had the right literary temperament, my father remained a poor businessman, constantly settling for too little compensation or loaning money to his authors, who were anything but good for it.

I had resolved to talk to my father about one issue in particular that could no longer be ignored—the agency's longtime deal with Rowohlt Verlag. Faragó's surprise visit temporarily delayed the discussion, but as soon as Leo agreed to disagree with my father, who returned to his office, I got up from my desk and walked the four steps it took me to arrive at his door. I had to act fast since I didn't know who or what might distract my father next.

"Dad, can I talk to you for a second?"

"Come in. Sit, sit."

He put the *Saturday Evening Post* he'd been reading back on top of a stack of other papers and magazines, including the *New Yorker, New York Times, Herald Tribune,* and *Publishers Weekly.* When he wasn't chatting with Leo or any of the other characters that took up his day, his nose was always in the papers or magazines, not books. He preferred the excerpts in the *Saturday Evening Post* or the *New Yorker* to the whole works. Although he loved publishing and books, I never saw him reading one.

"I think Leo is being too hard on Lazi," he said. "No one is saying he's a saint. But any man who won't give up chasing the Nazis is okay by me. Lazi continues to find new revelations about those bastards when everyone else says World War II is over. Over? Tell that to the victims. Saints are boring and so is their writing. Boredom is the root of all evil, as they say."

I didn't know where this was going, but with my father it could go on for quite a while, and I had business to discuss.

"Dad." I cut him off. "Are you aware of how much Rowohlt is paying us a month?"

"Sure."

"Three hundred a month."

"Right, three hundred a month."

"It's a very, very small amount."

"Well, it's something, isn't it? And it comes on time every month. That's worth quite a lot in this business. We had a French publisher who was paying us $500, but the problem was that we never got paid. They never gave us the money they were supposed to. With Rowohlt, the paycheck is sure and steady."

I felt my frustration level rising rapidly. Talking to Father was always complicated and roundabout. For him, choosing a morning pastry could inspire a lengthy monologue. He loved to reason things out to interesting arguments although not necessarily logical ones. I wasn't in the mood right now to ride the endless merry-go-round.

"It might have been good during the war, but it's not enough for the work we do—keeping track of all their foreign rights contracts here in the US and advising them on what American books to buy for their territory. We have to renegotiate our contract."

"Oh, Francis, I don't know . . ."

"Look, you can't make money this way. Rowohlt is not a charity. But it's turning *us* into one."

My father leaned back in his worn leather chair and gave me a look that was not easily discernible: part confusion and part dismay, yes. But did I also detect an undercurrent of pride? People get into the book business for different reasons. For my father, it definitely wasn't for money. Though it didn't seem to be about books either. It was always more about people than anything else.

Wherever he went, my father created a club. Before he married my mother, quite a number of people had keys to his apartment and stayed there unannounced whenever they were in New York. In fact, for the first year or so of my mother and father's relationship, people were constantly showing up who had the key but didn't know that he was now married.

There were many iterations of this hospitality: Leo, unaffordable loans to friends, and forgiving almost any character flaw. Even my father's fluency in three languages fed his social reach. I admired my father's generosity with his friends.

Born to Hungarian immigrants living in Glens Falls, New York, he learned to speak his parents' native language while spending his formative years in Hungary following what must go down as the most poorly timed holiday in history: When my father was ten years old, the family went on vacation to their native country. World War I broke out, and they were stuck there until peace was declared.

Later, my father attended Columbia, where he studied German, the language he, my mother, and Leo spoke much of the time. After university, he started his career as a press secretary for the successful actor, director, and producer Leslie Howard. He then worked as a story editor in New York for Warner Brothers during the late twenties, until he hung out his own shingle in the form of Sanford J. Greenburger, Literary Agent.

My father, Sanford Greenburger

Sitting across from me at his desk, my father put his hands up in defeat. The contemplative nature that kept my father meandering through the vagaries of life and in good company with his writers invariably bowed to my bolder American directness.

"Okay, fine. You're in charge of the numbers," he said. "I'll call Ledig and ask for an increase to $350."

"Let me call."

"Excuse me?"

"I'm going to ask for $1,500 a month," I said. "And bonuses if the books we recommend are successful in Germany."

A look of amusement sparked in my father's eyes and just as quickly went out. He knew I was serious and that I understood things he didn't. So we agreed I would talk to Heinrich Maria Ledig-Rowohlt.

Although the head of Germany's most prestigious publishing house was regarded as one of the great publishers of the twentieth century, having published everybody from Ernest Hemingway to Marilyn French (and he was friends with all of them: Baldwin, Nabokov, Havel), I was undaunted. Out of all the big names and personalities that came through my father's door, he was the one who became a mentor and more. There was something in the fantastic story of how he came to his position that I related to.

Ledig, whose name means "unmarried" in German, was the illegitimate son of Ernst Rowohlt, the founder of the Rowohlt Verlag publishing house—a fact that he was unaware of until he turned nineteen. A year or two before that, he had approached his mother, a well-known German actress, Maria Ledig, about his dream career.

"I don't know why, but I want to go into the book business."

"Well, let me see whether I can help," his mother replied.

She called the old man and said, "Look. Your son wants to work in publishing."

"Send him over," Rowohlt said. "But don't tell him who I am."

So off Ledig went to work at Rowohlt's publishing house, thinking a friend of his mother's got him the position. After a year or so on the job, he received a call that he was wanted at the big boss's office. Right away. He was scared out of his wits; this was autocratic Germany, where lower-level employees weren't summoned by the head of the company.

Once Ledig was inside the dark, imposing office, Rowohlt did not exchange pleasantries but barked out an order: "Sit in my chair."

"What?" asked Ledig, wondering what kind of torture he had in store for him.

"Sit in that chair!"

Germans do not disobey. Ledig walked around the other side of the desk and sat down.

"How does it feel?" Rowohlt asked.

That was how Ledig found out he had unwittingly entered into the family business. He worked side by side with his father, tacking his last name on after a hyphen, until the war, when the company ceased operations after the Nazis blacklisted it for its books by communists, Jews, pacifists, and other types of *untermenschen* whose works were un-German. Ledig, drafted into the army with which he served on the Russian front, was the first publisher to get permission after the war from American occupation officials to resume publishing books. Although printed on low-grade paper, they were wildly popular with Germans desperate for new novels. Rowohlt the father, meanwhile, set up his own operation in Germany's British zone, creating something of a literary father-son conflict. Eventually, though, they merged their operations into one, which Ledig took over after his father's death in 1960.

Even among his peers of top international publishers, Ledig cut an extremely elegant figure with his tailored suit and custom-made shirt that always remained crisp no matter how long his day. Ledig brought a sense of occasion to everything. He and his second wife, Jane, were the king and queen of European publishing. Jane, who came from an extremely wealthy family (her father, a British banker, put up the collateral for a fledgling company that became England's third largest British electronics firm), possessed a level of glamour and luxury that I thought only existed in the movies. She was always about the best of the best, buying couture dresses until they couldn't fit into her closet and wearing a different piece of jewelry every time I saw her. She also made sure every aspect of Ledig's existence was in high style. Later in life, when I visited them at their stunning eighteenth-century Swiss villa, Château de Lavigny, which I did often, I discovered the pleasures of the elegance

Courtesy of Foundation H. M. & J. Ledig-Rowohlt

H. M. Ledig-Rowohlt launching a book in 1968

with which Jane ran her household. Every morning, delicious hot coffee or tea, freshly squeezed orange juice, homemade pastries, and fine Swiss chocolate, all served on delicate china, were delivered to me while I still lay in my Porthault bedsheets. Jane gave the staff the guests' breakfast choice the night before because she didn't get up until noon, at best. (Jane tried her best to refine me as well; in the eighties I traveled to the château so she could introduce me to her Swiss bankers. But when I came downstairs for the lunch meeting she had planned, wearing khaki pants, a blue blazer, and no necktie, Jane took one look at me and said, "We aren't gardening. Hurry up and change." I ran upstairs and put on a dark blue suit and tie for the Swiss bankers, who, as it turned out, *were* extremely formally dressed.)

Whenever Ledig came to New York, I would act as his aide-de-camp: ordering flowers for whomever he had dined with the night before, picking up his shirts from the laundry, or procuring tickets to the best show on Broadway. I learned firsthand the habits of a man with the ultimate style and grace. Much more enriching, however, were the long conversations we used to have. I couldn't believe a man of such importance was willing to spend so much time talking to me. I discovered that his impeccable manners began with his extraordinary willingness to listen.

(Ultimately, Ledig and Jane became like second parents to me, helping me plan my trips in Europe right down to what were the "best" hotels to stay in in Venice, London, and Paris. The Connaught in London required a "personal" introduction, which Ledig provided me with. I learned many things from Ledig and Jane, including the difference between elegance and affluence. But most of all I learned how they valued people for their intelligence and personality.)

By the time my father and I had agreed to renegotiate our contract with Rowohlt Verlag, my relationship with Ledig had evolved into one with father-son undertones. Because of his generosity and obvious fondness for me, I had full confidence when I sat him down during his visit to New York.

"Ledig," I said. "Look. We're in desperate financial trouble here."

"You are?" he responded with genuine concern.

"We can't exist with the money that you're paying us."

After I showed him the numbers (for here was a man who, unlike my father, had some sense of what business cost), he agreed, and we got an increase from $300 to $1,500 a month, which helped for a while.

That was 1962. I was twelve years old.

．．．．．

I was a prodigy. A term usually reserved for child musicians or chess players, it perfectly described my early aptitude for business. I always had a job—or three. Money was my security blanket.

Working gave me a purpose. It grounded me in a topsy-turvy world that threatened to come completely apart when in second grade I developed a fear of elementary school. The phobia was not of crowds or cafeterias or chalk dust but of the very idea of school itself. I simply refused to go. I'd stay in bed, or sometimes my parents would coax me out of the house, saying, "We're just going for a walk." Then they'd walk me to the school, which was only two blocks from our house in Forest Hills, Queens. A hundred feet from the school, I'd refuse to budge.

The Board of Education assigned a child psychologist to find out the problem that kept me out of school for six months, but I guess he didn't get too far because the principal of my school asked me to come in for a conference. I agreed to hear the man out.

"Listen, Francis," the principal said to me in his office. "I know you had a really good time in kindergarten and were very close to your teacher. What if we gave you the job of kindergarten monitor, working with Miss Brooks? Would you come back on that basis?"

I thought that was an okay deal, so we shook on it and I returned to school, where I spent a couple of weeks assisting Miss Brooks until one day when the principal came into our classroom.

"It's time for you to go upstairs," he said.

"What are you talking about?"

"You've gotten over your fear. It's time for you to go to your regular classes."

"No way!"

He grabbed me and dragged me upstairs to my other horrible class where he forced me into my seat. At lunchtime, I escaped, ran home, and took matters into my own hands. Using the phone book, I found the number for the central Board of Education and called. After I asked for the president, I was connected to his secretary.

"I've been abused by the principal of my school," I explained.

People were sensitive to that word even back then. The secretary immediately patched me through to the president and I told him the story. My principal was investigated, but it didn't change anything; I still had to go to school.

I don't know what precipitated my strange relationship with school. Later in life, a therapist posited that I was insecure about my relationship with my mother. There certainly was a lot to be insecure about.

My mother's great desire in life, as far as I could tell, was to be a writer. It seemed to me she wrote for my entire childhood, although during that time she only published one book in 1973. *A Private Treason* was a memoir detailing her war years and why she chose to reject her native Germany when the Nazis came to power.

There was nothing in my mother's background to suggest such a rebellion. Born Ingrid Grütefien into a solidly bourgeois Berlin family (her father was a journalist and her grandfather an architect), as a young woman she made the bold decision to leave Germany in the thirties because she found the specter of Nazi politics anathema. Her leaving, and where that took her, defined the rest of her life.

After a short stop in Vienna—just long enough to start studying medicine, get married to another medical student, and divorce him— she left medical school and moved on to France, which by then had been invaded by the Germans. In a house in the Brécourt near Grenoble at the foot of the French Alps where Resistance fighters were hiding out, my mother fell in love with one—André Dubreuil. Their affair was the stuff of big-screen romance. Separation and reunion. Heroism and the constant threat of death. "We saw in the other's eyes that the fears each tried to keep to himself lay bared," my mother wrote in her book. "We reached for each other, but our embraces could not comfort, because they were forever perhaps the last embrace."

Their affair ended when André was tragically killed in the mountains of the Vercors while waiting on news of the invasion of Normandy right before the end of World War II. Still, he remained the love of my mother's life. And the father of her first child.

My half brother, André, never met his father, who died while my mother was in her first weeks of pregnancy. Still, the man remained a permanent shadow lurking around our house the entire time I was growing up. My mother and father fought constantly with, or over, my brother, whom she aptly called André since he was in her eyes the reincarnation of her dead lover. (My brother's legal name, written on his original birth certificate, was Patric-André. As explained to him by our mother, Patric, the K-less French version of Patrick, was chosen to represent the British-French armistice. But after my father adopted him, his name was officially changed to André Patrick Greenburger.)

My brother was a difficult kid, acting out all the time, but if my father tried to assert discipline in any way, my mother wouldn't have it. "He didn't mean it" was her constant refrain. One Sunday afternoon at the end of a weekend in the country, André, who was thirteen at the time, didn't want to leave, so he kept us captive by hiding the distributor cap from the car.

"He didn't mean it," my mother said as we sat hostage for hours while André refused to return the necessary part.

"What do you mean, 'He didn't mean it'?" my father shouted. "He could run us all over with the car and you'd still say, 'Oh, he didn't mean it.'"

Everyone knew what the fight was really about; André was the only remnant of a doomed and noble love. When my father attacked him, it was like he was attacking her dead Resistance fighter. In turn, my mother protected my brother at all costs.

As the sun fell to the tree line, sparkling through the reds and yellows of fall's leaves, my parents started to go after each other in the usual fashion. I couldn't stand when they argued and believed I had the magical ability to resolve the conflicts that popped up constantly. "Don't fight," I said with all the earnestness of my nine-year-old self. "Dad just needs to get home because he's got a big meeting tomorrow with someone from Gallimard. And Mom knows how André likes to fool around. I'll go tell him we need to get back and to bring the part he stole back."

And with that I ran off to make peace as I always did, my way of creating a role in a family where my place was always on the periphery. If I wanted to make my mother happy (and what boy doesn't), I should have just left her to her writing. The happiest I ever remember her being was on the publication of *A Private Treason*. Although she worked part-time at the agency doing clerical stuff, her raison d'être was her story and her writing. Because English was her second language, she spent many years writing and rewriting it with my father's help.

My parents were at their best while revising my mom's manuscript. A team with a common goal. Otherwise, they were at one another over André, money, and other disappointments. If I intuitively understood

My mother, Ingrid Grütefien

that my mother married my father because when she came to America with a young child she didn't know anyone, but that she wound up feeling compromised by the bargain, then my suspicions were confirmed by a comment she made to me over the lunch table when I was six years old.

"I have some adwice for you," she said, her German accent turning her Vs into Ws. "Don't let some woman marry you for your money."

That didn't seem too difficult since I didn't have any money.

"And," she continued, "*never* have children."

. . . . .

Even though my parents left me pretty much alone, choosing to focus their futile energy on arguing over how to handle André, I quickly got sick of our family dynamic. By the time I turned twelve, I had missed most of the fourth grade, preferring to devote my energies to the agency during the day and billiards at night. Still, the tumult of our neighborhood pool halls was no match for the *Sturm und Drang* among the members of my family.

I was lying in bed one night when I made a decision to give up trying to be an emotional part of our family. Nothing special happened, no apocalyptic fight, just the inevitably ordinary moment that always precipitates a big change. *I'm not going to do this anymore*, I vowed to myself. *These people are nuts, and if they want to drive themselves even crazier, they're doing it without me.*

I divorced myself from my family emotionally but not financially.

My father was terrible with money. His knack for mismanaging it, losing it, or not making it in the first place was an incredible source of stress within our family. He never gave my mother enough allowance to run the household, so after André, money was their second biggest source of argument. My mother would always go up to my father and say, "I need another twenty dollars." And he'd either have it or not. She never knew where she stood.

I had already taken charge of the bookkeeping at the agency, so organizing the family finances was a natural outgrowth. Setting my mother up with a fixed amount of money every week was the easiest thing in the world for me to do. I had always been phenomenal at arithmetic, not really higher math with its abstractions, but real numbers. They appeared in my head as clearly as objects in a room, making up a coherent interior. Because I created a picture in my mind, I could see the relationship between the basic data and the conclusion, and I knew when the conclusion was wrong.

"Look. I can manage the money," I proclaimed to my parents, whether they were listening or not, about my new role. "The rest, you guys have to take care of on your own."

No more Francis the peacekeeper or Francis the child. Francis the worker was the role I much preferred. The only time I was really truly happy in school was during sixth grade because my teacher, Mr. White, in charge of a lot of the school programs and also a bit of a drunk, was more than willing to hand over his responsibilities to me. I ran the audio-visual department, setting up the projector anytime a class showed a movie. As Mr. White's boy, I was the lunchroom monitor and ran the milk crew, organizing the deliveries of milk to the lower classes. I didn't get paid. Being in charge was enough for me.

What I decidedly wasn't interested in was homework. By 1963, when I was an eighth grader at Halsey Junior High School, my schoolwork was something I relegated to the daily ride on the F train after school from Forest Hills to 57th and Madison, the offices of Sanford J. Greenburger, where I arrived at four o'clock and remained until six thirty when my father, mother, and I would go home to eat dinner.

I loved the agency and literally grew up there. Even when I was a little kid, I would hang out for hours in the incredibly shabby office on 42nd Street my father had before moving to his spiffier digs fifteen blocks north at 595 Madison. During the thirty years my father spent on 42nd Street, the place never had a paint job. He used to sit in his leather tilt chair, cracked to the point where stuffing protruded, but when he tilted it back it would eat away at the plaster on the wall behind him. So by the time we left, there was a big hole in the wall.

The décor suited the agency's revolving door of characters, who were always scheming, breaking rules, and dreaming about the big payday. My father had one client, Max Werner (real name: Aleksandr Mihailovich Schifrin), who was famous for his prescience when it came to military matters. Exiled from his native Ukraine after the Bolshevik revolution, the self-taught military analyst landed in Germany, where he became widely known as the political editor of a socialist paper and author of more than a thousand articles.

When the Nazis came to power, he fled to France where, shocked to discover how ignorant the French military authorities were of Germany's plans for war, he wrote *The Military Strength of the Powers*. After sending a copy to Winston Churchill, he received a personal letter in return during the spring of 1939 that was uncharacteristic of the

Working at my father's literary agency in the midseventies

British leader known for his astute understanding of the dangers the Nazis posed. "I have looked into [your book] with some attention," Churchill wrote. "I think you greatly exaggerate the military strength of both Russia and Germany."

A year later, Max was on the run again after the Nazis invaded France. He came to the United States, where he wrote a column that ran in ninety American papers and signed with my father's agency. Max published a big best seller in '43 called *Attack Can Win*. In the September 4, 1943, issue of the *New Yorker*, Harold Ross wrote, "He has been pretty right from first to last."

My dad, with assistance from Leo, set out to help Max profit from his predictions. The three of them would sit around the office and cook up scoops based on whatever was hot in the news and sell the stories to the newspaper. "Hey, I've got a tip from one of my sources," Max told an editor from my father's phone, completely winging it. They were kind of soft things, but not that soft. And they were right more than they were wrong, so they got away with it. (I was only a toddler when Max died of a heart attack, so I have no way of verifying if the story is true, but from what I witnessed in that office, it sounds right.)

My father's agency was as far from a sleepy, quiet place of literary commerce as one could imagine. Through Ledig, who had formed a small international group of like-minded publishers that were all close friends, the Feltrinelli publishing house became a client. Giangiacomo Feltrinelli, son of one of the richest families in Italy, had four interests: publishing, bookstores, communism, and radical politics (which juxtaposed ironically with his father's passion for banking and real estate, including collecting villas, many fully staffed and filled with fresh flowers despite the fact that they might not be visited for years).

Giangiacomo published endless amounts of communist stuff, but he solidified the reputation of Feltrinelli Editore with *Doctor Zhivago*. More than a dozen Soviet editors, who condemned Boris Pasternak's epic that sweeps through the Russian Revolution and the rise of communism as

Staff at the Sanford Greenburger agency

"counter-revolutionary, shoddy work," banned its publication. In the summer of 1956, it was smuggled out of Russia to thirty-three-year-old Giangiacomo, who published it to epic success. Two years later, Pasternak won the Nobel Prize for his book that had been published all over the world in dozens of languages. It still, however, was not appreciated in the Soviet Union, where it wasn't published until 1987—the Soviet authorities forced the writer to decline the prestigious award.

In the late fifties and early sixties, Giangiacomo was one of the regulars hanging around Dad's agency, usually accompanied by his girlfriend, Inge Schoenthal. If Giangiacomo was a prince masking as the common man with his Groucho Marx-esque glasses and mustache (the first time I met him, at dinner at our house in Queens, he picked up a piece of lettuce that dropped on the floor and ate it, deceiving the housekeeper into thinking he was very poor), Inge was his opposite: a German Jew from ordinary means turned glamorous photographer who seemed to be everywhere and know everyone.

She had a particularly leggy photo of herself catching a fish with Ernest Hemingway and another laughing with Pablo Picasso. She also knew Winston Churchill, John F. Kennedy, Richard Avedon, Henry Miller, and many, many other powerful men. She also knew Ledig, which was how she met Giangiacomo.

It was 1958 and he had just split from his second wife. On a trip to Switzerland to get a new yacht, he made a detour to Hamburg to visit Ledig, who threw a party in honor of his Italian friend and colleague. Inge, invited to the event to take pictures, came "dressed to kill" and sat herself at Giangiacomo's table, where Ledig said they had "instantly taken to each other, and as they were leaving the party they hardly noticed anyone else."

Although she wore nothing but designer dresses, her political sympathies lay with the far-left Giangiacomo. He loved her and so did the Italian press, but they couldn't marry since he was still legally married to his second wife until he received permission in Italy to divorce (apparently he sought an annulment by claiming *impotentia erigendi et coeundi* or erectile and ejaculator dysfunction, which is how he ended his first marriage).

Inge quickly got used to living the high life (and her job in charge of relations with foreign publishers and authors) and didn't want to leave her tenure up to the vagaries of Giangiacomo's romantic interest. On a trip through North America in 1959, they got married in Mexico, but she needed something more solid than a south-of-the-border marriage certificate.

Enter Leo.

He became a consigliore to Inge in her quest to seal the deal with the radical publishing magnate. (Inge wound up playing a vital role in establishing and maintaining Feltrinelli Editore's literary brand. For decades to follow, she would protect the publishing tradition they created together through personal diplomacy and loyal friendships, even amid the endless scrutiny of bankers and "advisors." She did this first for her love of Giangiacomo but later for his heir apparent, their son, Carlo, who has been at the helm with the help of his mother since his father's untimely death. Her diplomacy knows few limits. To this day, she knows the first name of most of the staff of the Feltrinelli bookstores that are in every major Italian city.)

It was surprising that an international socialite would enlist the help of an unemployed émigré in fixing her love life, but I understood it. I often turned to Leo for advice about love affairs when I was a teenager. Despite the cigarette ash down his front, Leo had a way with women.

Although he was married *and* had a mistress, Leo was always extraordinarily friendly with the agency's secretaries. Fritzi, however, was one of those secretaries whose love went unrequited. Instead, she settled for Leo as an advisor. He told her to go to Europe and advance her studies in Renaissance literature, which she did. In Italy, she met a man who asked to marry her. Again, she asked Leo what to do, and he told her to marry him. So she married him. Later, when it wasn't going so well, she turned to Leo once more. He said, "Divorce him. Come back to the States," which she did . . . all the while carrying a flame for Leo.

In the time Fritzi had gone to Europe, Leo's wife, Frida (sister of Lise Meitner, a prominent scientist who was part of the team that discovered nuclear fission), and his principal means of support, had died. To make matters worse, his mistress of long standing also died, so Leo was disastrously short of money. His landlord came to him and offered to buy him out of his rent-controlled apartment, which he did, taking the money to live at a hotel for a while. But when that money ran out, he had no place to live. Fritzi, twenty-five years his junior, offered that he move in with her, but on one condition: He had to marry her. That was what she wanted and he needed a place to live, so they got married.

Leo was the perfect person to give Inge advice on her relationship with Giangiacomo, for he took a straight-ahead approach to love as he did everything else in life. He told Inge to get pregnant—and that was exactly what she did, giving birth to Carlo in 1962.

Giangiacomo liked to push the limits of "decent" society when it came to women and books. He was an ardent supporter of the avant-garde and politically extreme. He illegally published and distributed Henry Miller's *Tropic of Cancer*, which was banned under obscenity laws. He also published Che Guevara and Hồ Chí Minh.

Like his romantic entanglements, Giangiacomo's dangerous tastes in literature found their way into my dad's office. The most hair-raising experience had to do with Fidel Castro. Having befriended Castro (in a photo with the Cuban leader, Giangiacomo looks every bit the revolutionary with his mustache, thick black eyeglasses, and vaguely military-style shirt), he signed him up to write his memoirs not long after the Cuban Missile Crisis.

Because we were representing Feltrinelli in the United States, that meant we had become the American agents for Fidel Castro, which was like being Saddam Hussein's agent after September 11. People thought

Giangiacomo Feltrinelli with Fidel Castro

our country was going to be destroyed because of this guy. So when we were putting together a deal with the legendary publisher Mike Bessie (who had edited writers such as Aleksandr Solzhenitsyn and Elie Wiesel as well as founded Atheneum Books, the last major literary house started in the twentieth century), we had to do everything in code.

These were the days when business was done by easily monitored cables and telegrams. We couldn't have anyone figure out what was going on. If the word "Castro" appeared anywhere in the contracts, we would have been firebombed or who knows what else.

Fidel Castro's code name at the Sanford J. Greenburger agency became *Jesus Bart*, which is German for "beard." The contracts were signed by Feltrinelli and everything was going smoothly until one Saturday morning when my father and I got out of the elevator in front of the office, only to be met with ten men in dark suits, trench coats, and buzz cuts. These guys were definitely not looking to publish a book.

"FBI," one said, flashing the biggest badge I'd ever seen. "Are you Sanford Greenburger?"

My father nodded his head. Clearly, they had cracked the code.

"We'll need entry into your office."

## Chapter 2

# HIGH SCHOOL
# DROPOUT

• • • • •

C hildhood didn't suit me.

I had to come up with a way to explain this to my high school guidance counselor sitting behind her desk. It was clear to my teachers at Stuyvesant that my attentions weren't focused on school—I hardly ever showed up to my sophomore year classes and handed in homework even less—and now all this had come to the attention of the guidance counselor, who called a meeting in her office to discuss my performance.

"It's a privilege to attend Stuyvesant," the counselor said, glancing down at my appalling record. "This is one of the best high schools in the city and the country. Do you know how many kids would kill to be in your spot? You're obviously not a stupid kid, but you seem to be throwing this away, which is pretty stupid."

I'd been hearing the line about how great Stuyvesant was ever since I arrived. I had gained admission to the prestigious public Manhattan high school, even though I had missed part of my elementary school years, because I was good at arithmetic. Apparently, I was supposed to be eternally grateful for my good fortune, but to my mind the only difference between this school and others was the amount of homework.

"The students and teachers are the cream of the crop," she continued.

"No disrespect," I said, "but it seems to me that all the teachers do around here is give out an impossible amount of homework so that we're too busy to think. It's a colossal waste of time, which, I'm sorry, is not something I have a lot of."

"Oh yeah," she said, sending me a skeptical look from over her bifocals. "What more important things do you have to do?"

Actually. A lot.

Not only was I running my own business, but my duties at my father's agency, which had expanded beyond bookkeeping, occupied quite a bit of my time. My move from the quiet sidelines of managing the finances to the middle of the action had happened about a year earlier, when I was fourteen years old.

It had all started when the agency didn't receive payment for the touring rights to an infamous German drama, *The Deputy*. The 1963 work, which charged Pope Pius XII with remaining silent during the Holocaust, was probably one of the most controversial plays of the twentieth century. It had theological implications and international diplomatic repercussions. It was even alleged that the author, Rolf Hochhuth, was part of a secret KGB plot to slur the anti-communist Pope Pius.

Whatever it was, *The Deputy* became an international sensation after it was translated into more than twenty languages. As the representative of Rowohlt Verlag, which controlled the international rights, my father licensed the American theatrical rights to Herman Shumlin, a prominent producer who looked like Yul Brynner because of his size and shaved head. Shumlin in turn brought the show to the Brooks Atkinson Theater in a flurry of protests and press. Despite the outrage from Catholic groups, the play ran for 316 performances and earned Shumlin a Tony Award for Best Producer in 1964. Its success on Broadway brought the show around the United States after we arranged for another producer to license the touring rights with the royalties going to Shumlin.

One day while I was in the office and my father was home sick with the flu, I answered the phone to find an unhappy Shumlin on the other end; the producer of the touring show, currently playing in Chicago, wasn't paying up.

"We have to do something about this right away," he said in his trademark booming voice. "I want you to go to Chicago and collect the money."

"I will talk to my father and get back to you."

"No. I want *you* on a plane tomorrow."

I didn't know what to say. It was Herman Shumlin. I couldn't think of any bigger Broadway producer other than David Merrick. The son of a Colorado rancher, Shumlin had worked his way up from a high school dropout, then factory and railroad yard worker, to a press agent and finally award-winning producer. He gave Lillian Hellman (who had been reading scripts for him) her start when he produced *Children's Hour* in 1934—an instant hit—and launched the careers of many actors. As Hellman put it: Shumlin had "made many an actor into a star, and many a star into a decent actor." You didn't say no to a legend like that.

So after getting the okay from my father ("He wants you to go, so go"), I flew to Chicago the next day for a meeting with the deadbeat producer. Separating me at one end of the conference room table and the producer of the touring company at the other were seven lawyers representing both sides.

The producer, who knew my father and me personally, said to my set of lawyers, "Do you know how old your client is?"

They didn't have a clue. I was tall for my age and had a broad chest and full beard (all the rage in the early sixties). After they turned to me with uncomprehending expressions, I responded by pulling out the power of attorney that I had gotten from Shumlin, which authorized me to represent his end of the claim. Before leaving New York, I had learned that if somebody gives you power of attorney, you have legal authority—even if you are two years old. It's that person's decision whether or not you're qualified, regardless of age.

"I don't really see how that's relevant. I think this gives me the legal authority to act," I said, passing the piece of paper with my power of attorney around. His lawyers nodded and my lawyers nodded.

"Let's get on to the business at hand," I said.

The guy paid up and Shumlin was impressed. So was my dad, who soon after helped me start my own business exporting books after Karl Ludwig, a friend of Ledig's and an employee of Bertelsmann, a major German book club, approached my father with the idea to sell English-language publications to book club subscribers in Germany, where he believed there were enough English speakers to make the venture a commercial success. My father felt the deal was a conflict with his relationship with Rowohlt Verlag but said, "Maybe my son can help you."

It took a year or two after books came out in the US to be translated and published in Germany. That meant by the time they were out in Germany, the same books were going into paperback back in the States—and the hardcover publisher was "remaindering" its excess inventory. I saw an opportunity. Profit margins appeared in my head. I told Ludwig I'd help him out. The only hurdle left was to convince the American publishers.

During lunchtime at Halsey Junior High School, I skipped the cafeteria, headed to the pay phone near the nurse's office, and put in a dime.

"Dick Snyder, please," I said.

"Who may I ask is calling?"

"Francis Greenburger on behalf of Bertelsmann."

"One moment."

So far so good.

"Hello?" a gravelly voice said after a moment.

Going as deep into my register as possible, I launched into my pitch for Snyder, who would eventually go on to become a publishing legend. After he became president of Simon & Schuster in 1975 when it was a $70 million dollar company, he assumed a number of titles and transformed S&S into the largest book publisher in the world, with $2 billion in annual revenue. At the time of my call, however, Snyder was working in special sales and remainders.

"Look, I want to take five thousand copies of hardcovers off your hands," I said. "But instead of thirty cents per book that the remainder guys pay, I'm willing to offer fifty cents."

"What's the catch?"

"They're headed to Germany. This is a win-win. You're remaindering the book anyway. This will get it out of your market, so it's not going to compete with the paperback. And I'll pay you almost double what the remainder dealers do."

There was a pause while Snyder silently went through all the permutations of what could go wrong with this deal.

"Well, what are you looking for?" he asked, still cautious.

"Something popular. A best seller, nothing too heady. You know. The German market is saturated with that."

Snyder laughed throatily.

"All right. Harold Robbins."

*The Carpetbaggers* author was the surest bet in publishing. His track record was practically a best seller per year.

"Perfect."

"You're only getting twenty-five hundred."

"I'll take it."

I hung up the phone and looked at the clock on the wall; there was still plenty of time before math to make another call. I dialed the second number on my list. Bernie Geis ran an eponymous publishing house, financially backed by the likes of Groucho Marx and known for putting out racy, popular titles such as Helen Gurley Brown's *Sex and the Single Girl*. I knew the deal was good when I called S&S, but now I was doubly confident since I could tell Geis I already had half my quote from Snyder. It worked like a charm and Geis was practically pissed off that he could only unload 2,500 of *Valley of the Dolls* by Jacqueline Susann.

In math class, I tuned out the teacher's voice and crunched my own numbers.

1.25: Bertelsmann payment per book

-.50: payment to publishers per book

-.25: average shipping cost per book

× 5,000 books

=$2,500 profit

In 1963, three thousand bucks was a fortune. It was the cost of a new car, two years of tuition at Harvard, or half the average annual American income. And the whole deal only took me an hour. Doing geometry problem sets and diagramming sentences couldn't hold a candle to this. The feeling of mastery and accomplishment was astounding.

Bertelsmann was willing to do a similar deal with me, on average every three to six months, which meant by the time I was entering high school, I was drawing a serious salary. Especially for a fifteen-year-old. I was happy to have the money—really happy—not because I thought it'd change who I was as a person or prove anything to anyone else. Money for me was never about ambition. Even at fifteen, success for me meant not having to worry.

My dream was never wild opulence but rather the luxury of stability. The constant question mark that was my parents' checkbook balance made a lasting impression. During my freshman year in high school, I set a certain standard of living for myself and tallied what it would cost. What were the needs of a teenager attending public school and living in his parents' house in Queens? The answer was as urgent and direct as the desire behind it: girls.

My love of women started early. But even with my inflated sense of maturity, I was thrust into action earlier than I expected—eleven years old, to be precise. My family and I were spending the weekend at our second home in Colrain, Massachusetts, near the Vermont border, and had brought along the seventeen-year-old daughter of my mother's

German friend, who had also been in France during the war. Mara, a friendly girl with a box bob and reddish cheeks, had been living with my parents for about a month while she studied in the States.

The house in Colrain was truly a place of magical lawlessness. The charming but dilapidated farmhouse that my parents bought for $225 didn't have running water or electricity for the first few years. Although our life in Queens was by no means confined, the country offered other freedoms. Pool halls and edgy friends were replaced by mountains and trees. My dad and the usual assortment of strays he collected did a lot of the construction work themselves with me and my brother helping out whenever permitted.

As the sun went down on a long Saturday of home improvements and getting lost in the woods during Mara's visit, my parents and a few friends poured themselves cocktails in the living room while my brother suggested the three of us go up to his room to play strip poker. His interest was clearly seeing Mara undressed.

After enough rounds that we were more naked than dressed, Mara said she wanted a drink. Who could blame her? It was decided that I should be the one to fetch it. So I put on whatever I had taken off, went downstairs where my parents were hanging out, and stole a bottle of Teacher's scotch. After I reentered my brother's room with its two single, plywood beds propped up by books, we returned to the game and got drunk. Mara and I lost our clothes; my brother was more successful in keeping his. But of course in strip poker, depending on the circumstances, being the loser can also mean being the winner.

My brother wanted to win Mara, but for some reason she chose me, and the two of us, still naked, wound up in one of the beds in the cabin-like room. While my brother laughed from the other bed, Mara gave me instructions and we began to have sex. I lost my virginity while my brother cackled from the corner.

As if that wasn't enough family involvement, there came a knock at the door. It was my mother.

"Go away," I shouted.

But she kept banging on the door. "Open up!" she shouted back. "Open up!"

"No!"

My father, in bed and with no plans of getting up, shouted from the background, "I'm going to fine you five dollars a minute if you don't get out of there!"

Finally, my brother got up to let our mother in; Mara and I bolted under his bed. My mother yelled and demanded to know what was going on. We couldn't hide out there forever, so I decided to just go for it and ran out from under the bed and into my bedroom—totally naked. I got under the covers and prayed to die. Instead, I lived. The minutes felt like hours as I waited for my mother to enter my room and kill me, but she never came. I continued to live. Eventually I fell into a deep sleep aided by the drop in adrenaline and the Teacher's scotch.

In the morning, though, I woke up petrified. My embarrassment from the night before was magnified a hundredfold. What was my mother going to say? My fixation on that kept me from thinking about the even more terrifying prospect of facing Mara. I had no idea what to do. Unable to deal with what lay in wait for me downstairs, I stayed in bed until noon, an eternity. But I couldn't stay there forever, which seemed to come and go twice during that time.

After I headed downstairs, the first person I saw was my father lying on the couch. "You owe me for that bottle of scotch," he said without looking up from the local newspaper he was reading. I slunk toward the kitchen, the sick feeling in my stomach growing as I neared. But no one was there after I pushed the swinging door open. Room after room, there was no sign of my mother or Mara.

When later they returned, chatting busily as they unpacked the groceries from their shopping trip, both women hardly seemed to notice me. That disturbed me almost as much as my fantasy of a Visconti-esque melodrama. How could my mother be being so friendly with

Mara after catching us naked and guilty? I was more mortified than I had been upstairs in bed.

We returned to New York and that was that. There was no follow-up, romantic, punitive, or otherwise. It was like nothing had happened. A lesson in love. While it wasn't the greatest sex in the world, in my book it was a perfectly fine start; I was pleased to have broken the ice.

I vowed, however, that when I had my first girlfriend things would be a little more romantic than doing it while my brother watched. I got my chance a little more than a year later when I met Marie. Like so many other things, she came through the agency—her mother was a literary scout for a Dutch publishing company. When we started dating, I showed Marie the town. I would travel into Manhattan, pick her up at her Upper West Side apartment, and then together we'd head to one of the places I'd noted from Ledig's agenda of drink meetings when he came to town. I took her to the Grill Room at the Four Seasons and the Oak Bar at the Plaza because I knew that if the place was classy enough, they wouldn't card a thirteen-year-old who looked more like seventeen, and his fifteen-year-old girlfriend who looked just that. Out of all our haunts, our favorite was Top of the Sixes, a restaurant on the very top floor of 666 Fifth Avenue.

Walking into the restaurant's steely office building between 52nd and 53rd Streets felt important in itself. Isamu Noguchi's sculpture *Landscape of the Cloud,* fluid and lithe lines in the ceiling followed by a floor-to-ceiling waterfall, ushered us to the elevator where we traveled forty stories up to the top of the skyscraper. Top of the Sixes, or rather its view, was popular. The place was filled with couples on dates, and it wasn't unusual to cheer a proposal of marriage on any given night. I ordered the good stuff—champagne—in a romantic gesture that Marie rewarded me for with a marathon make-out session.

I had a big summer planned for the two of us. Her father had moved to Georgia after splitting from Marie's mother, who had to travel a lot for her work as a literary scout. All of that added up to a lot of alone time at her apartment.

That was where we were one warm June afternoon, tucked away in the back of the rambling West Side apartment, when things got a little heavier than usual. We hadn't yet slept together, but we seemed to be heading there when her mother suddenly appeared in the door. Whether we were so engrossed in what we were doing or the apartment was just so big we didn't hear the front door open, Marie and I were caught completely off guard—and naked.

As her mother screamed in Dutch at the top of her lungs, we both ran into the bathroom and locked the door. Unfortunately, I left my clothes outside. There was a lot of yelling back and forth in a language I didn't understand until Marie finally brokered an agreement where we could have the dignity of putting our clothes on without the presence of her mother. And then I left, quickly.

I called the next day, but, understandably, her mother wouldn't let me talk to her. When I tried back a couple of days later, I learned that Marie had been sent to Georgia. My summer of bliss was canceled.

After mourning the loss as much as any thirteen-year-old could, I moved onward and upward to a girl way out of my league. Benedetta Barzini—the daughter of Luigi Barzini, Jr., author of the giant best seller *The Italians*, and Giannalisa Feltrinelli, mother of her stepbrother Giangiacomo—was not just Italian royalty. She was a top model.

Luigi and Giangiacomo had a relationship based on mutual hatred. After his mother, the richest widow in Italy, married his new stepfather, Giangiacomo experienced unimaginable punishments, including being locked in a cellar for days with only bread and water (the experience caused a lifelong case of claustrophobia). His mother, Giannalisa, was no pussycat herself; she enrolled her son in the Italian Fascist Youth Movement and once scared her chauffeur by felling a deer with a shot from her gun taken from the backseat of her Rolls-Royce.

Despite the bad blood, I met Benedetta through my father's connections to Giangiacomo after she arrived in New York to start her career as a model. Although named one of the "100 Great Beauties of the World" in *Harper's Bazaar* for her black, almond-shaped eyes and mile-long neck, Benedetta was friendly enough. She was so approachable that I found the courage to ask her out, and for some reason beyond my comprehension, she said yes. I instinctively knew Top of the Sixes wasn't going to cut it. Champagne was like water for this girl. I had to take her to a real New York City pad.

Not long after I started my business exporting books to Germany for sale by Bertelsmann, I found myself with money that I didn't know what to do with. So I rented a pied-à-terre in Manhattan. It was a rent-controlled apartment for $45 a month on 73rd Street between Second and Third avenues. The deal was good, but the place was a wreck. I spent many weekends not sleeping there but fixing it up so it'd be habitable in case I ever did want to spend the night.

I finished painting and even bought a little furniture by the time Benedetta agreed to come over for an aperitif. Her slender arm linked through mine, we battled a chilly October wind coming off the East River. Each gust heightened my anticipation of walking into my modest yet cozy lair. I hadn't been there in about a month and, in my memory, the apartment had grown into a cross between James Bond's place and the sex den of *The Apartment*.

I opened the door cockily and walked straight into a fog machine. Benedetta protectively touched her hair. The place was filled with more steam than a sauna. While renovating the apartment over the summer, I had disconnected the radiator to paint behind it and apparently forgotten to reconnect it. Steam had been pouring out for a week, causing the paint to bubble and peel. The cheap furniture hadn't fared much better. My pied-à-terre was a worse wreck than what I had started with.

We laughed off the whole incident and went elsewhere. But that was the end of Benedetta . . . and the apartment. The Italian beauty started hanging out at the Factory and moved on to an Andy Warhol acolyte. As for my bachelor pad, two weeks after its meltdown, the landlord called to buy me out of my lease, which I agreed to do because I just couldn't face repainting it.

I had a confidence with women that well surpassed my age (the stewardess whom I met outside my building in Queens was pretty pissed off to find out, after a summer romance, that not only was I fourteen but I also lived with my parents). Like with business dealings, I assumed an air of maturity that had no correlation to experience. But girls were nothing like the numbers that popped into my head in neat rows. They were confusing but wonderful. I loved women, and I loved sex. However, it was never about flings or conquests. I considered it an honor when someone was willing to offer to me the emotional and psychological discoveries that came through the physical. My gratitude for this intimate female acceptance knew no bounds.

I wanted to be devoted to *a* woman, but this was the sixties and I was fifteen, so that goal was not easily achieved. The first to give me any kind of shot at boyfriend status was a lovely girl named Hanna. I had met her at Austen Riggs, a famed psychiatric facility. The perfect place to meet your first girlfriend.

I found myself wandering around the bucolic grounds of the open treatment center on account of my friendship with a young writer, David Berelson, whom I met through my father when he sold his coming-of-age prep school novel, *Roars of Laughter*. David was a complicated character. He had a lot of very strong opinions, all of which stemmed from either the *New York Times* or Johnny Carson. Anyone who dared to differ was considered a complete idiot. One had to forgive his foibles, considering his stepfather had murdered his mother and then killed himself while a seven-year-old David slept in his bed.

David's stepfather, Sheldon Dick, had been many things—literary agent, polo player, and photographer—but he could never escape his main title: heir to the A. B. Dick Company fortune. Even while traveling through the most destitute regions of the country to take photographs on behalf of the Farm Security Administration during the Great Depression, Sheldon, whose father founded the world's largest manufacturer of mimeograph equipment, "worried about the fact that he was a checkbook."

Later, he made a documentary on mining, but his biggest moment came in the spring of 1950 when Sheldon shot his third wife and David's mother, Elizabeth, and then telephoned the state police barracks to say, "We have just killed ourselves. Send an officer right away to the Sheldon Dicks."

Needless to say, David was scarred. But an inheritance of several million dollars meant that when he cracked up, he could easily afford the extremely expensive therapeutic program at Austen Riggs. He had already left when I agreed to make the relatively short drive from my parents' weekend place in Colrain to the stately facility in Stockbridge, Massachusetts, where he was visiting his girlfriend.

As I entered the institution's white mansion, affectionately known by its residents and staff as "The Inn," I quickly understood this was no mental hospital. This looked like the right place for James Taylor to kick heroin and Judy Garland to recuperate from a nervous breakdown. There was a formal dining room with iced tea in an urn in case your lithium made you parched, and the living room boasted enough square footage for twelve couches and a grand piano. It was the kind of place with chintz drapes, tennis courts, deck chairs, and a grand curving staircase that descended into the central hall.

That's where I first saw Hanna. We didn't speak but the image of her walking up the sweeping staircase, a serious and hesitant face lightened by a dimple on her cheek, was like a snapshot filed away in an album of memories. It remained with me.

A couple of weeks later, David called to ask for my help moving furniture for his girlfriend, who had arrived in New York with her roommate. I arrived at the apartment on 73rd and York to discover that the roommate was the girl on the staircase, Hanna. She was both intense and cute, a strange and fascinating combination. In return for carrying their stuff up the stairs, the girls invited me to Thanksgiving dinner at their place. I agreed on the spot, although I wasn't sure how my parents were going to take the news that I wouldn't be joining them for the holiday.

As promised, I returned on Thanksgiving to the tiny one-bedroom that was crammed with a dozen or so guests. Hanna hopped up to greet me. I hadn't eaten all day, but the buffet she pointed out was the last thing on my mind. She looked so lovely in her minidress.

Then she introduced me to her boyfriend.

I was upset, but only for a moment. The boyfriend, another Austen Riggs alum, was a chubby little nerd. Lording all six feet of myself (and full bushy beard), I thought I ought to be able to handle this. Sure enough, at the point that the crowd started to thin, Hanna asked me to stay a while longer.

"What about your boyfriend?" I asked.

"He left," she said.

I called my parents.

"I'm staying in the city with a friend. I'll be home tomorrow."

It was a wonderful night. And then a wonderful next day that turned into another night. I wasn't going anywhere, so I called my parents again.

When I called my parents on the third night, I got my mom.

"I'm spending the night in the city. But I'm not coming home anymore."

I had decided to move in with Hanna.

"I'm in love."

"What do you mean, you're in love?" my mother cried.

Despite my mother's initial alarm, my parents put up a small protest, consisting of me coming home to "talk about it," which was basically a good excuse to collect my things. My mother and father had always given me a lot of latitude.

When I was twelve, I accompanied my parents to a party held by a prominent literary couple in honor of a visiting English publisher at their posh Upper East Side apartment. A live trio played soft standards while members of New York's cultured elite mingled, drank, and laughed. I jumped undaunted right into the fray, no stranger to this kind of scene because of many a night spent socializing at the home of my parents' good friends Dagobert and Maria Teresa Runes.

Bob, as the Austro-Hungarian Empire expat was known in America, founded the Philosophical Library to publish the works of great European intellectuals, particularly in the fields of psychology, philosophy, history, and religion, after their displacement by the Nazis and World War II. He palled around with the likes of Albert Einstein and André Gide and once got into a fistfight with Picasso over the publication of the artist's only play, *Desire*, which contained pornography with vegetables. When Picasso asked Bob to print it on blue paper because "anything on 'Picasso Blue' will sell," Bob, a true man of letters, was so incensed at the crass comment it came to fisticuffs. Needless to say, there was always a great guest list at the Runes' parties, which were enhanced by the venue of their spectacular twelve-room triplex with double height ceilings at 44 West 77th Street. Partygoers enjoyed fine Viennese cooking (schnitzel, potato latkes, linzer torte, and gurkensalat) prepared by a Russian chef under the apartment's enormous windows that overlooked the Museum of Natural History. (In a true Viennese standoff, Bob and Mary never could agree on which curtains to buy, so they lived for fifty-one years without them.)

So I was perfectly at ease when I found myself at this Upper East Side party, sandwiched on a couch between a Channel Thirteen broadcaster and a very attractive woman. In fact, I was having such a good time that when my parents announced around eleven o'clock that it was time to leave, I responded, "I'm not ready to go."

Twenty minutes later, they reappeared.

"Time to go."

"I'm not leaving."

"Well, we're leaving."

And they did. At around two o'clock, when the party was wrapping up, I asked the hostess to "tell me where my bedroom is." I was not only under the assumption that somehow arrangements had been made for me to stay the night but also completely drunk. She apologized that there was no room for me but explained that a few of the guests leaving would drop me at the subway. I got on the subway and spent the rest of the night riding the E train from Manhattan all the way to Jamaica Center, the end of the line, then back to Wall Street. I bounced from end point to end point in a barely conscious state. By the third or fourth time around, the conductor pushed me off the train—thankfully in Queens— and I found my way home just as the light was coming up.

Why did my parents leave me at a party, drinking, while they returned home to bed? Perhaps they thought I could handle it. Maybe I was too strong-willed to fight. Or they were just too worn down by André. Years later, when I was old enough to realize that bad things can happen to you, I asked my mother how she could have let me do that.

"We didn't know *what* to do with you."

She was right. I was the definition of precocious: fifteen years old, my own business, and a live-in girlfriend. And that was why school did not fit into the equation. I just had to make my guidance counselor at Stuyvesant understand that.

I made my case. "My classmates and I are just in different places," I said. "I think I should leave, drop out."

She listened, took a thoughtful drag of her cigarette, and then said in her thick outer-borough accent, "You know what? I think you're right."

It wasn't vindictive or insincere; as a counselor and advocate, she recognized that, as insane as my story was, it was true. I respected her for having the guts to do her job. And I dropped out.

# Chapter 3

# TEENAGE LITERARY
# AGENT

· · · · · ·

My head was pounding when I walked through the agency's door. Although the fifties were over, there was still a lot of drinking going on—particularly in the tiny 64th Street apartment I lived in with Hanna. When she wasn't at her job at a graphic design studio or seeing her shrink, it seemed that we were often having a cocktail. Hanna drank scotch, Chivas to be precise, so I did too. Her other roommate, David's girlfriend from Austen Riggs, started her day with a breakfast of a water glass, filled half with Coca-Cola, half with gin.

The night before had been particularly brutal when some friends stopped by the apartment with some medical-grade pot. But if my father and Leo took note of my delicate state, they didn't say anything about it. As usual, they were locked in an overly analytic discussion.

"Laurie is leaving the agency," my father announced when he saw me.

Laurie Colwin, who had responded to a small ad I had put in the *New York Times* for a part-time assistant at the agency, had been a major step up from the low-key fellow who preceded her. Fluent in Yiddish (later, she translated for Isaac Bashevis Singer), she had been educated at Bard, the Sorbonne, the New School, and Columbia. Laurie loved chamber music and Jane Austen, but most of all she loved writing. (She went on to have her first short story published in the *New Yorker*, become a columnist for *Gourmet*, and publish a number of novels— including one loosely based on my father's agency.)

Although my mind ached from last night's excesses, as the realist of the group I instantly went to solving the problem of Laurie's replacement.

"You know, I met somebody who might be interesting for the office," I said.

"Please," Leo mocked. "Is it one of your wealthy friends from Stockbridge? We have enough cuckoos around here already."

Far from it. I was thinking of a classmate from Washington Irving Evening High School, which I'd been attending at night to earn my diploma. Heide Lange, the daughter of German parents who lived in Queens, was like most of the other people at Washington Irving: incredibly hardworking and admirably resourceful. Surrounded by students learning English or working full-time jobs, for the first time in my life, I actually enjoyed going to school. Everyone there struggled to get an education, which was fully respected by the teachers. They treated us like mature and highly motivated individuals instead of impulsive adolescents in need of homework to keep us in line.

With poor parents, Heide had to work to support herself. She earned $60 a week at her day job as a secretary at an engineering firm where she typed ninety words a minute. Laurie had been getting $40 a week from the agency to peck and hunt part-time. I ignored Leo's jab—for an extra twenty my father could have a full-time, fluent German-speaking speed typist. I got out the phone book. I didn't have Heide's phone number, but I knew her last name. So I started going through all the Langes in Queens, of which there were about fifteen, and asking, "Do you have a daughter named Heide?"

"No."

"Nein."

"No."

"No."

On the eighth call, I found Heide, who agreed to come in for an interview and, passing my father and Leo's unusual set of standards, was hired after an appropriate amount of "reflection" by my father.

I was far better at solving my father's problems than I was my own. While I liked living with Hanna, none of us liked living with three people in a small one-bedroom. With her roommate out in the living room, it was, to say the least, tight. So when Hanna found a studio on West 68th Street, between Central Park West and Columbus, in the building next to the one where she worked, I happily tagged along. In retrospect, I was a lot happier than she was. It wasn't as if she had agreed that I would live there. Under the nebulous arrangement, I was kind of looking for my own place, or something, but not finding it, whatever *it* was.

Despite my reluctant roommate, I entrenched myself even further in our new building by asking the landlord if I could rent two unused rooms I'd found on the top floor for an office. He was happy to make some additional money—$15 per room, per month—for rooms that were sitting empty. They didn't have kitchens or bathrooms but were a perfect—and affordable—office for my growing empire of publishing-related businesses.

In addition to the easy money as a buyer of English-language books for Bertelsmann in Germany, I had started a cookbook mail-order business with Bernie Brown, the owner of a bookstore on 58th and Madison where my father ordered all the books he sent to his foreign clients. I had gotten to know Bernie because I was in and out of his shop all the time. Having learned of my deal with Bertelsmann, he approached me about starting a mail-order cookbook business where we'd buy remainder cookbooks for a buck and sell them by mail order for $12.50.

The business didn't do very well, but that didn't keep me from going into business with Bernie again after he got a tip from a salesman that the primary wholesaler of boating books, which supplied all the marinas in the country, was going out of business. With nobody else in the market, publishers of this niche market needed somebody to sell into it. Again, we didn't do great, but now I had three book businesses—plus I was the New York representative of an Italian literary agency started by a friend. This hodgepodge fully justified my hiring a secretary. A beautiful redheaded one.

Theodosia, a friend of Laurie Colwin's, was of Italian descent but looked more English with her thick red hair, glowing white skin, and round, John Lennon–style glasses. She had the inexplicably unfeminine nickname Peter, but somehow it suited her. An engaging and open person, she was hired to do whatever I needed her to, which turned out to be not very much.

Although Peter was very friendly and nice, my girlfriend didn't care too much for her. There were a lot of obvious reasons for the animosity, but Hanna insisted that the main problem was Peter using our bathroom. The "office" didn't have a bathroom, and heading to Columbus Avenue every time she had to pee was out of the question. The purely residential Central Park West was okay, but Columbus was, to put it mildly, a slum. When Hanna forbade her from using our bathroom, Peter had to walk the streets dotted with flophouses, catcalling drug dealers, and stumbling junkies to find a dicey store where she could go.

The untenable situation finally came to a breaking point one spring evening. I don't know if it was the fact that Peter was just a little too attractive, or that after five months I still hadn't found an apartment, but Hanna completely lost it. Our arrangement had theoretically been temporary, but I wasn't eager to go anywhere. She, on the other hand, was extremely anxious for me to move on. She was afraid that if her parents found me in the apartment, they would stop paying for her psychiatrist, far and away the most important man in her life. It would have been pretty hypocritical of her parents, wealthy Catholics from Boston, to cut her off for shacking up with a guy, considering her father was the real-life version of *The Remarkable Mr. Pennypacker*. (For years, according to what Hanna told me, her dad had been absent for half the week, ostensibly on business trips. In reality, though, he was visiting his *other* family. He went back and forth between two wives with three or four children each without them knowing a thing until they figured it out.) It seemed the least he could do was pay for Hanna's treatment. Anyway, our fight that night came down to her psychiatrist or me—and her shrink won hands down.

"You're out of here," she screamed.

Then she began to throw all my stuff out the window.

My elegant Hanna, with her refined features, quiet demeanor, and conservative little dresses, was tossing my things from the third floor as I had seen women do in Italian movies. It was clearly time to go. I ran down to the street and started picking my stuff up (before other people had a chance to) while my junkie and drug dealer neighbors offered knowing glances of support.

The next day, I gathered all my stuff (as a sixteen-year-old, there wasn't too much of it) and went to look for a cheap apartment, which I found on 58th Street between Madison and Park. It was a fifth-floor walk-up, but the location was considerably less colorful than the Upper West Side and convenient to my dad's office on 57th and Madison. I hired moving guys to bring my limited possessions to the apartment, but having planned to spend the weekend with my parents in the country, I called Peter and asked her to deal with the move.

When I returned to the new apartment Sunday night I found Peter still there, and the draw of an interoffice romance was too strong to resist. She spent the night, then the next night, then the next. Basically, she never left, and so there we were living together just as unintentionally as I had moved in with Hanna.

I quickly found a vastly different life with Peter than the one I'd had with Hanna. Having grown up in the small town of Rhinebeck, New York, in a big Italian family that included an Italian grandmother and three aunts all within spitting distance of each other, Peter was a natural cook. When I returned home from a day at the agency and night school, I was greeted by the homey smells of a big pot of red sauce simmering on the stove or a roast in the oven. With Hanna, I don't even remember eating.

When my ex-girlfriend Marie came to stay with us for a few days that August, she enjoyed Peter's domesticity almost as much as I, and the two girls got along like sisters. Although I hadn't seen Marie since we were caught naked and guilty by her mother, who had shipped her off to a French lycée after deciding that Georgia was not far enough away, we continued to exchange letters, and when Marie returned to New York City it was straight back into my apartment (except this time, only as friends).

During her visit, she went to dinner with Peter, me, and an editor I knew named Claus Kimbel, a recent Yale grad (magna cum laude) and a very angry person. At a certain point that evening, Peter and I grew tired of Claus's tirades and decided to head home. Marie, however, accepted Claus's invitation for a nightcap and would return to the apartment later. But Marie never came home that night. Returning from work the next evening, I found a note from her: "Sorry I missed you. Headed back to Georgia."

That was all I heard from Marie until the following November when she sent a note that she was getting married . . . to Claus Kimbel. She wanted to know if Peter would be her bridesmaid at a small ceremony at St. Patrick's Cathedral. The whole thing was so completely bizarre— Marie hardly knew Peter, or Claus for that matter—that it warranted a long-distance phone call.

"Boy, what a surprise," I said to her. "When did all this happen?"

"I'm pregnant," she said.

"Are you sure you want to get married? You don't even know Claus," I said. "Have you thought about an abortion?"

Abortion, still illegal, was complicated but not impossible, especially if you had money. Marie, who was barely nineteen, had considered it, but Claus was adamant. He was Catholic, so they were getting married. No ifs, ands, or buts about it. Plus, her mother had said she wouldn't let her get an abortion.

"Your mother won't *let* you? You're the one who's pregnant," I said. "If you need help, I will do whatever I can."

"No, I'm going through with the marriage," she said. "Will Peter stand up for me?"

Peter did stand up for Marie, who married Claus in a side chapel at St. Patrick's with a small group, including her mother, looking on. But two days after the wedding, while they were on their honeymoon in Mt. Snow, Vermont, Peter and I were visiting my parents at their country house when Marie called. Marie, a real intellect, was friendly with my father and had become close to my mother, who picked up the phone. Whatever Marie said to her was enough for my mother and father to jump in the car and make the half-hour drive to Mt. Snow to rescue her.

They brought Marie back to my parents' house, crying and in complete distress. I didn't get the details, but it was clear she couldn't stand being married to Claus. At some point during the long night of hugs and tears, it was decided that Marie would stay with my parents until the baby was born. My mother was always protecting people in need. Happy to leave the problem for her to sort out, Peter and I returned to the city.

Ten days later, our peaceful existence was shattered by violent banging on our front door at two o'clock in the morning. Peter and I jumped out of bed, but whoever was trying to break the door down was too close for me to see through the viewfinder. Fortunately, I had a Fox Police Lock (I'd been robbed a couple of times already), because the bar that came down from the door was the only thing holding it up and keeping this lunatic outside. This had to be one of Monti Rock's jilted lovers, I thought. Who else would act so crazy?

Our neighbor and TV personality Monti Rock III was a very strange guy. Raised as Joseph Moses Montanez, Jr., in the Bronx by Puerto Rican Pentecostal evangelists, Monti was a classic tale of American reinvention. In the 1950s, he quit school after the ninth grade and became Mr. Monti, a well-known hairdresser at Saks Fifth Avenue, where he charged the small fortune of $50 for his celebrated blunt and asymmetrical cuts. At nights, when he wasn't cutting hair, he performed an act that had some singing and dancing but was mostly just him regaling audiences with stories about sex and drugs.

During his next phase, he put a "sir" before his name, Roman numerals after, grew out his hair, and wore white jumpsuits, makeup, and a lot of jewelry. His talent was still unclear, but he became a celebrity nonetheless, appearing on many talk shows, including *The Tonight Show with Johnny Carson* eighty-four times. And he happened to live right below our apartment.

Just as one might imagine with a guy who kept highbred poodles and donned a lot of gold lamé, his world was one endless party (several years later, he hosted a suicide party with a coffin and organ music for 600 people, where he downed a lethal combo of alcohol, Quaaludes, and amphetamines, although he didn't die). There would always be people, in the morning, afternoon, or middle of the night, pounding on his door and shouting, "Monti! Monti! Let me in! Let me in!" Sometimes they were women; sometimes they were men. But in our little building, there was a constant cry for Monti.

"Monti lives downstairs," I shouted through the door. "Wrong floor!"

"I'm looking for you," the man said.

It was Claus Kimbel.

*Shit.*

"What do you want? It's two o'clock in the morning."

"I'm going to kill you. I have a gun."

"Why?"

"I know Marie's in there. I need to talk to her."

"She's not here," I said. "Just cool down, and I'll open the door."

Even with the police lock, the door was barely holding. He'd almost broken the hinges, and I didn't want him to break down the whole door. Thinking I could talk him down, I let him in.

"You sit down over there!" he shouted at Peter and me. "Where's Marie?"

"She's with my parents."

"Get your mother on the phone."

I didn't see a gun but did just as he asked.

After my mother picked up, he started screaming into the phone, "You goddamn interfering bitch!"

If he thought that was going to scare my mother, he was wrong. She had experienced a lot worse than an enraged, drunken editor. I imagined her replying in her coolly authoritative German accent, "Marie vill stay here as long as she vants."

I hadn't been wrong about my mother. His wild emotions were no match for her steely will. Eventually he put the phone down, and then he started to cry. He was a mess.

"I'm sorry about your problems," I said, "but you know you're going to have to pay for the door."

• • • • •

"Hello?"

The voice on the phone was thin and crackling, as if it had traveled from the past. My father had never come close to the booming presence of, say, a Shumlin, but in the last year he had grown so physically weak that even his words were frail.

"Dad, I wanted to find out what time the movers should come tomorrow to the office to move your stuff."

"About that," he said. "I've changed my mind."

"You've *what*?"

"I've changed my mind," he repeated.

"The night before you're supposed to move, you change your mind?" I said in total disbelief. "We discussed this at *great* length. You agreed that the new office will be much easier to get to from your apartment. I already made a deal on the entire brownstone. And I bought all new stuff."

"I just won't be comfortable moving. I'm not going."

Despite my incredulity, and disappointment, I knew it was pointless to argue. I'd need to summon Aristotle, Spinoza, and Lincoln to have a fighting chance in this debate, and frankly I didn't have the energy; I had to move my entire office the following day to its new location in a town house on Lexington between 30th and 31st Streets. As I had gone over ad nauseam with my father, I rented the whole town house with the idea that the top two floors would be apartments, including my own, the beautiful parlor floor my father's office, and the ground-level floor my office. While taking on a whole town house was quite a risk for a nineteen-year-old, I was ready for the challenge.

My first real estate deal, which happened purely by chance, was a complete success. Back when Hanna and I first split up, I found a new office on 118 East 59th Street. I had been on the fence about the place because it had two rooms and I only needed one. "So, find somebody else to sublet it to," the landlord said to me. That afternoon I went over to Bernie's bookstore to deal with our boating book business, and there in the back was Robert Parker, a distant heir to the Parker Pen fortune, who just so happened to be looking for an office. I paid $50 a month for each room, and rented one to him for $100 so he was essentially paying for my office and his. *This is good,* I thought. *And easy.*

So for the next couple of years, I went between my father's office and mine, spending three or four hours in the morning at the agency and then dealing with my publishing interests at my office in the afternoon.

During that time, I continued to do the agency's books, but I also started to function as a literary agent after I found my first client from the slush pile I had been reading on a regular basis. One day I came across a play as strange as its title, *Stock Up on Pepper Because Turkey's Going to War*, which was written by some guy named Frank Zajac. It revolved around two bums, McKoater and McKeating, locked in a debate over the merits of the practical versus artistic sides of life. Very much in the vein of the Theater of the Absurd, it wasn't at all obvious, but still I liked it.

I didn't know anything about the author other than that he'd given a P.O. box on the Bowery as a return address. So that was where I sent a letter stating I'd like to try to sell *Stock Up*. Frank, who turned out to be a beer alcoholic in his thirties, carrying the plays he wrote on anything from napkins to newspaper in a brown paper bag from flophouse to flophouse, was thrilled.

Despite the fact that he was a Bowery bum, I went big with my first client and sent *Stock Up* directly to Joseph Papp. A theater dynamo, Papp had made a name for himself in the fifties by bringing Shakespeare to common folks through free shows at the Emmanuel Presbyterian Church on the Lower East Side and then at the 2,000-seat East River Park Amphitheater in the same neighborhood. He rarely directed modern plays and had never produced a completely new one before, but he had just taken over the old Astor Library on Lafayette Street for a new six-theater complex called the Public Theater, so I figured he'd need more material than *Macbeth*.

Even more absurd than the plot of *Stock Up* was the fact that Papp not only decided to produce Frank's play but also chose it as the premier performance at his new theater. My very first literary sale was an avant-garde play written by a wino to one of the country's most important theatrical producers! This was a cause for celebration. I called Frank and told him I was taking him out for dinner and drinks. "Meet me at Daly's Dandelion," I said, feeling pretty big.

Located in the shadow of the Queensboro Bridge on 61st and Third, Daly's was a fancy drink-joint frequented by the beautiful people, including a lot of celebrities, thanks to its owner, Skitch Henderson, the bandleader who'd followed Toscanini as NBC's music director before becoming the original conductor of the orchestras for *The Tonight Show* and *The Today Show*. Sitting at the bar, I thought Frank would appreciate my taking him to such a chic place.

Instead, he obsessed about the prices.

"I can't fuckin' believe how much this costs," he said, going over the menu again and again while we drank several beers.

"Don't worry about it. I'm paying for it," I said, growing increasingly irritated. "You want to get some dinner?"

"Look. I'm just not comfortable. This is not my kind of thing. Can we go to a regular bar? Is there any place near here?"

There happened to be a Blarney Stone a block or two away, so we went to the cheapo bar where you could get beers for a quarter instead of the two dollars they were charging over at Daly's.

Much happier now, Frank dove into our newest round of beers. At some point, not long after we'd settled in, a very flamboyant gay man walked in holding a fancy poodle done to the nines, and took the stool right next to Frank. It might have been a Blarney Stone, but it was smack in the middle of the interior designer district. We were just sitting there when, suddenly, I heard Frank say to the man, "You know what I would like?"

"No. What would you like?" the man asked.

"I'd like to have a big, fat dick in my mouth."

I spit my beer all over the place and hardly had the chance to recover before Frank and the man began negotiating how much it would cost for Frank to go back to his place.

"Two hundred," Frank said.

"Twenty bucks," the man with the poodle countered.

They were very far apart in their valuation of the deal, so for the next half an hour they went back and forth.

"It's worth it. I promise you won't regret it."

"I'm not going to pay that much."

They haggled for what seemed like forever until finally the man
with the poodle left. It was past midnight now, we still hadn't eaten a
thing, and I was extremely drunk. But just then, a couple of girls came
in and Frank said, "Oh, let's buy *them* a drink."

It was his night. We sat down with the girls for a while before taking
them back to my office, where Frank read his play out loud while they
giggled. I was drunk in a way that I rarely got, and I'm not quite sure
how, but I ended up going home with one of them. I had no idea what
happened to the other girl—or Frank.

When I woke in the morning, my head reeling, the girl asked me,
"What time is it?"

I looked down at my watch and said, "About eight o'clock."

"Oh, I've got to go," she said.

That sounded like a good idea, but in my perverse state, I asked,
"What's the rush?"

"My old man's getting out of jail today."

That was just perfect. She got up, dressed, and was headed for the
door when, unable to help myself, I asked, "What was he in for?"

"Murder."

"Well, then, you don't want to be late!"

Construction delays at the Public meant that *Stock Up* wound up pre-
miering at La Mama in 1967, and Frank's career never went anywhere.
Still, my father read it as a sign that I would take over his business—
when he was gone.

"You should come and work here full-time. You'll learn everything
and then one day take over the business . . ."

"I'm not sure that I want to just be a literary agent," I said. "I have
other things I'm interested in."

I liked the tradition of the agency, but I didn't necessarily feel it
was my calling. My wholesale boating books and remainder businesses
were going well, and my latest success subletting half my office space
made real estate an intriguing area of steady and easy profits that I

wanted to explore. It would have been nice to be a part of the agency, only not all the time.

"But I think I could build up the agency," I added. "I could bring in other people to work here so that you could find more clients and possibly—"

"You can't bring in other people," my father interrupted, waving me off like I was a bothersome kid. "A literary agency is a *personal service business*. You could do it because you're my son. But other people? No. That will never work. It's just not possible."

While I listened to him go on and on, following logic that only made sense in the confines of his agency, that old antsy feeling returned. The way he had been doing things for the last thirty-plus years wasn't so great for him; he barely scraped by on old relationships and demand for postwar European authors. What did he have to lose by giving a different strategy a try?

"Look. You've got to decide what you're going to do," he said. "Either you're going to take over my business, or you're going to do other things. You can't do both."

His lack of openness was frustrating, a kind of shutting down I witnessed in his eyes moving away from me and back to his papers. But I accepted it.

"I can't make that kind of a commitment, Dad."

In that moment I was conflicted in the sense that, like most good kids, it's comfortable to do what our parents want us to. Yet it was very clear in my mind that my father was asking me to commit to something I couldn't impose on myself. Freeing myself from this parental obligation was the right decision.

We remained close, but from that point on, we agreed that although I would continue to do his bookkeeping, he would go about his business, and I would mine.

He liked things the way they were, no matter how dysfunctional. So when, a few years later, after I got tired of running back and forth between our offices and came up with the idea for the town house where we could both run our businesses, I should have known it wouldn't work out. The new location would have made his commute from the apartment on 36th Street and Park Avenue, where he and my mother had moved to from Queens, manageable for the frail diabetic he'd become. But he didn't want to have anything to do with it, and I didn't push him. I simply stepped aside (just as I had done in the conversation about the future of the agency) and let him go along as he always had.

He still represented foreign rights in the United States for many European publishing houses, but in terms of living authors, my father only had one left. Like so much of the good my father and I experienced in our lives, Kurt W. Marek came, at least in a roundabout way, from Ledig.

The true story of the rise of Marek's literary career was stranger than fiction. As an editor at Rowohlt, he had pushed hard for an unusual book he described as "phenomenal" at a point when Ledig was just getting his publishing business up and running again after WWII.

"What is it?" Ledig asked.

"It's a book on archeology."

"Archeology?!"

This was postwar Germany where the citizens, starved for books, wanted romances, novels, philosophy even. But archaeology? Who was going to read that? For heaven's sake, half of the country was living in an instant archaeological zone after the Allied bombings. What they were looking for was an escape. Marek, however, was sure they'd be missing out on the opportunity of the century if they didn't publish it. Ledig wasn't exactly a pushover, but Marek, with his small piercing eyes and thick features, was a very strong domineering type (he'd worked for the Propagandatruppe during the war) who would shout in the way only Germans can, and so Ledig finally relented.

"The author wants a 20,000-deutschemark advance," Marek said.

"Are you crazy?" Ledig said. Not only was that a lot of money, a lot more in fact than anything they'd ever bought, but for a book on the study of old objects covered in dirt!

In the end, they compromised at some number that wasn't 20,000 but was still an enormous sum. Then Marek returned with his last outlandish demand.

"We should print fifty thousand copies to begin," he said, even though he knew full well that it was very hard to get any paper in Germany at that time.

"You're crazy," Ledig said.

Marek turned out to be not crazy but exactly right. *Götter, Gräber, und Gelehrte* by C. W. Ceram became a runaway best seller for years after it was published in 1949. *Gods, Graves, and Scholars* was essentially the history of archaeology but told as an adventurous and romantic romp through ancient civilizations. Readers went along for the ride as Heinrich Schliemann discovered the city of Troy, Lord Carnarvon and Howard Carter exhumed Tutankhamen's tomb, and many other quirky heroes unearthed abandoned marvels of culture. Over 5 million copies of Ceram's book were eventually printed in twenty-eight languages.

The book was such a moneymaker that it became Rowohlt's financial foundation. So all was forgiven when Marek revealed the true identity of C. W. Ceram: himself. (Ceram is Marek spelled backward with a C replacing the K.) In fact, despite his newfound riches, he continued to work at Rowohlt for a while, writing a couple of other books that did very well, until he moved to the United States, where my father, who had sold the American rights of *Gods, Graves, and Scholars*, started representing him.

When Marek, already famous by this point, decided to write a book on ancient North American history, everybody thought it was going to be the biggest book of all time—and it was my father who got to sell it. Knopf published *Gods, Graves, and Scholars*, but Harcourt Brace won *The First American* with a $250,000 advance, which was an obscene amount of money at the start of the seventies when they signed the contract. The commission alone—not to mention the worldwide foreign rights (except for Germany), which my father also handled—was enormous.

While this was the biggest deal he'd ever made, my father was fading. With his health deteriorating, he was no longer dynamic, and yet the messes his eccentric associates had always got him into continued to dog him. Lazi, the Hungarian Thief as Leo had dubbed him, reappeared one day, promising to make up for "all those bad times." He was almost done with a book to be published in England, he told my father, which was going to do very well. He was sure of it. He offered to assign part of the rights to the book to settle some old debts he had with my father. A week after the assignment of the rights, Lazi and my father were sued for libel. British libel laws are extremely tough, and my father lost the libel suit, which meant for the next twenty years he was to make monthly payments toward the claim.

Then came the news that Rowohlt, his biggest client, the publisher who had been one of the pillars of the agency for most of its existence, was planning on forcing my father into retirement. A letter had arrived stating that when Ledig next arrived in town they would need to discuss the company's relationship with the agency. My father was just barely holding on.

In June of 1971, Ledig came to New York and made an appointment with my father to talk about the contract, the future of which was not at all clear. I had no involvement in the agency other than our shared bookkeeper, who kept me apprised of my dad's situation—including the eroding deal with Rowohlt—as I operated from my office.

That was where I was when my parents' housekeeper called.

"Your father's passed! Your father's passed!"

Her hysteria was so confusing that for a moment I couldn't understand what she meant by "passed." Then, suddenly, I got it.

I ran the six blocks from my office to my parents' apartment, where I found my father lying on the couch, in his robe and pajamas, looking very still and white. He had suffered a stroke and died.

I was shocked, because even though he was in poor health I hadn't expected it. Only a moment of bewilderment, though. Then my practical side swung into action. Somebody had to sign a death certificate. I had to call my mother, who was at the agency. *The agency. Ledig.* I had to get the body taken out. A funeral parlor did that. Funeral arrangements.

A few days later, a service was held for my father at Frank E. Campbell, the Upper East Side chapel where many notables, from Igor Stravinsky to Ayn Rand to Tennessee Williams, were memorialized. It was well attended by the eclectic cast of characters who had populated my dad's life. Ledig and others spoke, including my father's lawyer, Hy Chalif, who took it upon himself to read a ten-page speech when the officiant asked if anyone else had something they wanted to say. My father would have been amused.

The burial was a much more intimate affair. At Christian Hill, a small cemetery near my parents' country house with its gravestones dating back to the early nineteenth century, no more than ten people gathered to lay my father to rest. Ledig, who never got the chance to discuss the contract, was one of those who stood around the open grave, his impeccable hand-made shoes sinking into the soft ground of early summer.

As I watched my father's coffin lowered by a flick of some switch by someone I didn't know, it all felt too easy. From the moment the undertakers from Frank E. Campbell had wheeled him out of his apart-ment to now, a lonely box abandoned by the mourners, making their way back to parked cars, including my mother walking arm in arm with Ledig, I had trouble connecting to the reality of the situation. My father's death was too antiseptic to be believed.

Once the last of friends and family had driven away, I turned to the gravediggers and told them they could leave too. Confused and concerned, they motioned to the hole in the ground that was empty save for my father. I ignored them and took my jacket off, grabbed a shovel, and began to dump the cold, wet earth onto the casket. The thud was hard, visceral. It cracked my protective shell.

More went in. As it collected in dark, dirty mounds at his head, then feet, a strange, inversely proportional dynamic occurred. The heavier the piles grew on top of him, the lighter I felt.

I always understood that my father's approval of me, and his constant concern, was simply an outgrowth of his love. His wanting to be helpful by giving good advice, though it drove me crazy, was a purely positive instinct. His pride in my abilities formed the basis of the self-confidence that allowed me to start businesses, sell books, make crazy friends, and love women at an age when most others were busy with homework. And yet, as the earth settled into a form vaguely resembling a mound, there was an easing. The recognition that he was gone, and I was on my own, released me from the burden of his influence. Without realizing it, I had always sought out his approval. His death freed me of the need.

When I put the shovel to rest, the weight of an angel, heavy with responsibility, lifted from my back.

*Chapter 4*

# REIMAGINING MY
# FATHER'S LEGACY

• • • • • •

I walked into my father's office the day after his death. My habit of self-soothing by searching for resolution compelled me to grieve through organization. He had left everything to me, but I didn't know what exactly that meant. So I planned to investigate and make sense, at least of my inheritance.

Among the piles on my father's desk, I discovered three businesses on life support: agenting, scouting American books for foreign publishers, and relicensing of older material. The last was made up of a few estates of mostly deceased authors, such as Kafka, that still produced revenue. As for foreign publishers, he had a few accounts, including the Dutch publisher A. W. Bruna and the Argentine publisher Emecé, but his biggest client by far, Germany's Rowohlt, was close to severing ties with the agency. That left my father's third business and one live client—Marek.

What there was plenty of at my father's agency were debts. My stomach churned with old memories of fights between my parents over grocery bills and cab money as I sifted through scraps of paper and letters that documented his many owed sums. His business strategy could

be summed up as borrowing from Peter to pay Paul. When he was desperate, which was often, he asked for a little loan from old friends and
colleagues like Bob Runes, whose Philosophical Library, though small,
was very profitable.

The money my dad owed Bob was nothing compared to a potentially disastrous, unresolved, and enormous dispute with Gallimard.
The French publisher, which had given my father his start during the
war by having him hold the American royalties of their widely read
writers, had renegotiated many of those original contracts so that the
American rights were turned directly over to the authors. Suddenly my
father found himself cut out of a commission on books important to
his business. He challenged Gallimard's action by holding on to his
commission on statements coming from American publishers for other
authors, such as Simone de Beauvoir, even though Gallimard was paying her estate the full amount of the royalties.

This had been going on unacknowledged for years, and during that
whole time he had never done any accounting on the money in dispute.
He would just keep the funds that came in, and say, "I'm not going to
send you anything until you account for what you owe me." If they were
right and the agency was wrong, we owed Gallimard *a lot* of money.

Even Marek, my father's cash cow, wasn't immune to his business practices. Years earlier, while Marek still lived in Germany, he
had asked my father to hold on to the huge sum from the American
edition of *Gods, Graves, and Scholars* because of his planned move
to the States. When he arrived and wanted to collect the money, my
father didn't have it. He'd, of course, spent a good part of it paying
off other debts.

My father's solution to that dispute was to put Leo in charge of the
negotiations. "Look. I know you collaborated with the Nazis. And you
know you did too," Leo threatened Marek. "If you make a big deal
about this, I'm going to expose you. We'll pay you a hundred dollars a
month, or whatever we can afford; and you'll get it eventually. You don't

need the money now, anyway." It was a miracle that Marek not only agreed but also remained my father's client.

The whole place was a mess. I marveled at how such a sleepy little place could wreak such financial havoc. There were only a handful of clients and only two employees, Heide and my mother. (Leo continued to come to the office every day to read the papers until his death about a year after my father's.) And yet the papers, notecards, and correspondence spread across my father's desk revealed a maze of complicated messes. No wonder, long before his death, he had stopped using his desk. Always overflowing with papers, it became a relic of his former self. Rather than clean it up, he abandoned his entire office and instead sat at an open desk next to Leo.

Despite the obstacles of debt and inertia, as well as inexperience, I decided to make his office my own as I endeavored to take over the agency. I not only cleaned his desk, I also replaced it. Out went my father's olive green army surplus desk that Heide and my mother had begged him to get rid of for years, and in came a sleek tabletop that sat upon two A-frames, reflecting the uncluttered look I preferred.

I was changing much more than just the interior design of the office. I planned to do all the things I had proposed to my father when he was still alive, and that he had rejected.

Sanford J. Greenburger Associates, Inc., as the new company was called, would definitely take up at least half my energy and focus. My real estate interests, which had grown beyond the town house I lived and worked in to include a host of other modest but lucrative deals, were too important to drop. But I couldn't juggle real estate, the agency, *and* the book businesses I had started as a kid. So I turned the remainders and boating book businesses over to Peter, who had been running them out of the Lexington Avenue office for a while now.

I then made an informal agreement with my mother in which I hoped to resolve the conflict that plagued my parents' entire marriage. I explained to her that in running this new agency, I would always provide her with enough money to live, imagining this was the purpose of my father's bequest. He had left nothing to my mother because he was afraid she'd hand it right over to my brother. Dad finally got to have his say regarding André.

(Things with my brother never got any easier even as he got older. If anything, they became harder. Around nineteen, he was married and his wife pregnant. A few weeks after the birth of their son, Michael, his wife disappeared—for nine months. During that time André, who was left to care for their newborn, got a divorce on the basis of mental cruelty. Even after his wife reappeared, Michael remained in the custody of my brother, who remarried about three years later. He and his second wife, Cathy, had another son, Holleran, in 1970. In 1974, several years after my father's death, André separated from Cathy and went to Alaska to work on the pipeline—with Michael, his girlfriend Pat, and collie Fang in tow. For two and a half years, it was a great place for him to make money because the job paid well and he put in endless overtime.

One day, though, I got a call from a childhood friend who had flown to Alaska to bring André to his home in Colorado. "André's been crying for days," the friend said. "I don't know how to help him."

"Bring him here," I said.

I took my brother, suffering from a PTSD breakdown, to an open-ward mental hospital in Connecticut where he spent a year, while I arranged for Michael to live with some friends of mine. By the time he left the hospital, André was better, but he still wasn't 100 percent.)

My mother didn't express any objection to my plan to run the agency. Her priority in life was her writing. After spending ten years writing and rewriting her memoir before it was published, she struggled with a couple of different novels whose completion were nowhere on the horizon. That was her driving passion.

While clearing the newspapers, threats of legal action, and IOUs from my father's desk, I found one lone book proposal. *Oh, My Aching*

My brother, Patric-André Greenburger

*Back*, a self-help guide to everything one needed to know about the back and fixing what ails it, was cowritten by Thomas Kiernan, a name I knew.

I first met the smart, sophisticated, and good-looking writer when he showed up at my parents' country house with his new wife, Ginger, who also happened to be Bob Runes's daughter. (On the way to their Vermont honeymoon, they stopped for a quick visit, and I remember thinking Ginger, in an incredibly tight pair of white jeans, was the sexiest woman I'd ever seen in my life. I was all of eleven years old.) The son of a distinguished lawyer from White & Case, the classic gentleman's firm staffed by plutocrats, Rhodes Scholars, and Ivy League grads, Tom enjoyed a very eclectic background. After graduating from Notre Dame, where he was none other than quarterback for its famous football team, he became head coach of the championship football team at Collegiate, an exclusive all-boys private school in Manhattan. Somewhere in between, he worked for the National Security Agency where, while following a lead on a theater director who supposedly was a spy (and had licensed a Kafka play), he investigated my father. Eventually he became chief editor at the Philosophical Library, and he and Ginger married. After their divorce, he decided to try his hand at nonfiction writing.

*Oh, My Aching Back* was good and an evergreen topic, so I called Tom up and after reintroducing myself said I'd like to represent him. Within a couple of weeks, I sold his book and was officially back to being an agent.

Tom turned out to be more than my first client; he was more like a one-man cottage industry. He quickly followed up *Oh, My Aching Back* with a book about Jane Fonda. Having lived with the controversial movie actress in between her famous husbands, he capitalized on his rare insight by writing a moderately successful biography. Following his straightforward strategy of writing about a subject that was topical, Tom could work on four books at the same time—and nothing was out of his range. He published everything from a biography on Yasser Arafat to a consumer's guide to psychotherapies. In the end, I sold more than a dozen titles for Tom.

Not every single endeavor Tom embarked upon was a success, however. While going after Alice Cooper as a client on the heels of a *Forbes* feature about the heavy metal rocker's incredible earning power, I became friendly with his manager, Shep Gordon, who also represented Raquel Welch. The bombshell actress, whose biggest claim to fame was "mankind's first bikini," which she wore in *One Million Years B.C.*, wanted to get started on a book right away but needed a writer. Tom could do it; he could do anything.

Tom flew out to LA to spend the weekend with Raquel to see if the chemistry was right. When he returned to New York Monday, I asked him how it went.

"Really, really well."

I immediately called Shep to share the good news.

"Raquel doesn't want to work with him," Shep said.

I was shocked by Shep's response after what Tom had told me, but I couldn't convince him otherwise. Raquel wasn't going to change her mind about this; she would not work with Tom under any circumstance. As soon as I got off the phone with Shep, I called Tom to see if we could figure out the discrepancy.

"Tom, I don't get it. Apparently she refuses to work with you."

"Oh, well," he said. "I guess I should have told you."

"Told me what?"

"It seemed to me that she wanted to sleep with me. I made it clear that I was happily married, and that wasn't going to happen. What can I do? On to the next."

Who knew if that was true, but he was definitely "on to the next." At any given moment, he threw ten ideas at me, and it was my job to figure out which ones had a decent chance of making it past the pitch. I went on instinct and the knowledge of different publishers' tastes developed over many lunches and drinks dates. I came into the agency not with a deep understanding of literature or writing (I had a degree in Public Administration earned at night from Baruch College, not one in English from Columbia or Yale) but instead an understanding of what was salable. My feel for the business of books was direct and results-based and ran contrary to my father's meandering, intellectual, or literary approach. I sold whatever viable material arrived at my desk, which turned out to be quite a wide variety, especially after I began working with George Bach.

A German native at the center of LA's human potential movement, George was one of the best-known group psychotherapists in the country. He helped to develop "marathon groups" where people met for twenty-four hours or more of intensive group therapy with the idea that the exhaustion and intensity of the session weakened the defenses of the members to allow for real emotional breakthroughs. For a little extra kick, sometimes the marathon sessions were held in the nude. This kind of work, which became known as encounter groups, turned into a cornerstone of the human potential movement, whose goal was the achievement of fulfillment, creativity, and happiness. Adherents flocked to the movement's geographic center, Esalen, located on the stunning cliffs of the Pacific Palisades in Big Sur, where the likes of Timothy Leary, Joan Baez, and Bob Dylan could be found roaming the property's lush twenty-seven acres.

George Bach in the midseventies

George already had a few best-selling pop psychology books under his belt when he sent me *Stop! You're Driving Me Crazy: How to Keep the One You Love from Driving You up the Wall*. He was something of a relationships expert, having introduced the concept of "fair fighting," a set of rules to facilitate communication even between hotheaded lovers. I didn't have to meet George, who lived on the West Coast, to know I wanted to represent him.

My instincts did not fail me. The day after I sent out *Stop!*, I got a call from Bill Targ, a renowned editor at G. P. Putnam's Sons who famously bought Mario Puzo's *The Godfather* in 1968 for $5,000.

"What's the *most* you'll take for this book?" he asked.

I knew he had meant to say *least*, but that kind of Freudian slip was music to an agent's ears.

"You know, he's a best-selling author," I said, "$125,000."

Although that was a hefty advance in the midseventies, Bill went for it.

"Okay. I'll offer $125,000, but you have to stop the auction."

I called George, whom I barely knew, with the good news.

"We've got this offer," I said. "But it's a preempt, which means that we can't take offers from others. It might get more from somebody else."

George, whose job it was to coax the most difficult emotions from the psyche, barked out a command in his German accent: "I order you to take the offer!"

It didn't take long for me and George to become great friends; it seemed whatever was going to happen with George always happened fast. Whenever he came to New York, he stayed with me, and I welcomed the visits that never failed to bring some kind of unconventional entertainment. It was during one of these trips that George told me he'd met an unbelievable woman. That wasn't so unusual. Although George was married and had a girlfriend/assistant whose presence his wife accepted, he was always meeting other women. His wife's nickname for him was GP, which stood for Genitally Preoccupied.

"I was at a sexology conference where a nurse gave a talk about her G-spot," he said. "Do you know what that is?"

"No. I don't," I said.

"You'll never believe it. It's women ejaculating. After she presented a paper, I went up to her and said I wanted to see it. She said, 'Okay, we'll go up to my hotel room and I'll show you. But my husband has to be there.'"

Sure enough George, the nurse, and her husband (a rocket scientist, no less) went up to her room, where she masturbated until she ejaculated.

"She's coming from Philadelphia tomorrow," he said. "I want you to meet her. She has to write a book about this."

The next day Beverly Whipple, a petite blonde with a prim style that made her look like a nurse, showed up at the office, where I signed up her project that I immediately handed off to Heide for a woman's sensibility. *The G Spot and Other Discoveries about Human Sexuality* not only became an international best seller, eventually printed in nineteen languages all over the world, but also marked a defining moment in the history of sexology.

George had the golden touch—and not just with women. Through him, I developed my next cottage industry: pop psych books. He was a font of fantastic clients because George was very big on not only promoting his own work but also promoting his colleagues. He had a regular poker game whose players were many big names in the human potential scene, including the world-famous Rollo May, and where I landed authors, such as Herb Goldberg. An early proponent of the men's movement, Herb wrote *Creative Aggression* with George, which sold over 1 million copies, and *The Hazards of Being Male*, which started off slow but found its success as a backlist book with another million copies sold over thirty printings.

Whether or not George's leads turned out to be best sellers (he also led us to the gigantic best seller *Drawing on the Right Side of*

*Your Brain* by Betty Edwards), they always wound up an adventure. A psychologist who with his partner had written a self-help program that promised to teach readers suffering from broken hearts how to fall out of love was a classic George acquaintance. After selling the book, I went to meet the pair out in Phoenix, where we met for lunch at the Arizona Biltmore.

Sitting poolside, we had already ordered and were talking about the publicity tour when I was startled by a totally unexpected sensation. Someone had grabbed my thigh under the table. The psychologist, across the table, was going on about a national TV appearance as his girlfriend grabbed my leg. I didn't know whether it was a friendly gesture or what to do. When our salads arrived, I put my napkin on my lap. I made it through lunch without any more incidents.

After lunch, they insisted I come to their apartment nearby. I wasn't sure what to expect, but getting to know my new authors was the whole point of the trip. During her tour of their place, the psychologist's girlfriend got progressively worked up about the fact that he was doing the author appearances on national TV without her. She began by hurling insults at him, which came faster and angrier until the crescendo: a direct warning to me that the psychologist had a side even darker than his black eye patch connoted.

"Come here," she said, commanding me to stand in front of a large closet. "You have to know what he's *really* about."

She flung open the doors and inside was an arsenal of whips, chains, gags, restraints, and other objects whose purpose I couldn't even imagine.

As the girlfriend continued her temper tantrum that might have been foreplay for her and the psychologist for all I knew, the irony wasn't lost on me that this big book being published and promoted as a sympathetic and sensitive portrait of romantic love and how to get over it had been written by serious practitioners of S&M.

· · · · ·

Down the long hallways of the huge, old house, a completely naked sixty-year-old man brandishing a whip ran after an equally naked twenty-year-old waif. Around the pool, a few editors and writers up from New York City smoked a joint. In the kitchen I was trying to come up with a remedy for my head, which pounded from the previous day's festivities.

Just a typical weekend in lovely Bedford.

The affluent, conservative Westchester town became the site of pure seventies hedonism after I rented one of its rambling mansions for a weekend house. It all began when a friend, who grew up in Bedford and loved its big houses, encouraged me to tour the swath of incredible mansions for rent. This was 1974 and nothing was selling because of the recession. The oil embargo's sky-high fuel prices meant the old-money families couldn't even afford to heat the stone or white clapboard mansions hidden along private dirt roads. The agency still wasn't turning a profit worth noting, but my real estate ventures, while not big enough to be considered serious business, combined to form a nice, steady flow of cash, which was a lot more than most people had at the time.

My friend was right—big houses were something to fall in love with. I was set to rent a beautiful stone mansion with two swimming pools and an amazing view afforded by the stately hill it sat upon at the center of fifty acres from the sister of Cass Canfield—the legendary publisher who ran Harper & Row on famously frugal advances and whose step-father was said to have invented the tuxedo. But at the last minute, she changed her mind. Apparently, some well-known pianist wanted it. So I proceeded to rent another estate in the middle of forty acres owned by a woman whose husband had been an ambassador. During the application process, I had to give endless references and received a five-page inventory of contents in the twelve-bedroom house, although there were no contents other than a mop and bucket in the basement.

I filled the main house and guesthouse rapidly and cheaply with finds from the many auctions around the neighboring counties where similarly rich families were unloading inheritances for a song and a dance. The austerity established by the Puritans who settled Bedford in the seventeenth century, and kept alive by many of its current residents, left no trace in my weekend home where people, protected by a half-mile driveway and a ring of thick trees, indulged to the fullest in sex, drugs (well, weed and alcohol at least), and rock 'n' roll. My friends were more than happy to make the hour drive from the city to swim naked in the pool, smoke grass in preparation for adult games of high hide-and-seek, and, of course, drink (drinking heavily was the one thing we shared with our WASPy neighbors). My guests reached for the Stoli in the freezer during breakfast; with lunch there were always gin and tonics and then wine; and once we'd recovered by late afternoon, it was cocktail hour. Bedford was a permanent hangover.

On any given weekend, I never knew who would turn up at the house. The guest list ranged from Ledig, my mentor and classy international publisher, to much, much less distinguished literary types. Sometimes the mix led to awkward scenarios that no amount of alcohol could smooth over. A client of mine, George Cockcroft, who wrote the well-known international novel *The Dice Man* under the nom de plume Luke Rhinehart, was a guest on the same weekend as Mike Franklin, an English publisher who had been remiss in paying him his royalties. It was an unfortunate and completely unplanned reunion. George, who lived upstate in a commune with his family and really needed that cash, told me, "Before I leave I'm getting the money from Mike." So all weekend long, the two of them played a game of cat and mouse with George stalking Mike through sitting rooms, gardens, and horse trails.

The year I spent in that mansion was wild, but at the end of it, I heard the Canfield house I had really wanted to rent was available again. With two swimming pools, it would be double the fun. But the Saturday before the Monday I was supposed to move in, I received a call from the broker, who notified me that "Mrs. Canfield has decided not to rent you the house."

Her change of heart was even more inconvenient than the last time she did this to me. The moving van was already booked for Monday morning; what happened?

"A vigilante committee from the community went to see her and told her you were an undesirable and that they shouldn't rent to you."

Apparently a half-mile driveway and ten acres of forest weren't enough to keep the town's most upstanding residents out of my business. I loved the housing stock, but Bedford wasn't the place for me. There was simply too much oversight.

An avid reader of the *New York Times*'s real estate section, I had noticed a home advertised in Ghent, New York, for more rent than normally associated with that area. And it had a private pond. I called the real estate broker immediately.

"Can you swim in the pond?" I asked.

"Oh, yes," she said. "There's a little road that goes by, but hardly anybody uses it. Frankly, you could skinny-dip in the pond. Nobody around here cares."

I didn't waste a minute driving up to see the place, which was a beautiful colonial, painted a surprising pink. The Pink House, as it was known in the area, was furnished impeccably with gracious country antiques, gleaming silver, and an incredible library. I took it right away, and the Pink House picked up where Bedford left off. While my country house continued to be a source of a lot of nudity and publishing-world antics, the funkier scene upstate somehow civilized the hedonism.

The Pink House wasn't the only thing rocking and rolling. By 1975, the literary agency had gone from a sleepy place to a vital player in the book world. (If the agency's Christmas parties were any measure of success, then SJGA was off the charts. One holiday party was so out of control that a lady from the building's cleaning staff who arrived mid-fete almost fainted. It was a cleaning lady's ultimate nightmare to see the office walls dripping with the remnants of a food fight, thousands of books strewn on the floor, and in the middle of all this an encounter between two people that is usually conducted in private.) Not that Sanford J. Greenburger Associates was a moneymaker by any stretch of the imagination. If we made $10,000 in net income, it was a lot. I could have made more money waiting tables.

Still, we were selling live authors' books, and a lot of them.

A big part was thanks to the addition of Jay Acton, an editor who I suggested join the agency when he talked about making the jump to the other side of publishing. Jay agreed, but he wanted to do business under his own name. So just like publishers had imprints, I set up the same model for agents and Jay became my first agent imprint.

Jay, raised in a suburb of Boston in an Irish Catholic family of moderate means, was always five steps in front of everybody else. By the time he was twenty-six, he had written and published five books and been an editor at what are now divisions of Macmillan, Penguin Random, and HarperCollins, as well as graduated from law school. (He also completed enough credits at Union Theological Seminary for a

With Jay Acton in the late seventies

master's degree, although he never delivered his thesis.) I don't know how it all fit together, but Jay knew how to land the big deals. His first client out of the gate was Helen Van Slyke, a onetime beauty editor at *Glamour* and vice president at the makeup company Helena Rubinstein, who churned out best-selling soapy romances faster than her former employer did lipsticks. From her ten-room Park Avenue apartment, she carried over her workaholic ways from her days as a cosmetics executive and produced 2,000 words a day, six days a week. With each novel taking about seven months, she had come out with one a year for the last six years to sell more than 4 million copies.

When she hooked up with Jay, her publisher Doubleday was paying her very small advances. They had given her maybe $25,000 for her latest book. We were flabbergasted by the deal. "They've got to add a zero here," Jay said.

Jay went straight to Doubleday and told them as much, but he simultaneously approached Berkeley and in two seconds got an offer for the $750,000 he wanted for Helen's next three books. The situation instantly erupted into a big political issue, because in those days Doubleday ruled the roost and thought authors should settle for paltry sums just for the privilege of being published by them. Its publisher, Sam Vaughan, considering Helen to be a friend and so feeling particularly betrayed, sent a letter to her in the middle of our negotiations that expressed his feelings in no uncertain terms: "So that my dislike of your agent is absolutely clear, if it wasn't for the laws, I'd settle this with a carbine."

Luckily, torching someone was against the law. Doubleday nursed their wounds pretty quickly and matched Berkeley's offer of $750,000. Jay's debut as an agent made a lot of noise.

Almost immediately, he sold his next project, *Nurse* by Peggy Anderson, to St. Martin's. The frank profile of an RN who reveals the hidden side of life in a Philadelphia hospital, including "snowing" terminally ill patients in terrible pain and fighting off male patients trying to trick nurses into sexually comprising positions, became a huge and surprising hit, selling 1.7 million copies and spawning a made-for-TV movie. Peggy, a former features writer for the *Philadelphia Inquirer*, wept when Jay sold the paperback rights for $137,000. (Having quit her job at the paper for a $2,500 advance to write a book about the Daughters of the American Revolution that never came close to earning out, she was subsisting on bean soup and counting the number of squeezes she could get out of a toothpaste tube when Jay found her.)

The success of *Nurse* was directly followed up with a memoir by Sparky Lyle, a left-handed relief pitcher in the Major Leagues, about the conflicts he experienced while with the Yankees. *The Bronx Zoo: The Astonishing Inside Story of the 1978 World Champion New York Yankees*, rushed out by Crown, spent twenty-nine weeks on the *New York Times* best-seller list and was the thirteenth best-selling hardcover book of 1979.

Within the span of one year, Jay had three books on the best-seller list—simultaneously. That was the stuff of legends. It was impossible to do better. Normally it takes two to three years to get a book written and published. And many agents spend at least a decade waiting for their first hit. Jay's reputation rightfully skyrocketed and at some point came to the attention of the horror powerhouse Stephen King.

King didn't have an agent when he made a deal with Doubleday in 1973 for his first novel, *Carrie* (initially thrown in the trash but later fished out by his wife, who convinced him to finish it). The publisher, which paid him a $2,500 advance, had put a clause into the contract, common in those days, stating no matter how much the royalties amounted to, they would only pay the author $10,000 a year on the theory that spreading out the payments made more sense for the writer's income taxes. But when the paperback of *Carrie* was a runaway success, earning more than $100,000 in back royalties, it was going to take King ten years to get his money.

When he approached Doubleday about changing the terms of his contract, they gave him the classic excuse: "If we change it for you, we'll have to do it for every author." King agreed to sign a three-book contract in return for $25,000 a year in royalty payments. But by his third book, he probably had more than a million dollars due from Doubleday over a forty-year payout.

This situation wasn't unique to King. In those days, Doubleday was a building with hundreds of employees. The large, powerful publishing house not only put a cap on annual royalty payments but also refused to improve the split of the royalties on paperbacks above 50–50 with any author. It was a measure of control, a way of putting people in their place. And nobody crossed them; they were that important. Agents talked about Doubleday's strong-arm tactics among themselves, but nobody wanted to take them on. That was until Jay came along.

Jay sought King out to see if he would be interested in new representation after his great strike with *Carrie*. They knew each other through *Cavalier* editor Nye Willden, who published a lot of King's work in the men's monthly magazine, and King agreed to work with Jay.

Within an hour of the word getting out to Doubleday that we were representing King, the corporate jet was on its way to Maine with an exec prepped to do a number on him about how terrible his new agent was. King got sufficiently spooked that he told Jay he wasn't ready to do a new deal—not just yet—and not to talk to Doubleday about anything he hadn't authorized. A high school teacher with a wife and three children to support, King didn't have a lot of money. He got $300 to coach the debate team, which was three weeks of groceries for his family. He couldn't afford for Jay to screw up his writing career.

Jay followed his lead and took a light touch, but Doubleday continued to bombard King every day with different lies, such as the absurd accusation that our agency was using him to leverage more money for Helen. Unable to handle the pressure, King became paranoid and was on Jay's case whenever Doubleday got in touch with him.

"I thought we said you wouldn't discuss anything without my say-so," King yelled at him.

"I *didn't* discuss anything with them!"

Finally, Jay decided to "fire" King. He didn't think the stress their relationship was causing was fair to the author or his family.

Without consulting me or anyone else, Jay called King up to say that he couldn't represent him any longer and put him in touch with Kirby McCauley, an agent who specialized in science fiction—earning the dubious distinction of firing the top-earning author of all time.

The agency's business was easy come, easy go. I never knew where we'd find our next hit. I certainly never imagined that an editor who did me a favor by taking a second look at a book of mine he'd passed on and publishing it to some modest success would sign one of the biggest powerhouses in pulp fiction to our agency.

Nick Ellison was a senior editor at T. Y. Crowell who went on to become a formidable presence as editor in chief of Delacorte. Under his watch, he published the likes of Irwin Shaw, Kurt Vonnegut, and Tim O'Brien. So I knew when Nick quit the buy side to join the sell side of the business, becoming another independent division of Sanford J. Greenburger Associates, that he would sign up strong authors. Still, no one could have predicted just how strong. Nick's first client was Nelson DeMille—the Queens native and Vietnam vet who, after leaving his job as an insurance fraud investigator for Liberty Mutual to try his hand at police novels, had become one of the top three best-selling male authors in the world.

Around this time, I expanded my publishing circle by joining the Independent Literary Agents Association and met some of my competitors who became lifelong friends, including Carol Mann, Al Zuckerman, and Maxine Groffsky, each of whom became their own legends.

Yes, by the end of the seventies, the agency was alive and well. Sitting at the desk I had substantially decluttered from my father's time, my mind couldn't help but wander to my reinterpretation of his life's work. My thoughts were divided. His pride in me fanned the self-confidence that permitted all my actions, regardless of my lack of

formal training or education. Yet our worldviews were so radically different as to make me wonder about the meaning of legacy. My father
had left me the ashes of an agency, an important tradition that I refused
to waste. But my vision was, in fact, the opposite of what his had been.
My father's fundamental commitment had been to an intellectual tradition that revolved around his European constellation. While I honed my
own literary instincts, with the additions of Heide, Jay, and Nick aggres-
sively pushing for the big deals, my commitment was to good business.
It was the Old World Clubhouse versus the American Upstarts, and as
far as I could tell, we were winning.

## Chapter 5

# COMING OF AGE IN
# THE REAL ESTATE
# BUSINESS

• • • • • •

As soon as I took the phone call, I regretted it. All of my authors had a lot of personality, but Jim was never happy about anything.

"I just read about your latest real estate deal in the newspaper," he said.

"Yes, the papers keep tabs on real estate trends and transactions," I said.

"I am not sure how can you be doing your job for me when you're busy buying up this city."

I didn't appreciate Jim's questioning my competence as his agent when I not only worked hard on his behalf but had also discovered him from the slush pile. Not long after my father died and I had taken over the agency, I put a small notice in the *New York Times* calling for authors to send in their work in an effort to drum up some new clients. Accepting unsolicited manuscripts was very unconventional for an agent, so starting the very day after the ad ran, I was deluged with all manner of books. Most were not worthwhile, but I did find a good, highly stylized, fast-paced thriller built around a political assassination. I liked the book and contacted the author to take on the challenge of selling his first novel.

A challenge is exactly what it became. I submitted the manuscript to publisher after publisher, but nobody was interested, claiming the thriller was "overly stylized," "not credible," or the classic "not for them." I went through twenty-seven rejections until I found an editor who didn't say no immediately. If the author would rewrite it, the editor would consider publishing it. Jim agreed and rewrote the book, which I resubmitted to the editor, who nonetheless declined it.

Most agents would have certainly given up at this point, but I can be extremely stubborn when I have a hunch about something. So I continued to submit Jim's book—to another nine publishers. On the thirty-eighth submission, however, I was beginning to get disheartened; this was the second round with Little, Brown, albeit to a different editor. But not only did the editor buy it, he paid 10,000 dollars, a very generous advance for any first novel and especially one that had been rejected thirty-seven times. *The Thomas Berryman Number*, Jim's first book, published in 1976, won an Edgar Award for best first mystery. It was a nice little success story (a parable on the merit of dogged determination), but it hardly warranted him calling the shots in *my* career.

"Look," he said. "You have to decide whether you're buying buildings or selling books, because I can't have an agent who does both."

"You know I always give a hundred percent to get your deals done," I said. "You're number one on my list."

"Sorry, Francis. If you want to keep me as a client, you'll have to give up the real estate business."

I didn't need to think two seconds about my answer. There was no contest. I wasn't going to let any author, not even James Patterson, put an end to my real estate ventures.

"I can't do that."

What had started as a deal to sublet the extra office I had rented for my book business at 118 East 59th Street evolved into a calling as strong as, if not stronger than, the literary agency.

My first real estate deal opened my eyes to the fact that there was quite a bit of money to be made from renting small one-room office spaces. Back in 1965, it was hard to find small offices with cheaper rents for small businesses, which made them something of a commodity. Commercial landlords, fixated on renting large offices, were leaving good money on the table that I was more than happy to collect.

Within a month of subletting the offices on 59th Street, I noticed an ad for some walk-up offices on the corner of 58th Street and Lexington. They were 7,500 of basically worthless square feet to the landlord because of their location on the second, third, and fourth floors of a commercial building without an elevator. The expensive first-floor rental was worth ten to fifteen times more than the upstairs. Employees of IBM or Pan Am weren't going to hoof it up four flights of stairs. But what about all the little guys in this city of entrepreneurs, independent businessmen just like me? Surely they needed office space too. Cheap office space. The landlord had no problem with me dividing up the space and renting it out in smaller pieces. What did he care? It was a dead loss to him.

His dead loss was my opportunity. I made money renting out the three floors to a variety of tenants, including a locksmith, a design studio, a man who I had no clue what he did, and a psychiatrist, who surprised me by taking almost an entire floor. "I've been working with an experimental treatment for drug addiction," he told me when he came to see the space.

"What kind of treatment?" I asked.

"It's a new substance that we're testing out," he said. "It's called methadone. There won't be any drugs on the premises except for the methadone we'll be dispensing to people who come to the clinic." It didn't bother me, especially since he was going to pay a big rent, which he did, on time, every month (there were a lot of people on drugs in the sixties). In fact, a couple of times, he accidentally paid the rent twice; he was well funded.

I followed my success on 58th Street with a similar venture about a block away—to similar results. I was filling a gap in the rental market for one-room offices that I had discovered when I looked for one for myself. I knew that if I could provide that type of space, there would be demand for it, because I also knew there were many other people like me in Manhattan.

Discovering an unmet need in the market is a tremendous start to any business. An effective way to find those opportunities hiding in plain sight is to consider one's own experience. When, as a consumer, you find what you need is hard to source, that is a clue it could be a good business to start. Once I stumbled upon the need for one-room offices, I test-marketed the strategy by leasing one of my original offices. When I found someone wiling to pay double what I had paid for a two-flight walk-up, I declared my concept a success and repeated the formula again, and again, and again.

My father, an avid follower of my real estate dealings, introduced me to a friend of his who was a partner in a small real estate company having trouble finding tenants for an office building it owned on 28th Street. The seven-story elevator building was a big step forward in my move into the small tenant market. I chopped the offices into 200-foot spaces, put an ad in the *New York Times*, rented out all of the space, and made a nice little profit. It wasn't rocket science, but it did take perspective. I had found a niche that had gone unnoticed by most people in the business.

The owner of the real estate company was sufficiently impressed by my success to include me in a deal to buy a loft building at 29 West 15th Street. The money for the down payment came from a group of investors, who would receive a fixed return. Then he and I shared in the profits above the fixed return for our management services. Everything was moving so fast. Within a year I'd gone from subletting an office for a little extra cash in my pocket to sharing the profit of an entire building. But the whole deal was almost derailed when we discovered that two of the tenants were the Young Socialist League on the second floor and the Marxist Information Service on the fourth. I couldn't have cared less, but they did not sit well with my staunchly anti-communist partner. I saved the deal, though, by arguing its merits not on First Amendment grounds but on economic ones. "We shouldn't be concerned about who the tenants are but whether they are able to pay the rent," I said. "And they are."

The members of the Red Brigade weren't the only colorful characters on 15th Street. A belly dancer on the top floor, who ensured that the building got extra attention from the novelist I'd hired as an assistant for my growing real estate business, put on a real show when I brought a prospective tenant to see the space. We were trying to get into her loft because she had fixed it up nicely, but there was no answer at her door. So I suggested we climb down the fire escape from the roof and look through a window. When we got down to her unit, we saw much more than the apartment. There was the belly dancer having very flexible sex in the middle of the floor. We decided not to disturb her and instead headed back down the fire escape—but the prospective tenant was "interested" in moving into my building. It didn't take much imagination to figure out why.

Throughout all these deals, I discovered that I loved buildings—not just their unique architecture or the income they could provide, but also the life that teemed inside. Managing offices and apartments in New York City was not for the faint of heart. Big gambles, inherited disasters, sluggish bureaucracy, and irrational demands made the whole field maddening. Among the crumbling edifices and crazy tenants, however, I felt at home. There was a lot to conquer, improve, fix.

Never was that more true than in 1971, when most people in New York City were looking to get out of, not into, the real estate business.

Rent control, introduced by the federal government during World War II to battle the nationwide housing shortage, was the major reason why. When Robert Wagner was running for his third mayoral term in 1962, he wooed voters, the vast majority of whom were renters, by handing control of rent regulations from the state and federal government over to the city, where they grew even tighter. The result was a crisis for property owners, who couldn't maintain buildings as their expenses escalated but rents remained static. Despite the unsustainable formula, in 1969 the city passed a rent stabilization law that brought most properties built after 1947, which had been previously exempted, under regulation as well. A year later, the shortfall of investment in housing ran into the hundreds of millions, and the annual rate of tax delinquencies was rising exponentially.

New York City was littered with abandoned buildings. A place that had been the center of so much was falling into decay as owners were eaten alive by their investments. Many, unable to pay their utilities, maintenance costs, or taxes, lost their buildings to the city. Disillusionment replaced whole fortunes that vanished through unreasonable rent regulation. Nobody wanted to get near the city's buildings . . . except for me.

Real estate was in a terrible state, but it was also very, very cheap.

Without any basis for my certainty, I was convinced the situation had to get better and that if I got in at such low prices, I'd surely make money by fixing up the buildings and increasing rents. I had a perfectly good business model founded on sensible growth and plenty of youthful optimism. What I didn't have was cash. Even the down payments for squatter-filled wrecks were out of my range. So when Phil Rudd, the owner of one of the original office buildings where over the years I had turned more and more floors of large work spaces into smaller ones, told me he'd invest in property with me if I ever found anything interesting, I found 23 Barrow Street.

The five-story walk-up with fifteen apartments was a typical Village tenement (although with three-piece, separate bathrooms instead of toilets in the hallway or showers in the kitchen, it was considered a "luxe" tenement). After factoring in the selling price of $70,000, the rental income, and my estimation of the expenses, I decided that 23 Barrow would give investors a 10 percent return on their money and was as good a place as any for me to start as an owner. Phil, a few investors, and I had hardly just purchased the building when I experienced my first landlord crisis—one that was far more serious than a leaking roof or rats in the basement. The tenant, a young lady holding her hands together tightly as she sat across from me, arrived at my office to offer her complaint in person.

"I was raped in the hallway," she said, "by a professional."

My heart leaped to my throat in horror. Totally unprepared for anything of the sort, I realized the problems of buildings are the problems of people. I didn't know exactly what to do or to say except to ask what she meant by the term "professional."

"He had a jar of Vaseline."

I offered my sympathies and said I would do what I could to make the building safer. The professional rapist hastened my decision to sell 23 Barrow, where I was already struggling to pay the bills and my investors their return since I had underestimated the expenses (something everyone always does but that I didn't have the experience to know). I solved the building's financial and criminal problems by selling it to a policeman, who paid enough for me to give my partners 10 percent on their initial investment and improved security with his presence.

Although my first purchase could hardly be called a great success, I was ready to buy more. It was like the entire city was a giant fire sale full of deals that I couldn't resist. In the second half of the 1970s, some elevator buildings were going for $200,000 in cash. Together, Phil and I went on a buying spree in the Village that included 54 Carmine

Street, 17 Grove Street, and 90, 100, and 102 Bedford Street. We also shopped uptown, purchasing a building on 33rd Street between Second and Third Avenues, eventually venturing to the no-man's-land known as the Upper West Side.

Amsterdam Avenue and 80th Street was basically the Wild West, which explained why six buildings with a range of ten to twenty apartments each were up for sale for a total of $60,000. The price, incredibly cheap even for New York in the seventies, was a pretty accurate reflection of their state. There were drug dealers who used the hallways for business *and* didn't pay rent, a mountain of back taxes, hundreds of building violations, and no chance of getting a mortgage. Anyone who wanted to buy the property had to show up with a strong stomach and a check for $60,000.

502 Amsterdam Avenue, another building I bought for $25,000, near the six buildings at 80th & Amsterdam that I bought for $10,000 apiece

This was either an opportunity or a suicide mission, but we decided to go for it. The very first thing I did after dropping off the check was to hire a bunch of guys from the Nation of Islam (NOI) to bring some order. I didn't know much about the African American religious-political group except that, for whatever reason, all the men seemed to be very big, very strong, and very serious. The NOI insisted its adherents follow a healthy diet and physical fitness regimen that precluded pork and, more importantly for my purposes, alcohol or drugs. In each building, we gave a representative of the Nation a free apartment and a little money to make sure that people didn't use the lobby, hallways, or stoop as a place to party or do business.

We weren't looking for a war, just a few diversionary tactics to avoid total chaos. The NOI members didn't need to rough anyone up; their judgmental presence (and army of brothers) offered enough of a deterrent. So did our less-than-macho super, who washed the sidewalk down with a hose every hour in a passive-aggressive maneuver that kept the drug dealers from loitering in front of the buildings. "Oh, excuse me . . ." he said politely, holding his hose. Pretty soon, they figured it was easier to stand on the other corner.

In the hunt for deals, no neighborhood was off-limits as far as I was concerned. I loved to explore Manhattan's grubby, decaying, and always changing boundaries. While walking among the shabby prewar gems of Central Park West, the graffitied tenements of the Lower East Side, or the art deco–influenced canyons of Wall Street, I developed a real estate person's catalogue of buildings. I was a quick study, absorbing without effort the histories of architecture and ownership. The way in which properties transformed as neighborhoods were reconceived fascinated me.

From an investor's point of view, it was hard to be sure if those changes were lasting, but they were certainly real. I saw for myself how people were moving into the longtime rag district of SoHo—the neighborhood south of Houston Street—when one night another real estate investor and I decided to explore the industrial streets ourselves. We landed on dark and empty Spring Street, where it was hard to imagine living in the large loft buildings, which until then had been primarily used for manufacturing. Other than one or two lonely bars, the area was a complete ghost town. There were no coffee shops, grocery stores, dry cleaners, or anything else associated with civilized existence, only sooty industrial buildings with loading docks instead of entryways. Looking up at the dark picture windows above, I wasn't so sure this place was inhabitable.

Just then, however, a beautiful woman with wild black hair and the kind of clingy jumpsuit favored by disco sets came out of one of the buildings.

"Do you live here?" my fellow explorer asked her.

She pushed a black curl behind one ear and gave us a wary look, either because she thought we were going to offer to buy her a drink or fine her, since living in those manufacturing zoned buildings was illegal.

"Is there a problem?" she asked.

"No. No problem," I said. "We're just looking at the buildings around here."

"Can we see where you live?" the other real estate guy jumped in.

I looked at him like he was crazy, but she took us up to her place and showed us around and I got the appeal of the raw loft immediately: wide plank cedar floors sturdy underfoot, heavy beams impressive above, windows big and open all around, and space. So, so much space. It was a perfect place for an artist to live and work. In the loft of our host, an abstract painter, she could easily go from bedroom (a mattress on the floor and record player) to her studio (the huge canvases in process on the other side of the space).

So when a pair of buildings was offered to me about a year later, there was no question I wanted them. Looking at the two six-story walk-up tenements located on Spring Street between West Broadway and Thompson, most investors saw lousy rental income from residential tenants paying about $35 a month and not much more from stores like a mom-and-pop cheese shop on the ground floor. What I saw, however, was the heart of a new art district.

I made an offer of $75,000 for the two buildings, which was accepted by the lawyer on the condition that we meet before making a deal. At his office, the lawyer surprised me by asking, "Well, what do you want?" I was confused: He said that *he* wanted to meet *me*. I almost said as much but something stopped me. Real estate is about a lot more than just numbers. Buildings are places people have loved, believed in, and suffered over. As the lawyer waited for a response, I figured out that I should want *something*.

"This is an offbeat neighborhood," I said, improvising. "It's going to be hard to get a mortgage. If I can even get a mortgage, it's probably going to be a low one."

I asked if he would give me a second mortgage for $20,000, and I'd arrange for a first mortgage (which I had been planning to get from Phil since I didn't think any bank *would* lend the money for this kind of place). The lawyer agreed and we shook hands.

As it turned out, Phil didn't want to invest either. A couple of days later, we toured the buildings, where we were yelled at in Italian by an elderly lady living with about a hundred cats and just as many images of the Madonna in her tenement apartment before the cheese shop owners insisted we take a hunk of provolone with us. Phil shook his head in disbelief.

"You know, Francis, we've owned some crappy buildings together," he said. "But this one is too crappy for me. I'm out."

"You don't understand, Phil, this neighborhood is going to be like Times Square one day."

Maybe I was overstating it, but I did believe shops and mainstream residents would follow the artists to SoHo. Phil didn't budge from his position. Although together we'd dealt with drug dealers and complicated tenants, I couldn't convince him. (This was the first of many disagreements I had with Phil, which eventually had to be resolved in the worst litigation of my career that felt more like civil war than a lawsuit. Phil had what I regarded as completely irrational or fictional points of view that bordered on psychotic paranoia. It took the talents of an extraordinary litigator and good friend Herb Teitelbaum to overcome the army of aggressive litigators Phil employed.)

Luckily, I did find a bank willing to give me a mortgage of $55,000. That combined with the lawyer's second mortgage meant I didn't have to put any money down at all for the buildings, which eventually did turn to gold (the cheese shop that rented for $150 a month at that time brought in around $22,000 in 2014, and the apartments where people paid $35 a month rented anywhere from $2,500 to $4,000).

If the Spring Street deal was crazy, I didn't know enough to know that. I hadn't grown up in the business like so many of my peers who were part of real estate dynasties. Making my own way meant there was no one to tell me to stop buying. By 1974, there were so few buyers that I would usually be the only offer or close to it. Brokers, who found me easy to deal with, started to bring sales to my attention. Instead of worrying that I was the only one in the game, I snapped up properties as fast as I could.

It was around the time I bought Spring Street that I also bought a building (346 East 20th Street, a typical purchase of mine, had gone through foreclosure and was riddled with deferred maintenance issues) from an affable and charming man named Milton Newmark. He had a funny way of peppering an exchange as mundane as a real estate deal with Old Testament references that, frankly, were over my head. Still, his clear, open expression was that of a straight shooter. So when he said if I ever needed an investor for a new real estate deal, I returned to him shortly, just as I had done with Phil Rudd. Only this investment, a group of fifteen very nice buildings in the West Village, was far bigger than any deal I had done before.

In Milton's office at 500 Fifth Avenue—a slender and sumptuous sixty-floor art deco building on the north side of 42nd Street—light streamed in from an unobstructed view of Bryant Park as he reviewed my calculations. The purchase price of the group of buildings in the West Village and Meat Market was $1.5 million, but the seller was willing to give me a mortgage for $1.2 million. That meant I still needed $300,000, which was $300,000 more than I had. I watched Milton work through the numbers (in his sixties, he was still a handsome man whose bright eyes and white hair and beard were striking against skin tanned from winters spent in Florida). I didn't have a clue as to what he was thinking. I hardly knew the man. Suddenly he picked up the phone.

"Abbott, it's Milton," he said. "I've got a deal; you're in for one-fifty."

After a few words about his plans for the upcoming Jewish New Year, he hung up and immediately made another call.

"Art, Milton . . . . You're in for seventy-five."

Then he put the phone down, looked at me, and said, "Okay, it's done."

He hadn't even told me he wanted to do the deal before it was "done." His pronouncement was particularly startling, because here I was, a twenty-four-year-old stranger, for whom he'd found $300,000 within ten minutes. It would take me a while to learn that Milton, brilliant and generous, immediately picked up on my potential that I didn't yet know I possessed. Because he didn't care about labels or appearances, only talent and honesty, he wasn't afraid to act upon it. So my age and scruffy beard didn't dissuade him from becoming my instant and, ultimately, enduring champion. (Maybe my underdog status helped, since Milton was the enemy of pretention. Once while at a snooty French restaurant, he decided to rebel against their affectation by dropping his coat on the floor next to his chair. The maître d', who nearly had a heart attack, asked to take the coat, to which Milton said, "No, leave it there.")

I made the offer on the group of properties, which the owner, Arthur Jacobs, accepted, adding that he expected me in his office to look over

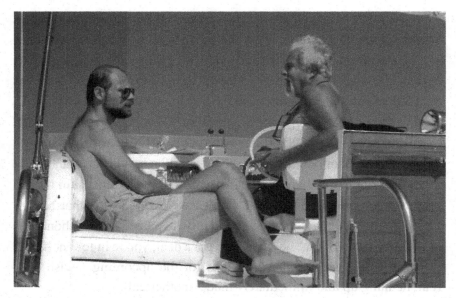

With Milton Newmark in the late seventies

the rent records. I was so unschooled in the real estate business that I hadn't thought to do that but didn't let on. "Of course," I said to Arthur, who presented me with about half a dozen boxes when I arrived at his office to do my due diligence.

"It won't be necessary for me to go through all of these . . ." I said, thinking he was simply making a show that there was nothing to hide with years of records covering his conference room table.

"Surely, you'll want to thoroughly assess your purchase," he said, cutting me off. "Unless you aren't concerned with the financial stability of the buildings."

His insistence disoriented me. It was contrary to most sellers, who would consider it at best a bother to go through rent records and at worst a problem that something objectionable might ruin the deal. I thought about it from his perspective; an elderly man about to take back the mortgage on his buildings in order to sell them, he had to make sure I was a responsible operator who wouldn't burden his wife and family with foreclosure if I didn't make good on the mortgage after he died. I had to look through every one of those rent records carefully to prove to him I knew what I was doing and could be trusted with his family's inheritance. "I just didn't want to inconvenience you," I said as we sat down for a three-day history lesson of each apartment—how much the tenants paid, any complaints, repairs done.

At the signing, I felt victorious. The major work had been done, and all that was left was to pass the stacks of papers that each represented one building around the conference room table for everyone's signature. Milton, a lawyer, came with me to Arthur's office for the signing, even though we already had a lawyer representing us in the transaction, in order to read over the contract.

A natural-born philosopher and trained trial attorney, Milton had fallen into real estate by chance. He grew up in the Bronx to immigrants from Poland who owned a pair of fish stores, one run by his mother, the other by his father. Milton's father might have been the one to drive the horse and carriage packed with ice to Fulton Fish Market every morning at 4 AM but his mother, Regina, who spoke many languages and did the math for the business in her head, drove the family's ambition and Milton's career (his philosophy professors urged him to join their profession but she insisted he become a lawyer). It was her idea to buy a building, which eventually turned into the family real estate company called New Regime in a nod to her name and leadership style.

At the signing of the West Village deal, Milton picked his head up from a document and said, "How about lowering the interest rate?"

*What?* The outrageous last-minute, out-of-the-blue request came as a huge shock to everyone. You don't renegotiate the interest rate at the signing. Certainly not after three days of poring over records. We had all agreed to the deal before us.

"No," Arthur said without blinking.

To my horror, Milton, who could be an imposing figure, wasn't done with his rogue negotiations.

"I see here that if we are late paying the mortgage by just ten days, you have the right to call the mortgage in default."

"That's right," Arthur said.

"We should have at least thirty days."

Okay, now I was convinced that Milton had lost his mind or at least wanted to sabotage the deal; what he was asking for was not an industry standard and he knew that.

Arthur didn't dignify Milton's request with an answer but instead slowly started to gather the stacks of papers on the table and fill his briefcase. He was old and tired; he didn't have time for this.

He picked up his coat and said, "If you're so concerned about how much notice you will have if you don't pay the mortgage, that must mean you don't intend to pay it, and that means I'm no longer interested in this deal." Then he walked out.

That was it. Milton had taken a blowtorch to our joint venture. In the conference room, emptied of contracts or a negotiating partner, I was devastated and confused. What I didn't understand was that Milton didn't intentionally destroy the deal but was compelled to assert himself out of some sort of ancient, unspoken, and competitive instinct. Arthur, every bit the patriarchal Jewish male, called his bluff. I, meanwhile, was stunned and bereft.

After we'd all left the conference room, I asked the broker to get in touch with Arthur. But the old man wouldn't even pick up the phone that day or any for the next couple of weeks. I decided it was a lost cause, but Milton, out of guilt or perhaps the same strong-headedness he showed at the signing, called a meeting in his office of the investors, Abbott Simon and Art Travis, otherwise known as his best friends. They had been close since their days in Syracuse, where Abbott and Milton attended college, and Milton moved into Art's family home so that he could keep kosher. A poignant combination of worldly and provincial, mixing great financial success, wide cultural acumen, and the fraternity of landsmen, the three men were all extraordinary in their own way. Art, at the point of retiring when I met him, had been a top garment executive and one of the pioneers of manufacturing in the Far East. After he left his last job and we started working together, he took up classical clarinet, which he had played in high school, and would give wonderful concerts for his friends and family.

Abbott, another lawyer, was a true Renaissance man. He had been a music critic and knew a tremendous amount about art, but he was also extremely politically active, namely as a peace activist. He was a member of the American Student Union, a national student group founded after the merging of communist and socialist student organizations in 1935. As legislative director of the affiliated American Youth Congress, he was arrested during a protest in which they booed President Roosevelt on the White House lawn during the Stalin-Hitler pact. It was through the ASU and AYC that Abbott met and became a very close friend of Eleanor Roosevelt's (just how close is a matter of speculation, with a rumor that his invitation to sleep at the White

Abbott Simon, Art Travis, and Milton Newmark

House was more than an official visit). Later, Abbott was indicted in the McCarthy hearings and became an advisor to the prominent African American civil rights activist W. E. B. Du Bois. Popular among many different circles, Abbott didn't find any contradiction between his left leanings and making money in the real estate business. His interests and passions were fluid.

"We should offer Arthur $50,000 more than we offered last time and see what happens," Abbott said.

"This isn't a matter of money," I said. "He lost confidence in us. The money isn't going to change anything."

"Let's do it anyway," Abbott said.

"Okay, but I doubt it's going to work."

After the men had settled on the plan, they began to discuss lunch with almost the same strength of opinion. During the debate between diner or deli, Milton leaned back in his chair, interlacing his fingers, and asked me, "Have you heard the story about the bag of gold and the man's head?"

"Definitely not."

"If you have a bag of gold and throw it at a man's head in order to kill him, but the gold falls at his feet and he uses it to become wealthy, have you done a good deed or a bad one?"

"I have absolutely no idea," I answered, pretty nonplussed by this point. "My knowledge of the Bible isn't too great, Milton."

"Francis, it's an enigma!" he said, energized by the expansion of my mind. "Something to puzzle over."

Milton's riddle might not have had a real answer, but the letter we sent Arthur with an offer of a $50,000 increase sure did. Abbott was right; the sum was enough of an apology for Arthur to put the deal back on and turn my growing real estate interests into more than just a side business.

One day I had two buildings and two employees. Then I had five and five employees. Then it was twenty buildings and as many employees. As the seventies came to a close, I housed both my real estate and literary businesses in the same office. My now ex-book client Jim Patterson hadn't been totally incorrect about my attentions being divided. While books had their fair share of drama, gambles, and surprises, the ones in real estate were a lot more costly. As I managed my growing property interests, I was often stressed. On paper, I was a millionaire. In real life, though, I was skating on razor-thin margins that a busted toilet could threaten. But I preferred to remain on the edge as I kept my buildings running rather than sell any of them before they grew to the much higher value I had a hunch they would one day achieve.

## Chapter 6

# SEARCHING FOR CASH

• • • • •

W hy don't you sell one of the buildings? That'd solve your cash problem," Abbott said while he, Milton, Art, and I relaxed in the book-lined den of Milton's Manhattan apartment.

It was the usual dose of wisdom and ribbing I got from the patriarchs, but this particular topic made me uneasy. Hundreds of heavy tomes of biography, philosophy, history, Jewish thought, and Milton's other intellectual passions stood in judgment of my inexperience as the discussion came around to how I could hardly pay my bills.

"I'm not a great seller," I said. "It's not in my DNA."

"You like to hold on to things," Milton said.

"Yes, I like to hold on to things."

The seventies might have made me a millionaire on paper, but I still didn't have any cash. Being a landlord had only gotten tougher as the decade progressed. Although New York was bankrupt in the mid-seventies, increasing rents was not politically acceptable, and those in charge of rent regulations started reinterpreting them in a very negative way for landlords. For example, the law said an owner had the right to increase rents when apartments became vacant to comparable rents or market rate of similar units at the time when the rent-controlled tenant moved out. But then the city invented a Byzantine interpretation of the law that stated market value for a unit had to be calculated by taking the average of rents charged in the building for the last five years for comparable units—even though rents were artificially low because of the regulations. It was a catch-22 that spelled bankruptcy for many landlords.

That was only the start in the city's kamikaze mission to make real estate a terrible proposition. After taxes were raised disproportionately to income increases, the coup de grâce to the market came in the form of the '73 oil crisis when OPEC put an end to decades of cheap energy. World oil prices quadrupled within just a few months, dampening the nation's economic growth, fostering inflation, and absolutely obliterating profits on most rental properties.

Even the margins on my buildings, which I had bought very cheaply, were uncomfortably small. If a $75,000 property made 10 percent a year in net operating income of which $5,000 went to pay the mortgage, I was left with about $2,500 in profit. That barely covered the maintenance issues that inevitably cropped up. If somebody's toilet broke, I'd be scrambling for the funds to cover the plumber. My current situation was hairy, like most of New York's housing stock, which was in mass abandonment or extremely poor condition. To put it mildly, business looked bleak.

When you are out doing business on your own, the fears are endless. In the case of real estate, the anxiety starts with closing on the property. *Will I have enough money for the transaction? Will the bank or my investors come through the way they promised?* And making the acquisition is just the beginning. The next round of worries comes with the business plan. Whether it is the amount of rent charged, improving the occupancy of the building, or bringing down operation costs, you are constantly putting your judgment up against the marketplace. The ability to predict outcomes is what defines a successful track record. An entrepreneur in charge of reaching these goals is constantly haunted by concerns, many of which are totally unpredictable. Who could have predicted that in the 1970s, oil would go up fivefold and begin absorbing

100 percent of real estate profits—or more? It is a constant battle to produce business plans optimistic enough to produce a reasonably high result but conservative enough to absorb the inevitable curveballs—like the skyrocketing price of oil.

Tough economic times often put character to the test. The stress of making a business work during a downturn can lead people to rationalize making immoral or illegal decisions. During this period of real estate in New York, the temptation of landlords to cut corners that broke the law or came very close to it was great. Many pretended the law on determining decontrolled fair market rent value hadn't changed or ignored it outright—and they got away with it because their tenants weren't sophisticated enough to know any better. I remember when I brought the topic up with Milton, saying that a lot of owners were taking a very liberal approach to the city's new interpretation of the law.

"Then they don't have real estate," he answered swiftly and sternly. His response puzzled me. Another of Milton's cryptic parables.

"Whether you cut off the heat in the dead of winter or you create a legal quagmire by not following the intent of the law," Milton said, "by doing that, in effect, you no longer have legitimate property. That kind of thing always catches up to people. You'll see."

Of course, Milton wasn't just ethical but also right. Decades later, there was a stark example of this that involved a developer who took advantage of the interim loft status for people who had moved into commercial lofts that weren't originally zoned as residential to turn them into legal dwellings. The city would issue an interim multiple-dwelling status and then after the building was brought into compliance, it would grant legal residential status. Well, this developer, enticed by the money to be made on apartments in previously industrial areas like Williamsburg, converted buildings that weren't zoned residential into living lofts, rented them up, and *then* went to the city to request this interim status. In his case, there was no work to be done to bring it up to code because rather than a bunch of people homesteading in previously industrial lofts, he had turned it into a profession. Eventually, the city caught up with the developer's methodology and took his property away from him.

Milton taught me early on that you might get away with bending the rules for a little while, but eventually you destroy what you have. I certainly didn't want to break the law in order to keep my real estate investments afloat during a trying time. I hadn't become rich to become a crook.

Ironically, I hadn't come too far from my father's example. Without any cash or credit, I was always scraping it together. Getting a mortgage was one thing (though not easy, doable—sometimes), but if I needed money for working capital, like paying a plumber, sometimes I found myself approaching friends and family with my cap in hand—just like I'd cringed watching my dad do.

In 1978, I caught a small break when banks invented personal checking accounts with overdraft privileges, which were tantamount to small, personal lines of credit. This couldn't have come at a better time for me, and I didn't hesitate to take full advantage of the opportunity. All you have to combat the endless and inescapable fears of entrepreneurship is your judgment and creativity in finding alternative solutions when Plan A doesn't succeed. Adaptation and resilience must be as constant as the anxiety. With this in mind, I walked into six different banks on the very same day and filled out an application for a personal checking account at each. I didn't want any lag time during which the banks might communicate with each other and figure out my total potential credit exposure.

It worked, and they all approved my applications. One bank gave me a credit line of $7,500, another $5,000, a third $10,000. So, suddenly, I had about $40,000 in credit, which meant I could finally pay my bills when they were due. In some ways, it was just a more official version of the way my father ran the agency, borrowing from Peter to pay Paul and keeping his liabilities from sinking the entire business. In one of my father's greatest gifts to me, I learned from him the important skill of managing debt, which is fundamentally what the real estate business is all about. The credit lines were good, but they only bought me a little bit of breathing room. I needed a long-term strategy.

Milton's wife, Sandra, popped her head into the den where Milton, Abbott, Art, and I were sitting to ask if we needed anything. We all shook our heads. After the lavish spread of smoked fish, bagels, blintzes, cakes, and more that she had put out for the lunch in honor of the Jewish center where Milton taught ethics to the youth group, I couldn't imagine ever eating again. Before she closed the door, Abbott quickly complimented the color of her freshly painted walls, which I hadn't even noticed. Sandra, an assiduous home decorator, beamed. Abbott was always great with women.

"I've become involved in something that might be interesting to you," Abbott said after Sandra exited. "Co-oping."

I didn't know anything about the process of converting existing rental buildings into cooperative housing owned by the tenants. The first co-op in the United States, the Randolph on West 18th Street, was built in 1876 and followed by several other "home clubs," as they were known, that gave wealthy people the benefits of home ownership without all the responsibilities. Through its history, however, the city's private cooperatives were mostly defined by exclusivity and luxury. They were located in good neighborhoods and filled with the "right" kind of residents. I wasn't sure how I fit into the picture since I didn't own anything remotely like that.

"I just finished the legal work for a guy co-oping a building on Fifth Avenue," he continued. "What you do is something called a non-eviction plan where people can either choose to buy their apartments or stay renting in whatever deal they already have. Whenever a rental becomes available, you renovate and sell it for quite a nice profit. You only need 15 percent to buy in order to convert a building from rental to co-op. If you offer a nice discount on the price of the apartments, you'll get your 15 percent easily. Well, maybe, not *easily*."

Milton and I smiled; nothing in real estate was easy.

I did the math. Most rental buildings by this point offered at best a 4 percent profit. By co-oping, I would be dealing with tens of thousands of dollars in sales rather than hundred-dollar rents. I imagined the scenario of tenants trading in low rents for discounted apartments: You offer a one-bedroom, worth $50,000, to a tenant for 40 percent less than market value, so that if he wanted to sell it the very next day, it would put $20,000 in his pocket. For most of the people in my buildings, that was more money than they'd ever seen or might ever see. But would they go for it? Would they even be able to go for it? I owned tenements in the kind of neighborhoods most people who owned co-ops wouldn't dare venture into after dark. Co-oping one of my buildings would be nothing short of revolutionary. I started to get interested.

"Why don't we co-op one of the buildings that we have in the West Village?" Abbott said. "I can do the legal work."

Sinking back into one of Sandra's tasteful velvet couches, I eyed Abbott with some skepticism. Was this plan born out of his interest in maximizing the long-term value of our real estate portfolio or rather his constant need for money? With his expenses exceeding his income, Abbott was always broke. Part of that was based in tragedy: His wife, Priscilla, had suffered a severe stroke in midlife that required her to live in a costly institution. But Abbott also loved the finer things in life—art, restaurants, opera—and was so anxious to get money that he'd take 10 percent less for his legal fees if he could be paid immediately. To him, a lower cash price was always worth more than the wait. Still, he'd been right about jump-starting the failed negotiations with Arthur Jacobs by offering another $50,000, which I had also doubted. One thing I was sure about: The rental approach to real estate was a slow uphill battle even in the best of circumstances. Perhaps co-oping would work.

"All right," I said. "Let's try it."

We chose 21-23 Bethune Street, a small building we'd bought from Jacobs, and put in a co-op plan. True to his word, Abbott handled all the legal paperwork necessary to co-op the walk-up situated on a pretty brownstone block between Greenwich and Washington Streets in the heart of the West Village. I didn't know what to make of the very controlled industry governed by the attorney general, so all there was for me to do after we submitted the plan to the state and the tenants was wait. And wait.

For ninety days, the period during which the tenants had the right to buy their apartments at a discount, there was nothing to do because no one was buying. Nobody was even willing to talk. Radio silence was all we received from the residents.

Then on the ninety-first day, we heard word in the form of a five-page letter filled with vitriol aimed at us although addressed to the attorney general. The copy sent to my office called the plan fraudulent and an outrage. The four-story red-brick row house built in 1937 was not only falling apart under our watch, the letter charged, our plan didn't disclose any of the conditions. Most egregious, however, was that the plan didn't discuss the impact that Westway would have on the buildings.

What did Westway, a $2.1 billion proposal to put the West Side Highway below 40th Street underground and build a park above, have to do with our co-op? The highway, like so many other parts of New York, was falling apart (a section of it near Gansevoort Street actually collapsed). In 1969, city planners came up with the idea to bury it, which became a cause célèbre with those fervently for and against it (during the sixteen years the plan languished on community boards, the *New York Times* printed over 1,000 articles on the subject). Passions on Westway ran high, but the actual highway ran two blocks away from Bethune Street—and so whatever the future of the plan, the effect on the building would be zero.

The legal standard for a co-op's offering book is that it must disclose anything a buyer needs to know in order to make an informed decision about whether to buy the apartment or not. Owners have to describe such things as the physical condition of the property through an engineering report, the rights of those who wish to stay renters, and the organization of the boards that will run the co-op. But the standard of what an informed buyer needs to know, of course, is very flexible. In the opinion of the tenants of 21-23 Bethune, that included Westway. What was next? A fiscal analysis of the city? Odds on who was going to win the next election? It could have gone on and on forever.

I knew from then, there was no point in trying to negotiate further. But just in case I didn't get the point, the author of the letter didn't leave any wiggle room for interpretation. He made sure the intentions of the residents were 100 percent clear.

"We have absolutely no interest in buying apartments from the Sponsor," the letter stated.

What had seemed like a miracle solution—to sell these apartments as a way to make them a viable investment—had proved too good to be true. It was one thing to form co-ops on Park Avenue and quite another in the Village. The naysayers had been right—it just couldn't work in this kind of building. I plunged to the low point of entrepreneurship, when you face the prospect of returning to the well for inspiration even though you are in a state of complete discouragement.

"This thing is dead," I said to Abbott over the phone right after reading the letter.

"Come on, Francis. Don't give up so easily," he said, laughing. "We're just getting started."

Abbott was not the kind of person to quit on anything: New York real estate, lost souls, and even the world peace he began working for as a kid and continued throughout his life and long after it had ceased to be a chic goal.

The tenants stayed true to their letter, and not one bought an apartment. But Abbott was right as well. Not too long after the letter, one tenant moved out, which gave us the right to sell his apartment. I found a buyer easily enough. When another apartment upstairs became available, we sold that as well. The two apartments represented more than 15 percent of the building, enough for us legally to close the plan. Under the non-eviction plan, all the renters had the right to stay in their apartments at the rents they were paying, but only six months after getting shut down by them, the building on Bethune was an operating co-op.

As quickly as it arose, my disillusionment vanished. When a business plan works, I not only acknowledge it but embrace it. Feeling that we were on to something, I was excited to push the concept by applying it on a much wider basis. There was no time to sit back and enjoy the success of Bethune; I wanted to scale it up.

And just like that, we were off and running in the co-op business. Right after Bethune, I got a great deal on three newly renovated brownstones. The rents for 141, 143, and 145 West 85th Street weren't high enough to make sense as rental properties, so I converted them to co-ops right away. The process proved that it worked in Upper West Side brownstones as well as West Village tenements.

Despite the characteristics that made each building unique, they all shared a similar path to becoming co-ops. Generally I sold half of the apartments to existing tenants eager to buy them at the "insider's" discount for the possibility of serious profit. The other half either didn't have the money for a down payment or the increased monthly outlay for the mortgage. No matter how good a deal was, it was no good to someone who had been paying $100 in rent for the last thirty years and couldn't afford anything more. The way the economics worked: If half the tenants bought apartments that provided enough money for me to pay for 100 percent of the building, then, slowly, over many years, as the renters moved out or died, I could sell their apartments to make good money, possibly *very* good money.

But before any of that happened, I first had to get my co-op plan approved by the tenants, and that was never easy. In managing all the different interests of a building's population, I always had to bleed before they were satisfied. It wasn't until they saw blood, or what they thought was blood, that they were ready to make a deal. 333 Central

Park West was a classic scenario. I had a very long and difficult negotiation with the tenants of the elegant twelve-story corner building
where I knew a couple of the people who lived there—including a
*New Yorker* editor and Warner Books publisher Larry Kirshbaum.
Caught between their leftist backgrounds and the possibility for enormous profits, they negotiated until the last hour of the last day before
our deadline to declare the co-op plan effective to the attorney general's office. They held out until midnight when capitalism finally won
out; 60 percent of the tenants bought their apartments, many of whom
made millions off them.

The hardest people to negotiate with are those who don't know what
they're entitled to. That's because they often expect too much. This was
all very new. Even for those savvy about co-ops, what I was doing was
totally unheard of. Earlier in the seventies, there had been a wave of
co-oping prewar elevator, doorman buildings, but no one had co-oped
walk-ups, tenements, and other properties in transitional locations. For
me, an entrepreneur, discovering this wide-open market was like striking oil. Just like when I figured out that I could make money by turning
big offices into smaller ones, co-oping lesser buildings was a wide-open
field that I had practically all to myself.

Indeed, lots of folks thought what I was doing was insane. While
having a drink with Laurie Colwin—the writer who'd charmed Leo
and my father when she worked at the agency years before—she said,
"You'll never believe what happened."

"You know, I live in the smallest apartment in the world," she
explained. "Two hundred square feet in this dilapidated building in the
West Village. And guess what? Some lunatic who bought my building
is co-oping it. How can you co-op a postage-stamp dump? How is that
possible?"

"Where do you live?" I asked.

"34-36 Bethune Street."

"I've got to be honest with you, Laurie, that weirdo is me."

I might have been a weirdo, but it wasn't because of my real estate decisions. I knew something that Laurie and the market had not yet fully embraced—which was that one could basically convert any Manhattan building, regardless of its character. After reaching that judgment, I also figured out that with my co-op formula I could pay a higher price for buildings than most people looking at them as rental properties (if anyone wanted them at all). At the time, buildings generally sold for five to seven times gross rents. With my strategy, I could afford to pay nine or ten times that. There weren't that many buyers for New York City real estate to start with, but at that point I would have my pick of almost any building that came on the market.

As always, my problem was cash: I didn't have enough of it to buy all the buildings I wanted. But I had never let that stop me before. There was no way I was going to let it now that something so potentially big was ripe for the taking. My father, who always bragged about how good I was with numbers, would have liked the creative solution I came up with.

Typically when buying buildings, I did it like anyone else, taking out a mortgage with a down payment. Then after a couple of years to sell the apartments, I'd get the money back to pay off the mortgage. When I saw this opportunity unfolding, however, I didn't even have enough money for the down payments. So I approached owners with an unorthodox deal that was hard to refuse: I offered upward of 50 percent more than they could sell their building for to a normal buyer, but they had to wait two years to get the money while I co-oped and made the money back. For a million-dollar apartment house, I agreed to pay a million and a half, with a $100,000 deposit, with the understanding that we wouldn't close for two years until the tenants had closed on their apartments and I had recouped the remaining $1,400,000. The theory (later known as "a stretch deal") was simple: You can name the price if I can name the terms. If a price is exaggerated, but I can create a deal structure that permits me to delay compensation or make it conditional to profitability, then I will pay it.

I put a big ad in the *New York Times*—which had worked so reliably in finding tenants for my small office rentals—saying that I would pay these high prices and was deluged almost immediately with responses.

There were a lot of deals to be had, but that didn't mean they were easy to close. Although, to me, the math was simple and stable, this was cutting-edge stuff, legally speaking. And folks in real estate, especially those parting with their properties, tend to be pretty conservative. My offer, too tempting to ignore, made some sellers very, very nervous.

One of my most anxious was a real estate investor named Joe Saleh, who in addition to producing films also converted the underground powerhouse for Manhattan's short-lived cable car system into the Angelika Film Center. Born in Iran, Joe had a Middle Eastern trading mentality that made the rich price I was offering for 35 West 90th Street, a beautiful art deco doorman building, irresistible. He liked the money but was concerned about the deal.

Joe had only agreed to it after getting counsel from the legendary real estate lawyer Jack Weprin, a consummate dealmaker whom some called "God" because everyone looked to him for advice. Jack arrived at his office every day by 7:30 AM to hold what he called his "psychiatric hour," where he slipped off his shoes (never to be replaced for the rest of the day) and took calls from clients before the official day started.

In Jack's Times Square office, it seemed as though Joe needed a psychiatric hour or two. Jack knew me and was comfortable with the unusual nature of the contract. But Joe couldn't sit still while the lawyers hashed out all the different permutations of what would happen if anything went wrong. Because there was no precedent, the negotiations went on and on. Meanwhile, Joe kept pacing around the office, getting more and more agitated. Everyone's patience was wearing thin as normally happens during marathon closings, but Joe's manic movement and nervous interjections began to migrate from annoying to deal breaking.

"What do you mean, 'if the offering book is not comprehensive'? What must it be?" Joe asked.

"Is it assured that the tenants will agree to this co-op?"

"How many of these have you done again?"

Hy Schermer, the independent broker who had sold me the building, recognized that Joe was getting cold feet and that if he didn't calm him down, the deal would fall through. Hy was always fast on the uptake. His career in real estate started while he was working as a laborer on a building, and a man passing by asked if it was for sale. Hy said, "I'll find out," and that became his first brokered deal. He also happened to be a semiprofessional poker player, which came in handy during the tense closing. Hy, who knew that Joe enjoyed the game, announced that we were going to play poker in the other room while the lawyers worked on the papers. Joe acquiesced, and so for the next four hours, while the lawyers finished the contract, I lost a couple grand to Joe. But that was a cheap price to pay in the business of buying 101 apartments just steps from Central Park.

I was excited to be breaking ground in the often wonderfully and always aggravatingly complicated landscape of New York real estate with something lucrative not only for investors like me but also the city's residents. Co-oping was both a financially viable and politically elegant solution to the problem of fixing the wreckage of rent regulation, and I would devise any scheme necessary to keep going. But finding the money to continue converting buildings posed an endless challenge. I often wondered what I could do if I had limitless funds.

# Chapter 7

# BANKS IN THE GO-GO EIGHTIES AND THE GROWTH OF A REAL ESTATE EMPIRE

• • • •

You know who has all the money?" Milton asked apropos of nothing.
"Who?" I asked.

"The banks."

We were in the car driving out to the country, and Milton had the faraway look of a philosopher. Although he often quoted Leviticus, Milton was also a pragmatist. If he was breaking the silence of our drive with such an obvious thought, there had to be a good reason.

"Banks are beached whales," he continued. "They have all the money, but they can't do anything with it. They have to find competent people to give it to. That's where you've got to go if you need money."

Milton's Zenlike statement turned out to be, ultimately, true. That *is* where the money comes from. But at the start of the 1980s, when bank loans for New York real estate were hard to come by, the suggestion was somewhat of a radical one. Learning to relate to banks and getting them to know me was a novel strategy.

I began my quest to follow Milton's advice in 1980 with a bank only two blocks away from my father's old office. I asked the Irving Trust Company on 57th and Madison for a $50,000 credit line, and to my amazement, they said yes. Two short years later, the money couldn't keep up with my growing real estate company. But Irving Trust wasn't comfortable increasing my credit line, so I turned to M&T, a relatively obscure bank up at 63rd and Madison, which gave me the princely sum of $200,000. Milton had proven his sagacity again; the banks did have a lot of money and, unlike just a few years earlier, were more willing to lend it to me.

Not long after M&T opened up its generous line of credit, representatives from Chemical came to my office, upon Phil Rudd's recommendation, in order to offer me money from their bank.

"How much would you like?" one banker asked.

"Well, how about a million?" I answered. It was a ludicrously high number, but with unsecured credit lines from two other banks, I didn't have anything to lose.

"No problem."

*No problem?* Well, if it was really "no problem," as these bankers offered, I also needed it fast, since I was in the middle of a deal and could use the money for a contract deposit.

"How long will it take you to approve it?"

"You got it."

"What do you mean I have it? You just walked into the office."

"It's within our authority; we're approving it."

"What if I want to draw on it tomorrow?"

"Just sign a note and we'll give you the money."

"Wow."

I was blown away by the sudden ease of it all. This, however, was just the start. A young officer soon suggested she organize a credit facility that put all my buildings together and let me borrow as much money as I needed as long as the loan-to-value ratio of all the buildings in the facility were within certain limits. By now I had twenty different co-op buildings, worth a lot more than when they were initially purchased, for which Chemical would give me credit.

The bottom line: A twenty-four-year-old officer put through a $50 million credit line for me. I now had 100 percent of the purchase price and fixed costs of any building that I wanted to buy.

The closing dinner to celebrate my new deal with Chemical was fittingly held at La Côte Basque. We celebrated long into the night and had our fill of French food and wine among the glittery society set. A year or so later, Chemical raised my line to $100 million.

And just like that my days of scraping together the funds to buy buildings were gone. Suddenly, the broke seventies were over and the world was rich. In 1978, I had $35,000 from seven different banks. Less than five years later, I had $100 million from one.

I was on high octane, closing on new properties all the time (indeed, while waiting for our table at La Côte Basque, my lawyer arrived at the bar so I could sign the contract on a Central Park West building). Nothing seemed beyond my grasp—not even the Crystal Building at 47 West Street. The property, built in 1912 and named after the original family that owned it, was actually three buildings on one tax lot: a twelve-story tower capped by a green mansard roof and internally connected to the seven-story structure at 74 Washington Street, as well as a three-story building at 50 West Street. I had no idea what I would ultimately do with the property that sat close to the Brooklyn Battery Tunnel, but at 90 percent occupancy it was profitable, so I put in an offer of $2 million. If it went through, this would be the single biggest deal of my career. Unfortunately, I learned the owner had agreed to sell it to somebody else for the same amount as my offer. When I relayed the disappointing news to Milton, he offered to get Sarah Korein, a legendary figure in New York real estate, to put in a word for me with the owner, whom she knew.

Although not well known outside real estate circles, Sarah had as impressive a roster of properties as any of her contemporaries who regularly made newspaper headlines. Among her holdings were One Penn Plaza, which was the fifth-largest office building in the city at the time; the modernist landmark the Lever House; downtown's first big tower at 120 Broadway; and the former Delmonico Hotel where Bob Dylan "turned on" the Beatles to marijuana and which Donald Trump bought for $115 million in 2002. Even more impressive than her portfolio was the fact that she was 100 percent self-made. The German native raised in Palestine started her empire by buying a six-story apartment house for her family members to live in East Flatbush, Brooklyn.

Milton was one of Sarah's most trusted confidants. (Their relationship was so close that Sarah offered him and his wife an apartment in one of the two Central Park South apartment towers overlooking Columbus Circle that she owned and lived in, which he accepted.) Because Milton asked, she called the owner of the Crystal Building—at five o'clock the following morning. That direct style, bordering on abusive, was typical of the ruthless dealmaker disguised as a little Jewish grandmother. "You will sell the building to Greenburger," she said over the phone to the owner, "or I will take all of my business away from you."

This was no idle threat; Crystal and his partner managed many of Sarah's buildings. The owner agreed to walk away from the original buyer if he asked for any changes during the contract negotiations— and it's unheard of not to negotiate a contract—and sell it to me, but on the condition I get him a check that day and arrive at his office to sign the contract, no questions asked, as soon as he telephoned to say that the other buyer was out. I was grateful for Sarah's intervention and agreed to all terms.

When I got to the office that afternoon, however, I quickly realized that her help came with a price.

"You! Sit down," Sarah, a stout woman pushing eighty and surrounded by a large entourage of men in suits, barked at me in the German accent she'd never lost.

She had arrived an hour earlier than me to take control of "my" deal and negotiate the contract. The complete violation of her agreement with the owner was a classic Sarah Korein double cross. After he blew off the other buyer, she started renegotiating. And once she started in, there were a hundred points—all totally against his interests.

The lawyers continued to grind away until eleven o'clock at night when I decided I'd had enough.

"Sarah, I'm going home," I said.

"We'll be partners," she announced to me.

"I'm not sure about that. Can I have my contract and check back?" I said, pointing to the two items still lying on the table. "I'm leaving now."

"No. I'm not giving them to you."

"Fine, Sarah. You keep it."

In the morning, I got a call from my lawyer, whom Sarah had asked to meet at noon in the restaurant at the base of her building. Neither of us knew what to expect, since with Sarah anything was possible. Later, at the Italian eatery where she lunched every day, Sarah took out the contract for the Crystal Building that had been made out to her and signed it over to me.

"Tell Greenburger," she said to my lawyer, "it was only a joke."

The Crystal property was a serious step forward in my career, but fundamentally I wanted to own it because it was a good deal. No matter how much money was at my disposal, finding value, particularly value overlooked by others, would always form the core of my interest.

Value—something priced moderately with a good, definable reason why it will go up—can take many different forms. It can be a building whose purchase price is inexpensive compared to its replacement costs. (In the real estate climate of the post-2008 recession, I purchased a building in Cherry Hill outside Philadelphia that was almost empty in a very soft market. But at a price of $30 a foot for something that would cost $200 a foot to build new, the property was what we call "cheap bricks," and I knew we could quickly fill it up with tenants for a lower price than the neighbors, which is exactly what happened.)

Another opportunity for value is to identify buildings that have extraordinary potential because of the changing nature of their location. (Decades later, not long before the recession of 2008, I bought a retail condo property in London Terrace, a complex built in the thirties, on the corner of 23rd and Tenth Avenue. Although a vibrant and chic art district had sprung up in that area, 23rd Street, oddly enough, had not come up. The district ran from 20th to 23rd Street and then jumped to 24th Street, where it started again. My rationale for going after the piece of retail property was that even if 23rd was a little gritty, how could it not become valuable considering its surroundings? With all those fancy gallerias going back and forth, it was only a matter of time before that corner became prime real estate. Ultimately, the whole area matured, including this strategic corner, occupied by Chase Manhattan Bank. Over the course of ten years, the rent on the property we bought for $2 million went up 500 percent. We put a $6 million mortgage on the original purchase at a very low interest rate, so not only did we put $4 million in our pocket, but for $180,000 a year in interest we make $900,000 in rent. That is the real estate market when it gets really, really good.)

Back in the early eighties, to me there was no bigger gem hiding in plain sight than Clinton Hill Apartments. I came upon the twelve-building complex of 1,200 rental units that towered over the rest of the low-lying, historic neighborhood of Clinton Hill, Brooklyn, while I was still in the process of beefing up my credit lines. The property, which because of rent control didn't earn enough to pay the mortgage, let alone the maintenance, had all the makings of a perfect co-op conversion, except for one thing: The tenants were primarily African American.

Clinton Hill Apartments

Designed by Wallace K. Harrison (the architect who also created
Rockefeller Center, Radio City Music Hall, Lincoln Center, and the
United Nations), the apartments were built between 1941 and 1943
as housing for workers at the nearby Brooklyn Navy Yard. Reflecting
many neighborhoods throughout the city, the complex shifted dramatically from white to black during the fifties. By the time Secretary of
Defense Robert McNamara closed the Navy Yard in 1966 and sent
9,000 of its workers packing, the apartments were predominantly occupied by African Americans. Clinton Avenue, filled with magnificent but
crumbling mansions built in the nineteenth century when the area was
home to the families of industrial titans such as the Pratts and Pfizers,
was particularly feared. The nearby commercial strip, Myrtle Avenue,
gained the moniker of Murder Avenue.

For Sydney Levy, head of a syndicate of 800 investors who owned the property, the complex was nothing but a nightmare. He had bought it in the early fifties when it was still profitable, but because of the rent-control laws the economics of the complex had completely changed. While the property generated only $40,000 a year in cash flow before debt service, the interest payments on its mortgage alone came to $350,000 a year. Levy's biggest fear was that he would die and his wife would be left to deal with the mess. When I proposed a two-year option during which I'd try to co-op the complex, he thought I was nuts *and* said yes. The conventional wisdom at the time was that black people wouldn't buy apartments. But I never found conventional wisdom a very useful tool. Did African Americans not want to buy apartments, or had no one given middle-class black people the same chance to invest in their homes as afforded their white counterparts? Walking around Clinton Hill, I found enough upwardly mobile families to give the neighborhood my own moniker: the Black Forest Hills. It wasn't just a sales pitch—I really saw a parallel between the Brooklyn community and the upwardly mobile Jewish one in Queens where I had grown up.

In Clinton Hill, I identified the need for working- and middle-class families in New York City to own their own apartments, which was not that common in those days. If I could offer the apartments inexpensively enough to the middle-income families that lived there, I was sure they would prefer to own their own homes. In a sense, I would be transferring the benefits of my value-hunting skills to the complex's tenants if I bought Clinton Hill at a cheap price, enabling me to resell it at an inexpensive price, which would motivate middle-class families to buy in. The political forces in the community recognized that the complex couldn't survive under the limited rents that the rent-control laws allowed but didn't have the will to change the laws. The result was that the complex was deteriorating, and because it was such a large presence in the community, the neighborhood was deteriorating with it.

This economic transaction would bring new monies into a very important but bankrupt housing complex and influence the future of the whole area. Both as a businessperson and as someone with a desire to serve my community of New York City, it was truly a win-win.

Still, I was anxious the night we introduced the plan to the tenants. With the project's politically sensitive mix of race and housing, I was concerned about any misperception that this was an eviction plan. (New York state law allowed two different kinds of co-op conversion plans: one that required all residents to buy or lease their apartments or be evicted, and a non-eviction plan, where tenants could either buy or stay indefinitely as renters.) To make sure everyone understood what was happening, we decided to hold two meetings so that neither became overwhelmingly big. Splitting the groups along the two campuses of the complex, we invited the south campus bounded by Lafayette, Green, Clinton, and Waverly Avenues to the first meeting. The north campus would be on another night.

Walking to the front of the nearby Masonic Temple's large auditorium where we held the meeting, I was not only keenly aware of my whiteness but also surprised by the turnout. We expected a turnout of maybe 100 people, but more like 500 showed up. However, I had a secret weapon: Abbott. One of W. E. B. Du Bois's close supporters, Abbott Simon brought some influential African American figures to lend credibility through their presence. After laying out the facts, I braced myself as we opened the meeting up to the audience.

The first question was: "Well, if we want to sell our apartments, do we have to share that money with anybody?"

Tenants were familiar with city-sponsored co-ops for low-income residents, who could not keep the profits if they sold their apartments.

"No. There's nothing like that."

The second question was: "What are we going to do about them?"

"Who is *them*?"

"The people that live at the northern end of the complex."

I had worried that the tenants might be intimidated by or worried about eviction, and it was just the opposite. There was a perception in the southern end of the complex that the people who lived in the northern end were made up of a lot of "troublemakers," and they were disappointed my plan didn't include a way to get rid of *them*. As far as I could tell, the residents of the Clinton Hill co-ops were no different than most middle-class white tenants.

There was very good demand for the vacant apartments we started selling to gather our necessary 15 percent of apartments for a co-op plan to become effective under New York state law. That made me hopeful as we began the search for a bank to put a new mortgage on the buildings. First, I approached Equitable, which held the existing loan, about assuming it. They not only refused but wanted to get out of the loan so badly they were willing to take 60 cents on the dollar for the $6.5 million loan. If we paid them off, we could have an instant savings of more than $2.5 million. With 1,200 apartments, the bargain-basement mortgage per unit plummeted even further.

Over the next couple of months, with demand and value driving me, I approached scores of banks, but not one would touch the deal with a ten-foot pole. I couldn't even get bankers to take a car out to Clinton Hill to look at it.

I was climbing the walls. Obsessed. Surely someone out there would appreciate the good deal I had created. I left no stone unturned in the hunt. If there was an advertisement in the paper for a bank giving out toasters, I sent a letter to it. Banks in Nevada. Banks in Wyoming. Banks wherever. But I couldn't find anybody.

I hadn't yet contemplated complete defeat but was nearing that point when out of the blue Len Druger, head of credit policy for Citibank, rang me up. "If you want to try to convince me to make this loan," he said, "come to my office at three o'clock tomorrow." I was beyond confused—Citibank had already passed on the loan for Clinton Hill—but I said I'd be there.

In his office, Len's only question was whether the project had the support of the Brooklyn political establishment. (What I found out later was that a Queens congressman and leading liberal Democrat named Benjamin Rosenthal had publicly criticized Citibank for redlining black neighborhoods. So Len had to come up with something to demonstrate that they weren't. The Clinton Hill co-ops were the perfect opportunity.) Because of the sensitivity of the project, I had sought out many of Brooklyn's leaders to tell them about my plan and ask for their support. They all felt the conversion would stabilize the neighborhood, and I was able to give Len the assurance he wanted.

"I'll call you in the morning," he said.

I got my financing. Citibank provided $6 million, which was enough to pay off Equitable, get a new mortgage, and provide $500,000 to $1 million for improvements to the buildings. We put in $1.5 million in equity capital and also got state money so that we could offer 90 percent buyer financing for first-time homebuyers. Still, there were many who wanted to buy but couldn't afford the inside price. So we came up with an innovative solution: an alternative purchase plan where tenants would buy at a price reduced from the insider price, and when they wanted to sell their apartment, we would be given the first option to buy it back according to a predetermined price schedule that still afforded them a nice profit.

Citibank was trying to make itself look good by financing the conversion, but I wound up getting a lot of the good press. AFFORDABLE CO-OPS: AN EXPANDING MARKET read the headline of a New York Times article from 1984, which featured the project and quoted me as saying, "In 1983, probably half our apartments sold to people with incomes in the $25,000 to $30,000 range."

When the plan was declared effective in 1984, there were 300 closings, including many long-term tenants, who paid about $4,000 to $5,000 a room. Two years later, one-bedroom vacancies sold for $55,000 to $60,000. Clinton Hill, considered an important deal in the co-op movement for its effect on reclaiming distressed neighborhoods and the revival of historic Clinton Hill, was an unmitigated success.

This was just one of our many successes. At the start of the decade, I owned about a dozen buildings and had two employees. By 1984, my real estate company, Time Equities, Inc. (TEI), had grown to sixty employees, whom I consolidated from offices all over the city into one at 55 Fifth Avenue. At first we took one floor, but we expanded in relatively short order to two and then three floors, so that by the eighties we had close to 60,000 square feet.

The growth during the go-go eighties was out of control. At its height, I was buying a building every two or three weeks with 250 employees converting thousands of units from rentals to co-ops or condos and managing as many as a hundred buildings. I had sales, marketing, construction, and design departments, as well as legal, rent, administration, accounts, and acquisition departments. Having all those in-house resources, unusual for a real estate company, let me control my own destiny as I established priorities for the companies. I didn't want to go outside to professionals who might have different priorities, different agendas, and also, frankly, in some cases, extraordinarily high fees.

I wasn't intimidated by growth and responsibility. On the contrary, I thrived on it. Though I recognized the risks associated with hyperexpansion, particularly in a business as labor intensive and time consuming as co-op conversions, I couldn't resist the lure of a loudly humming company. The only problem was that while Time Equities was mushrooming into a full-blown corporation, I had basically no corporate experience. I barely knew the titles and job descriptions of the positions you were supposed to have at a company the size mine had grown into.

When Art Travis found out I had twenty-five people reporting to me, he declared me insane. "Management theory says you should have eight, max," he said. "You need a COO."

"What's that?" I asked.

"Someone who is going to do half of what you do."

I wasn't sure if the people I had working for me—folks with strong personalities who brought unique and invaluable contributions, such as Roberta Axelrod, who was head of our co-op and condo conversion department; Stuart Bruck, who led the mortgage finance group; Sam Gordon, who ran our design and construction department; Scott Klatsky, retail leasing; Phil Brody, my general counsel; and Dottie Biondo, my controller—would agree to report to someone else.

"If you get the right person, they'll be happy to report to him," my investor assured me.

Despite my desire to have a range of in-house experts, I was never opposed to outside opinions and readily took up his advice. In my search for a chief operating officer, I went the recommended route and enlisted headhunters, who brought in a few "professional" executives. But they just seemed like bozos to me. A good business partner is as special and hard to find as a spouse.

I didn't think I ever got luckier than the day I met Robert Kantor. Both a lawyer and accountant, Bob entered real estate through a college roommate named Bill Becker, who invited Bob to come and work for his father's accounting firm, which he used as a way to attract investors for real estate deals. In the early eighties they were doing some similar things to what I was doing, such as a few co-op conversions, but on a smaller scale. One day, they were due in Lake Placid on business when at the last minute Bill suggested Bob stay back to finish working on some legal matters at the office. The small plane Bill was flying crashed, leaving Bob the task of figuring out what to do with the business and making sure that Bill's wife and three young children were provided for. Bob eventually married Bill's widow, Jane, and raised her three kids, becoming as devoted a father as anybody could ever be. (Eventually, both of Bob and Jane's sons, Bryan and David, came to work at TEI and are now valued colleagues and partners.)

I first encountered Bob when he was selling 221 West 82nd Street. His operating partner on it turned out to be a very difficult man who refused to maintain the building properly. After numerous violations, a judge ordered Bob to sell the building within a forty-eight-hour period or a receiver would be appointed to take it over. Contract negotiations started at noon and went all night. We signed the documents at nine o'clock in the morning, and they were in court an hour later. The hurdles didn't end there. A complicated problem arose after the attorney general's office decided it didn't want the operating partner having interest in a mortgage on the building. That was part of my deal, and without it I wasn't sure I could go ahead with the plan.

I came up with a technical solution around the problem involving a wrap mortgage. If I were the holder of the wrap mortgage, and so responsible for the underlying mortgages, the AG would most likely go for it. When Bob called me to discuss the matter, he suggested the exact same solution. There weren't too many people who could have come up with that idea. Smitten, I wondered about Bob for my COO.

I couldn't ask him whether he wanted a job because I was buying a building from him. So instead, I asked him if he knew anybody who would be suitable for the job. If he wanted to blink, he could, and that was exactly what he did.

When he came into the office to talk it over, there was immediate chemistry, so we cut to the chase.

"I'll take this job on one condition," he said.

"What's that?"

"I don't want to discuss salary. I'll work here for six months, and then we'll discuss salary."

His proposal made me nervous. I didn't want him to come up with some salary I couldn't meet after I had integrated him into the firm and was dependent on him. So I warned, "Don't have unreasonable expectations."

"I assure you, I won't determine the salary. You'll determine the salary. But I want you to see what kind of job I can do before you do that."

Who could argue with that?

I didn't need six months to see Bob's value. A couple of weeks later, I offered him a fair but appropriate salary given his many talents. Because he was a CPA, Bob was able to get a handle on my wildly out-of-control accounting department. As a lawyer, he also took charge of the twenty lawyers in our legal department, which was bigger than a lot of smaller law firms. In his first month, we were in the thick of the Clinton Hill co-op project, making all kinds of necessary improvements to the buildings, including replacing the windows in each of the 1,200 units. In the middle of the construction, my employee in charge of it came to me. "We have a problem," he said. When he'd seen the original plan, the mullions looked narrow to him, so he had made an executive decision to make them a quarter inch wider. Now Landmarks was saying our mullions weren't how they should be, which they weren't, and we were perilously close to missing a three-week deadline for the upgrades.

While witnessing me absorb the million-dollar error and figure out a way to get the correct size mullions installed in time, Bob made his first recommendation to me. "I think you should sell everything and close the business," he said. "This place is crazy."

He wasn't wrong—it was crazy—but we didn't close. Under Bob's supportive and sometimes skeptical guidance, we continued to grow even bigger. Art had been right. Everybody fell in love with Bob and soon preferred to report to him than me. Bob has a remarkable personality in that he's brilliant and modest. Only someone who confidently knows what he brings to the table could offer a deal like the one he did me where I decided how much he was worth *after* he accepted the job.

His unusual combination of humility and self-assurance made for an incredibly complementary relationship between us. I was a successful young person in the high-profile business of New York condo and co-op conversions. Almost every day there was an article in the trades about me or my business. It took an in-check ego like Bob's to be okay with that and push me to be better at what I did. He proved to

Isabelle and I (center) with Jane and Bob Kantor

be an extraordinary leader without ever making me feel like we were in competition.

Hiring management—or in my case a COO—is a transition any growing company has to face, and those that don't face it risk future growth. My advice to those with expanding businesses is that they must first make a decision about how they want to allocate their time and structure their business so that they have a balance that reflects that. Managing people is a major responsibility and takes a major amount of time. What I noticed as Time Equities ballooned but before Bob came on was that my role had shifted from a doer to a teacher. I was uncomfortable in the shift because I like doing. I love to conceive of projects, convince banks to invest, be part of the marketing strategy, and so on. While I enjoy helping my employees establish priorities, make decisions, and manage their workflow, I only want to do that about 50 percent of the time. Bringing in a COO allowed me to rebalance my own agenda so I could become a doer again.

Finding Bob was an extraordinary stroke of luck for me, and the timing just as lucky since he arrived on the cusp of my ultimate transaction—the purchase of Tudor City. I had made my fortune in being disciplined in avoiding the trappings of flashy real estate. But the massive complex of thirteen apartment buildings decorated with gargoyles, heraldic arms, and boar's heads that overlooked the United Nations and East River fell into my lap.

Tudor City

My involvement with the property began when another real estate investor, Phil Pilevsky, brought me in as a partner to buy one of the complex's buildings called the Manor. Built in what was then the slaughterhouse district by Fred F. French in the late 1920s and early '30s, the nearly 3,000 apartments in Tudor City gathered around four small parks between First and Second Avenues and 40th and 43rd Streets, and were, according to an original sales brochure, "planned not for millionaires but for people of taste and refinement, people who appreciate the importance of environment."

At the time of our deal to purchase the Manor, Harry Helmsley owned most of Tudor City with his partner Alvin Schwartz. This wasn't my first time dealing with the famed scion of real estate, whose vast holdings included the Empire State Building. Many years earlier, I signed a forty-nine-year lease for 25 West 43rd Street after Harry disagreed with Charlie Benenson, his partner on the office building, over its management. In that deal, as in all deals with Harry, he said no to every point and rarely conceded anything.

No matter how much he played the hard-nosed business type, Harry was a softy compared to his wife, Leona. Much later, after Charlie and I had become very close friends, Charlie invited me to his wedding. (Although he was well into his senior-citizen years, he and his longtime girlfriend decided to tie the knot because they wanted to buy an apartment in an exclusive co-op that frowned upon applications from couples living in sin.) At the wedding at Charlie's Greenwich, Connecticut, home, I was seated next to Harry, who never missed an opportunity to sell something and was in the middle of a pitch on a piece of land in Fort Lee, New Jersey, when suddenly, Leona appeared out of nowhere. Staring down the lady who had been seated on the other side of Harry, Leona asked her, "Who are you?"

"What do you mean?" the woman asked. This wasn't some dance-hall girl; Charlie's friends were a who's who of real estate, finance, and art.

"Why are you sitting there?"

"Because this is my assigned seat."

"No it isn't," Leona said. "Get up."

The woman obeyed. Most people did when it came to either of the Helmsleys' demands. There was one exception, however. John McKean, a resident of the Manor and a major thorn in Helmsley's side, had made it his life's work to stop the building of a high-rise on parkland in the middle of Tudor City. During the seventies and eighties, McKean, a former real estate executive, thwarted Helmsley by filing lawsuits and working with city government. He wouldn't stop at anything, once using a bullhorn to call tenants down to form a human chain against the bulldozers that Helmsley had sent to begin work at the very uncivilized hour of seven o'clock in the morning on Memorial Day of 1980.

When I approached the tenants' committee about our conversion plan, McKean was, of course, the head. Devoted to his mission, McKean stated during the negotiations that his committee wouldn't allow our plan to go through unless he was "guaranteed" that the parks would be protected. We didn't own the parks or anything else other than the Manor in the complex. To attend to McKean's request, we had to approach Helmsley, who responded by offering us the rest of Tudor City. He was sick and tired of its parks—and tenants. If we bought the whole complex, he said, we could do whatever we wanted with the parks.

Helmsley's proposal was a big shock—and involved a huge amount of money. The Manor alone was $12 million; for the rest, Helmsley wanted $150 million. Even with my line of credit, I still didn't have the money for this large a deal. The contract deposit alone was a gigantic sum. So we went back to my original business model where we'd give him the down payment but wouldn't have to deliver the other $130 million for a couple of years, during which we would file the regulatory offering plan with the attorney general's office, get it approved, and negotiate with the tenants. (Incidentally, the way I got the cash for my part of the down payment was by borrowing on the collateral from the office building I had leased from Helmsley and Charlie that had increased in value dramatically in the time I had operated it.)

There were a lot of risks associated with converting Tudor City. Dealing with 2,337 apartments and possibly losing $20 million if it didn't work out was problematic enough. But one of the most complicated issues with Tudor City was that the largest buildings in the complex were predominantly made up of studio apartments—and tiny ones at that. Laurie Colwin had thought I was a nut to co-op her small apartment in the West Village. Would anyone want to buy a 350-square-foot apartment in Midtown that made Laurie's look like a mansion? My prior experiences convinced me that all kinds of people wanted to own all kinds of housing particularly if it was in good condition and in a good location. It was a big gamble: If they didn't sell, I'd lose $10 million and be ruined at the ripe age of thirty-six. But I had broken through the tenement barrier and the African American barrier. Now came the tiny, tiny studio barrier.

The Sunday morning we opened the Tudor City sales office, I came in early and left a red rose on Roberta Axelrod's desk. I was pleased with how she handled everything, including her great job arranging three model apartments. This was more necessary than usual, as some of the spaces were so small (under 300 square feet) that purchasers needed to see how they could be lived in. She installed Dwyer compact metal kitchen units because the units, originally designed for hot plates, were too small for a standard kitchen. And way before it was fashionable and commonplace, she had California Closets show how the storage spaces could best be utilized. She also enlisted Andrew Dolkart—a member of the Landmarks Preservation Commission and now director of Columbia University's historic preservation program—to give free walking tours of Tudor City to prospective buyers.

Still, Roberta (just back from maternity leave after the birth of her son, no less) had her work cut out for her. When I told her we had to sell 300 vacant apartments in one year, she looked at me like I was crazy.

At that time, we estimated it would take seventy shows of an apartment for one purchase.

"We can't get twenty-one thousand people in and out of the sales office," she said.

"Don't worry about it, Roberta," I replied. "I know you'll figure out a way to do it."

And she did. Roberta commandeered a freight elevator and had it fixed up so no one would have ever guessed that it had primarily been used for garbage disposal. She ran it express to the sales office, which was open seven days a week, to get people in and out quickly without disrupting the residents. In the end, we sold over 300 vacant apartments.

At thirty-six years old, I was self-assured and foresaw limitless possibilities, not because I owned one of the biggest apartment complexes in Manhattan or had hundreds of employees, but because of my instincts. They went decidedly against the mainstream, but they had yet to prove me wrong.

## Chapter 8

# THE PAIN OF BLACK MONDAY AND THE JOY OF A BABY BOY

· · · · ·

Iwas never all that comfortable with marriage. I found that the pressure to make a romance legal intensified with women when the relationship began to have problems, and my position was that if the relationship wasn't working, marriage wasn't going to help. Marriage should be a celebration, I reasoned, not a solution.

Karen, a beautiful Australian lawyer, was the first woman who, if not leading me to reconsider my aversion to the formal institution, at least got me thinking about settling into a more stable union that included children.

I noticed her immediately—a red flower in her long, dark hair— when she walked into one of my favorite restaurants, Gotham, in the winter of 1984. She sat down by herself, which was a little unusual on a Saturday night, so I sent her a drink and soon she had joined me and my friends at dinner. As it turned out, Karen had only arrived that very day in New York to start work at a large law firm.

Karen was still on my mind the following morning as I finished up last-minute business before leaving on my Christmas holiday in St. Bart's the next day. Until then I had been eagerly anticipating the trip; but now I wanted to see Karen again. I had an idea that seemed a little forward, even for me, and before I had a chance to contemplate its weirdness, I was calling her.

"Do you want to go away with me to the Caribbean for ten days? I'm leaving tomorrow," I said. The request was a little unusual for a girl I'd only met the night before, but I figured, what the hell? She asked for ten minutes to think about it, which was fair enough, and then called back to say yes.

When we were on the plane to St. Bart's, I said, while really happy she decided to join me, I was sort of surprised since she didn't know the first thing about me. "As it turns out, I'm a good guy," I said. "But God knows, I could have been Dracula or something."

"Most people make decisions by thinking about why not to do something," she said. "They worry about all the bad things that could happen. I try to think about what good could happen."

I was in love.

For several months, we spent most of our time together, and we got as far as discussing the idea of having a child. But one day Karen announced that her previous boyfriend of seven years she had left back home was coming to see her, and she needed a week to decide how she felt about him. At the end of that very long week, she made up her mind that I was the one she wanted. The fairy-tale ending wasn't to be, however, because not long after, Karen hooked up with someone from her firm at the office Christmas party and we broke up.

I had grown very attached to Karen and was heartbroken. I decided the best way to mend was by going out with other women, *a lot* of other women. That spring there was Toni, Blythe, Star, two Judys, and Isabelle, a French architect who had also just landed in New York for work.

Twenty-four, French, blond, and beautiful, Isabelle wasn't the choice of a man ready to settle down. But I had returned to my bachelor habits. I thoroughly enjoyed being with her as she discovered America and relished taking her along on a trip in 1986 to see a Texas developer. With the real estate market having crashed in Texas (a foreshadowing of things to come for the rest of the country), he hoped I could save him, and a visit to Dallas would inspire the rescue. Isabelle and I had only been dating for three weeks, but she was game for the trip although she had no idea what Dallas in the eighties meant.

The developer, a former member of the air force and dead ringer for Bill Clinton, had charmed a lot of people into giving him a lot of money to invest in real estate, and was going bankrupt. But that didn't stop him from picking us up from the airport in a stretch limo with a bottle of champagne cooling in ice. Isabelle, a doctor's daughter from southern France, was incredulous at the display of excess everywhere we went. From the 32-ounce rib-eye that would have fed a dozen French people to the teased hairstyle of the developer's wife to the helicopter he flew us around in to show me his properties, here more was definitely more.

I continued to date other women, but I wanted to protect Isabelle, quietly intense and inward, as she grappled with New York City. I found an apartment for Isabelle to sublet in one of my buildings on 16th and Seventh Avenue. And when I went away for the weekend, I asked a friend of mine, who also lived in the building, to watch out for her.

In retrospect, the friend, Izzy Abrahami, was an odd choice for the role of protector of a very beautiful and very young French woman.

Izzy was expansive, to say the least. An Israeli of eastern European descent, one of his proudest moments was when Golda Meir called him the "shame" of the Jewish people because one of his plays was interpreted as sympathetic to the Arabs. Izzy was a proponent of breaking down barriers, particularly sexual ones.

In this arena, Izzy, who was twenty years older than me, brought a new level of openness to my life. Nothing was out of bounds for him, not group sex or walking through the St. Regis completely naked, which was what he did when I invited him to the high-class hotel for a party I was hosting in honor of Ledig Rowohlt.

Izzy and a novelist friend of mine, Ken Fishman, decided to streak the party. This was the midseventies, when streaking, which is supposed to be done rapidly, had come into vogue. But as luminaries from the literary world sipped cocktails and exchanged snide comments behind each other's backs, Izzy and Ken milled about without a stitch of clothing. The two of them caused quite a stir amid the hotel's formal rooms. "If I looked like you," Philip Roth said to Izzy, "I would pick up the pace."

(Despite Roth's comment, Izzy was a lifelong nudist. One of his favorite vacation spots, even as an old man, was Cap d'Agde, a nudist colony in the south of France. It was the most depressing vista of middle-aged people in gold chains and nothing else walking around a high-rise and shopping center complex off the beach, but Izzy, his wife Jozey, and his filmmaking partner and very good friend Erga thought it was heaven.)

Nothing if not a faithful friend, Izzy loyally followed my directive to look after Isabelle while I was away. He didn't want her to be lonely, so he invited her to his apartment where he introduced her to a friend, who six weeks later proposed to Isabelle, who eventually said yes.

My diversionary tactic of dating lots of women was starting to wear thin and not just because I had lost one of them. After spending a long twenty years as a bachelor doing whatever I pleased, I was ready for a family. Suddenly, I saw all the women in my life in this light, and one stood out clearly from the rest for the warmth I felt would make her an ideal mother.

One of the Judys—Judy Willows—was a special spirit. From the moment I met her at a cocktail party at my neighbor's house in the country, she radiated acceptance and conviviality. She made everybody feel welcome no matter the circumstance. The ultimate host, she whipped up a lunch for twenty on ten minutes' notice. She had a million friends and a big laugh. I wanted to have a child, and I decided I wanted to have one with Judy.

Judy and I hadn't told anyone our plans to marry when I escorted her through the gigantic limestone arches of the municipal building. Judy, her beaming expression mirroring the open disposition that had made me fall in love with her, glowed more than usual as she wrapped the fur coat I had bought her against the last of the chilly morning air.

I had arranged for a judge I knew peripherally to officiate in his chambers, but the somber faces of the people waiting to go through the metal detector to deal with some aspect of the justice system didn't break our euphoric mood. We were starting our married life together! I was a little nonplussed by the security guard's rough manner that seemed out of line in a civil institution, but Judy and I pushed on and into the elevator. We had more important things to concern ourselves with.

Judy and I

Once on the correct floor, we began our search for the judge's chambers. As we walked the hallways, the most bizarre group of characters lined our path. There was a guy with a large scar running down his face, a shaky man with hollowed-out cheeks, and two teens who eyed us like we were prey. I felt Judy—from Winnipeg in the extremely wholesome Canadian prairies, where she had been raised in an evangelical Christian family—stiffen against my arm.

The scene outside the judge's chambers wasn't much better. We picked our way through a line of tough-looking folks until a bailiff stopped us. "No cameras allowed," he barked, pointing at the Canon in the hand of our witness, Roxy, Judy's best friend from Winnipeg.

"Where are we?" Judy looked up at me.

A woman, also wearing a fur but not much else, rolled her eyes under blue-shadowed lids.

"You're in criminal court," the bailiff said.

My getting married surrounded by hardened criminals wasn't a comment on my feelings; I just hadn't realized that our officiant was a criminal judge.

•  •  •  •  •

By the time we were getting married—at criminal court—Judy was pregnant with our son Alexander, whose birth on May 27, 1988, was more transformative than I could have ever imagined.

The arrival of this tiny boy was an unanticipated revelation. I understood life—the meaning of being born, growing up, and dying—in a completely different way. I had amassed all these buildings, but what was I going to do with them when I was gone? The purpose was to pass it on to him. Children are our immortality. My efforts would take on a greater meaning with Alexander as my heir.

So there I was, in love with my son, who grew more magical with every passing month. With a halo of blond curls and a beaming expression, he looked like an angel. Wherever we went, people stopped to remark, "What an extraordinary child."

And we went everywhere with him. Judy, who loved to travel as much as I, was undaunted by taking a toddler to Europe or the Caribbean on a moment's notice. I loved having him, even if some of our hosts didn't always feel the same way. Despite his beatific aspect, he was still a little boy. Around the time Alexander had just learned to walk, we took him to visit Ledig and Jane in Switzerland. Theirs was a formal household, and Judy was never formal about anything, so Alexander ran through their home with his two-year-old exuberance, leaving Limoges teacups or a $100,000 crystal-something-or-other teetering on the verge of destruction. At Inge Feltrinelli's castle, Alexander threw up on a sixteenth-century rug.

Alexander could have broken the whole world for all I cared. With him, the simplest moments—having his little face greet me as I woke early in the morning, playing one of his favorite games in the pool where I tossed him high in the air and together we plunged into the water, reading *Goodnight Moon* to him every night—filled me with satisfaction and love. Children require attention and involvement. This takes you out of your self-orientation and makes you invest in another person who can only pay you in one currency: love.

My son's entrance marked a halcyon period in my personal life—accompanied by one conversely dark in my professional life. If anyone had asked me in 1990 what the chances of my business's survival was, I would have said one in one hundred. I still consider it a miracle that we didn't go bankrupt.

The swift and brutal transformation of what had been the go-go real estate boom of the eighties into economic devastation began with the Tax Reform Act of 1986. Prior to January 1, 1987, when the government's new tax regulations went into effect, a lot of investing in real estate had been driven by generous tax benefits. A tax deduction was given for accrued interest on a mortgage, which the owner owed but

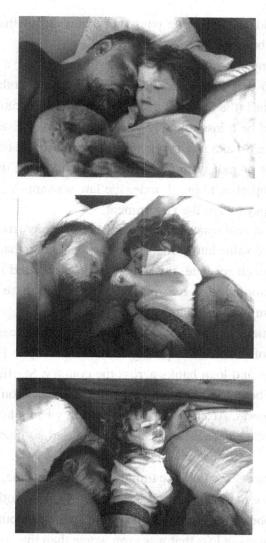

Through Alexander, I came to understand life in a different way

didn't pay. Many real estate deals were made where a seller, and not a bank, provided the mortgage. These sellers, often real estate promoters, got a certain amount of accrued interest that permitted the buyer to take deductions in excess of their actual cash payments. This "accrued" interest would, in theory, be paid years later out of the profits of the resale of the building.

For example, a million-dollar mortgage earned a deduction for $60,000 at 6 percent interest that was paid and another $60,000 of accrued interest (the $60,000 accrued didn't have income up against it, so that would be a loss to apply to something else). Even if real estate investors didn't make any money on the actual real estate, the tax savings put a lot of money in their pockets. In addition, the rapid depreciation of properties allowed under the law was another way to reduce income and pay less to the government.

So a lot of real estate deals prior to 1986 were driven not by their true economic value but by their tax value. Deciding that it was missing out on too much revenue, the government eliminated these tax loopholes in a swooping tax reform. By taking away these tax benefits, it radically changed real estate's value.

The dramatic and swift reduction in the worth of real estate touched off a chain of events that quickly led to catastrophe for hundreds of small savings and loan banks across the country. Starting in the eighties, they had been lending money very liberally based on the fair market value of property. After the Tax Reform Act, when a lot of those loans were underwater because values had decreased so much, the value of the banks was also severely undermined.

Then, when it seemed like things couldn't get worse, came the worst crash in stock market history. On October 19, 1987, otherwise known as Black Monday, the Dow lost 508 points, which accounted for 22 percent of its value—a loss that was even worse than the crash of 1929 that kicked off the Great Depression.

Suddenly, the country's entire economic system was under siege. Government planes landed in small towns and dumped scores of bank examiners to commandeer and close down local banks. Customers had to leave; employees had to leave. After depositors received checks for their guaranteed amounts, the government took over any remaining assets. This happened over and over, spreading misery like a crop duster of economic woe.

Time Equities had a couple of tax-oriented deals, but most of my real estate transactions were based on the basis of legitimate economic value. (One of our tax-benefit-based deals—214 West 96th Street, which I purchased for about a million dollars with accumulated interest of another million over a ten-year period—today is worth $30 to $40 million; so, needless to say, it easily paid the interest that was accumulated.) But it didn't matter that New York property values in general had increased greatly in value, unlike the Southwest, Southeast, California, and other go-go markets. Real estate had become a bad word.

The collapse rolled through the entire nation as the savings and loan crisis escalated. In the winter of 1988, financial analysts estimated that taxpayers were looking at anywhere from a $50 to $100 billion bailout to deal with more than 500 bankrupt savings and loans. The banks stopped making loans to those who wanted to buy apartments (or they made the requirements practically impossible to meet), and co-oping, the core of my business, was based on people getting loans.

I and the two other large co-op sponsors in New York City tried to hold at bay the huge wake of bankruptcy and commercial ruin headed directly for us by offering purchasers our own loans that we financed from the banks still willing to make loans using other properties as collateral. But the downturn proved too ferocious and fast for us to beat back. By February of 1989, Congress was working on passing a $156 billion S&L bailout package.

That was it. The banks wouldn't lend one cent. To anyone. All the tributaries that kept our business running went completely dry. Co-oping is slow; it can take five years or more to turn over a building from a rental and make enough to cover the costs of the conversion. But banks pulled the plug on their lending while we still owed over $100 million on co-op projects in process. In the moment that banking seized up, all our lenders were paid up to date—we were never a day late about anything—but we didn't have the money to pay more than a couple of months or so of interest on our projects going forward without new sales occurring.

Walking around the office in October of that year, I felt the despair over the situation in the faces of those who worked for me. It was like watching people try to run a race without oxygen. I had to get out in front of this thing somehow. I couldn't watch everything we had worked so hard to build come tumbling down because of financial circumstances that had nothing to do with the desirability of our investments. I had made a fortune by the time I was thirty, and at forty years old was facing ruin.

I decided the only viable plan was to try to talk reason with the fifteen or so banks with which we had loans. Many people in my position would probably have tried to avoid dealing with their lenders, but I find when you confront problems and are transparent about them with others who are involved, you can sometimes resolve things in a way you never imagined. I always tell my employees, "If there is a problem, my phone rings 24/7. If it's good news, send it to me by snail mail." Some try to cover up problems or manage them alone. Yet people often don't think clearly about who controls the solution to a problem. If someone doesn't have enough money to pay his rent, he will try to borrow money from family or get another loan from the bank instead of trying to negotiate a deal with his landlord. Identifying who controls the problem should be the first attempt in solving it. Then, what participation can you get from that entity or individual?

In my case, there was no question of who controlled my problem of looming bankruptcy. But how much I could negotiate with the banks remained to be seen. In boardrooms with sweeping views of the skyline, hushed carpeted offices, and spaces capped by vaulted ceilings of another era, I made the same plea: "I can understand why you don't want to lend money to new projects, but these are projects you already have on your books. Wouldn't it make more sense to continue to lend to the buyers and use the money to pay down the project loans? You're shooting me in the head, but you're shooting yourself in the foot."

The responses of the banks ranged from absurd to horrifying, like a mashup of a Kafka novel and Kubrick film.

"You're not late in any of your payments. Why are you telling us this?" our incredulous point person at one bank asked. "You are one of our best borrowers."

"You've turned the water off! What do you think is going to happen?"

At another bank, Crossland, it was hard to get the representative, consumed with a barrage of problems already in progress, to pay attention to our impending one. He paced around the room as if we weren't even in the room, waving a sheath of papers that listed all of Crossland's outstanding loans. "This is unbelievable," he ranted before we had said a single word to him. "Nobody's paying! Over half of my borrowers haven't paid me this month. I don't understand what's going on."

It was hard to understand how the banks couldn't understand what was happening since it revolved around their actions. But too often people are so immersed in the micro—what's happening on their spreadsheets or in their cubicles—that they miss the big picture, which in this case was total collapse.

Our biggest lender, Chemical Bank, had a clearer picture of the precariousness of our situation and ordered us to hire a special outside firm to audit all of our properties and produce a report from which the bank would determine its actions. Chemical had been very good to me, giving me that first unfathomable million-dollar line of credit, so I heeded their orders and hired a famous real estate auditing firm. While teetering on the brink of bankruptcy, we wound up paying in order of $50,000 a week in fees to this firm, which in turn overran our offices with twenty-five auditors, who spent their time doing things like checking how each tenant's name in a building was spelled.

The government, shutting down banks left and right, was an even worse negotiating partner. In many cases, we couldn't make a deal with the government after it took over a bank because there literally wasn't anybody to talk to. After spending a year negotiating a renewal on a performing loan on a hotel and office building, we had a room filled with paper a foot high for a closing the next morning at 10 AM when we received a phone call that the bank needed to postpone the closing. The next day the bank was taken over by the FDIC, which reneged on the loan.

When the government did take action to deal with the enormous failure of almost half of America's savings and loan institutions by enacting the Financial Institutions Reform, Recovery, and Enforcement Act of 1989 (FIRREA), it only worsened our situation with a host of new absurdities. The new federal law stated that if a government-controlled bank had an outstanding obligation to complete a building under construction, it no longer had to honor its side of the bargain (to give the builder money to finish the project), but the builder was still obligated to pay the bank back. How were we supposed to pay them back with a half-completed building? Construction deals across the country, of which I had a couple, came to a screeching halt.

Real estate headed into a depression, and I wasn't far behind. Despite my best efforts to have numbers guide deals, the industry has never been a rational one. Real estate is often driven by passions (and people with large checkbooks and often little knowledge). But as it started to sink, the irrationality peaked into mayhem. While many were scrambling to save their own necks, however, my staff struggled to maintain the integrity of Time Equities.

When he could have easily jumped to a safer industry or company, Bob Kantor explained to his wife, Jane, that he was going to remain loyal. Roberta, my longest employee, worked tirelessly to keep the co-op and condo associations we had sponsored from freaking out. A very bright lawyer, Bob Herman, used his knowledge from having been a special advisor to the attorney general to propose something highly unusual for a real estate company trying to stay afloat. Although we hadn't defaulted on a single payment, he suggested we alert the attorney general's office of our potential problems. His reasoning was that our impending financial difficulties, or inability to make future payments, were real enough to make us noncompliant with the regulation that co-op sponsors are financially capable and responsible. That meant reporting to over a hundred buildings we had sponsored that we were in bad financial health.

"Are you out of your mind? You can't do that," Bob Kantor argued. "You will create panic and destroy the whole co-op and condo industry if you do."

"It's the law," Bob Herman said.

I usually don't have much trouble making a decision, once I've done enough research. But with two very valued advisors giving me opposite advice, the process was extremely tough. I finally concluded that whatever the consequences were, we had to follow the law. I always say that character is defined not in good times but in difficult ones. That's when it is critical to be honest and ethical, because that's when it's hardest.

At the attorney general's office, we predicted our imminent financial crisis, and just like many of the banks, they couldn't quite understand why we were telling them prospectively. After scrambling for a week, they reached the same conclusion as Bob Herman.

When there is a problem, people often underestimate it because, in minimizing it, the problem becomes easier to face. They create a partial solution for part of a problem. But that only delays the discomfort. The sooner one alerts those that the problem affects, the more it gives the other party a chance to be ahead of the issue. In the case of the attorney general, we approached them before something happened that would make them look bad. Our amendment plan wouldn't stop the financial crisis rocking co-ops across the city, but at least the AG would be on top of it.

We worked with the AG's office to create a disclosure amendment that would explain the change in the market and the potential effect of that change on a co-op or condo's financial condition for anybody who was thinking of buying an apartment. We listed every co-op we owned shares in, whether there was a negative carry, and whether we were in default on any of the loans. We helped make policy when the AG didn't even know there was a problem, and I'm proud to say the amendment quickly became an industry standard.

Bob Kantor, however, was also right. A couple of days after we released the amendment, I walked out of the office to hear someone hawking papers with the headline CO-OP KING BANKRUPT! READ ALL ABOUT IT! Having converted more than 10,000 New York apartments to co-ops, I had earned the nickname, and now the amendment had earned me a much less royal distinction.

My life had become like a bad movie, where the main character, down on his luck, sees doom everywhere. At the Alfred E. Smith Memorial Foundation Dinner, where the country's leaders in business and politics gather each year for a white-tie charity dinner benefitting the Catholic Church, Donald Trump came over to my table at the Waldorf Astoria and said, "Gee, Francis. I understand you're having a hard time. Sorry to hear that."

Why was Trump coming over to offer me his sympathies? I hardly even knew him. Well, a month or so later, he announced his own troubles. Trump was coming to see what it smelled like. And it didn't smell good.

Although I was sure of the rightness of filing the amendment, the public scrutiny it brought didn't help as we continued to go through the nail-biting negotiations with all of our lenders. Our basic agreement with most of them revolved around turning over the profits from the properties we owed money on in lieu of interest payments. Some banks wanted to sell the property, which we did at whatever price they quoted.

We did whatever the banks told us to do whenever they told us to do it. Still, we had to work out each deal separately, and the anxiety piece came with the fact that if any one of them failed, it would have undermined everything. *Everything.* If we failed to work out any one of our loans, that would be it. Time Equities would go bankrupt.

Success was far from assured, and there were many close calls. European American Bank was the only one to sue us. We couldn't work out an agreement with the bank because the bank simply wouldn't talk to us. In the scheme of things, our loan with them—$5 million—was not that big. But it was an unsecured loan, so if EAB got a judgment against us, it could levy all our assets within ninety days, forcing us into the bankruptcy we were fighting with everything to avoid. "Pay us or that's it" was the sum total of their position.

It was maddening. A five-million-dollar loan with a bank on Long Island was going to take my entire business down! But that was the way it looked until we were saved in the eleventh hour by the most unlikely of characters, a mortgage broker named John Reynolds.

I had met John in the mideighties through his real estate firm, which was started by his father in the early part of the century and advised the Catholic Archdiocese of New York in real estate, among many other things. Extraordinarily thin and tall, he was a dapper dresser, always with a handkerchief in his pocket or a hat on his head. He was also married to a beautiful and elegant actress, Betsy von Furstenberg, who starred on television and Broadway. Despite his tidy appearance, John had gone through some very messy times. A recovering alcoholic who had once gone on day-long binges that left him lying in the streets, he was a devotee of Alcoholics Anonymous. In all the time I knew him, he went to at least one or two meetings a day and was proud of the fact that he'd recovered from the depths of his disease with the help of AA and his wife.

Through his charm and expansive personality, John knew everybody in the real estate business. But occasionally he was prone to fits of rage. He educated me as to how alcoholics have a lot of anger and how part of recovery is trying to deal with that anger. John had varying levels of success managing his own. Once when he and Betsy bought an apartment on Central Park West and a small apartment adjacent to it, he started to connect the two without board approval, which in New York City is almost as important as God's approval.

The board put a stop to the work immediately and then put John through a long approval process that got longer every time it was bumped at a board meeting for other business. With each passing meeting, John got more and more steamed up until he found himself riding in the elevator with the board president the day after another meeting. When he asked about the status of his approval and was met with the fact that the board still hadn't been "able to get to it," John grabbed the other guy by the lapel and slammed him against the side of the elevator so hard that the cab stopped and the two men were trapped inside for an hour. "And I still need approval for my stupid renovation." He laughed about it later.

For the most part, though, John was the biggest charmer around— and that was exactly what he did when he met the new president of the European American Bank at a party, fresh off the boat from Ireland for his new job in New York. "I'd like to come and see you on Monday," John told the new president. "I have some business to discuss." John called me at one o'clock in the morning after the party to say he had opened a door, and sure enough that introduction eventually led to us working out a deal with EAB.

I always think about the line Sam Zell, one of the great real estate investors of my generation, used during the late eighties when real estate was in a depression: "Stay alive to '95."

Easier said than done. The world was littered with individual real estate investors and entrepreneurs wiped out by the S&L crisis. All of the other leaders in the New York co-op and condo industry were having serious financial difficulties. That included Marty Raynes, who paid aggressive prices to buy large Manhattan apartment houses of the type

traditionally used as co-ops; Aaron Ziegelman, who purchased buildings in neighborhoods he knew in Queens and Upper Manhattan; Gerry
Gutterman, who bought high-end buildings, then spent tremendous
amounts of money over-improving in order to sell them at stratospheric
prices; and Trump, who was only building new buildings.

Between 1990 and 1994, we shrank from our peak of 250 employees on three floors to sixty employees on one floor. Without people buying apartments, there was no work for the sales, legal, or conversion
departments. I tried my best to treat everyone who worked for me with
respect, but the best I could do under the financial pressure was give
them some time to try and find new jobs.

I reluctantly turned over most of the Clinton Hill sponsor apartments we had used as collateral to borrow money for other projects to
the banks involved. When we went broke, we tried desperately to get
different financing that would allow us to carry them, but in the end we
gave over the title to Citibank and two others.

We still owned a bunch of apartments that didn't have loans on
them and so continued to attend Clinton Hill co-op board meetings that had become vicious. Before the collapse, everybody at the
meetings was smiling because the apartments were worth $125,000,
several times what we had sold them for. After the world fell apart,
however, people weren't so happy since they couldn't sell their apartments to anyone except drug dealers paying in cash and the building was falling into serious disrepair since the co-op couldn't borrow
more money for improvements against the value of the property. After
the board president broke with one voting block and had dead animals placed outside his door, he feared for his life and abandoned his
apartment.

The white-shoe lawyers representing the banks, already uncomfortable in deepest, darkest Brooklyn at a meeting stretching past eleven
o'clock at night, were greeted with similar animosity. "We don't want to
hear your bank bullshit," tenants shouted.

This went on for a year while Citibank spent a lot of money renovating their 150 new apartments and figuring out whether to rent them or not when out of the blue I received a call from the bank asking to come see me—that very day. When the officers showed up, they announced that they didn't feel Clinton Hill co-op apartments was the type of property that should be owned by a bank and decided to transfer them. Would I be interested? Of course, but before I could ask the price, one of the representatives said, "And we'll pay the transfer taxes."

I was disoriented. When I made the original transfer of the apartments *to* Citibank, I had to pay about a million dollars in transfer taxes. Quickly it came together; they were talking about transferring the apartments for nothing and paying the expenses!

"Will you accept the offer?" the bank rep asked.

"Why wouldn't I?"

"There's one condition."

"What's that?"

"You have to sign the papers by tomorrow morning."

"I'll sign them right now."

I told Bob Kantor about it just to make sure I wasn't crazy. He couldn't believe it either. If the apartments were conservatively worth $50,000 apiece, then Citibank had just given us a $7 million gift.

If I thought that was strange, things got a lot stranger a couple of days later when Chemical Bank, one of the other two banks to whom I'd transferred over the Clinton Hill apartments, called: "We heard you made a deal with Citibank. You know, we've been very good to you, Francis. We've cooperated with you in solving your problems. And we feel, as your lead lender, we should get the same deal."

Now I knew it was the world that was crazy.

"You want the same deal as Citibank?"

"Yes."

"You have been very good to me. Of course I'll give you the same deal." Another hundred apartments just like that.

It wasn't too long later that the third lender, FGH, a Dutch bank, called wanting the same deal. The banks didn't want to be associated with the bankruptcy of a predominantly black, working-class building. If they stopped putting the money in, they could be considered as forcing the co-op into bankruptcy, but they didn't want to put money into a place that might be going bankrupt. In the end, the banks decided the safest thing to do was give back the shares.

When all was said and done, I ended up with about 350 apartments, which was worth something along the lines of a $15 million gift (as property values improved and Clinton Hill, like the many other parts of Brooklyn, turned into a very desirable place to be, the gift was more like $100 million).

Some say you make your own luck. I don't know. I felt like I had more than my share of good fortune during that time—even when I put it all on the line, risking more than was smart or rational.

Around the start of the troubles in 1988, I put some money in my wife Judy's name so that it wouldn't be exposed to my creditors if the worst happened. Although it ensured we would have enough to live on, for some reason in the depths of my financial problems, which were astronomical two years later, I decided to invest a substantial part of it, because, well, I could never resist a good deal.

Back in 1985, I had encouraged a good friend, Michel Zaleski, to go out on his own into what was then the new business of leverage buyouts. As a young associate at a boutique shop, he wasn't privy to a share of the huge profits the firm made off the deals he put together. My confidence in his abilities came in the form of a $10 million investment with his new firm that he started with Ned Sherwood. With the ZS Fund, Michel and Ned proceeded to do what they had promised: In five years, they bought at least ten companies in everything from retail to insurance to textbook printing and made their investors like me a robust profit.

A couple of Michel's investors, Bill Friedman and Gene Philips, also owned a real estate company Southmark that they built (with help from Michael Milken and his junk bonds) into a $10 billion conglomerate and the nation's largest publicly traded real estate investment firm until they went bankrupt in 1989. I immediately jumped on the 10 percent shareholder stake that Southmark held in the companies owned by the fund. Figuring that nobody involved in the bankruptcy proceedings really understood what these partnership interests were, I contacted the receivers and offered them a modest amount to buy their interests. I was deep in the middle of my own financial problems, but they gave me favorable terms since no one was buying anything. I didn't even have to pay all cash for the interests, but I did need some cash. That's when I decided to raid part of the money I had given to Judy to keep safe for our little family.

It could have all gone very, very badly, but a year later, one of the companies that Michel bought went public and hit the jackpot. I paid about $2 a share in the original purchase of Sun TV, a Midwestern appliance retailer, which went up five times to $10 a share the day it went public. But luck really shined her face down on me when a well-regarded investment advisor decided Sun TV was a wonderful buy and recommended it, sending the stock soaring to sixty bucks a share.

Every time I looked in the newspaper, my initial $500,000 investment mushroomed until it was worth $25 million. Michel kept selling as much stock as he could on behalf of the group, since investors can only sell a certain percentage of stock after a new company goes public. Sun TV eventually collapsed back to $2 a share and went bankrupt, but not before Michel had sold about half of our investment and I got about $15 million out of it.

That money, which the banks weren't entitled to because it was in Judy's name, was critical in keeping me afloat and helping me turn Time Equities around.

Judy was instrumental to the whole operation, not that she knew anything about it or cared. I remember getting a call from Michel one day asking, "What do you think of the last Sun TV check I sent you?"

"What check?"

"The check we sent to you about three weeks ago."

"How much was it for?"

"Two million."

"Two million?"

Judy, who was perpetually disorganized, had stuck the envelope with the check into a random pile of papers somewhere in the house. I was glad to retrieve it and gladder when I saw Alexander bound out of his room to run into my arms.

*Chapter 9*

# TRAGEDY AND REBIRTH

. . . . .

Then came the blackest day of my life.

Judy, Alexander, and I were at our beach house in Quogue, Long Island, that I had bought in 1985 to spend summer weekends when we didn't go up to the country. I had woken up early to play tennis at the club down the road with one of the owner's associates, Jeff Forster. It was something I did often. Alexander was still asleep when I left him in the house with Judy and the au pair.

I was in the middle of my game when one of my houseguests ran toward the court. Something had happened. I should return to the house immediately.

When I arrived, there was an ambulance in the driveway.

Alexander had woken up, unlatched the lock to the staircase, gone down to the first floor, walked across the parking lot where he somehow also opened another locked gate, took the steps down to the pool, and jumped in.

I followed the ambulance to the hospital, where they tried to resuscitate him until finally the doctor said it was over.

He was two years old.

I got back in my car, my mind racing with the impossible facts. How could he have opened both gates? He was so little. Did somebody leave the gate open somehow? Where was the au pair? What was Judy doing? I didn't know what to do or what to think. I didn't want to think because all I could think about was that my son was gone.

Alexander loved the water. Jumping into the pool while I stood waiting to catch him was one of his favorite things in the whole world. He could jump in for hours and hours. When he went to the pool himself, he had no idea that he didn't have his floaties on or that he couldn't swim. That he drowned doing something he loved was too much to bear.

I avoided driving to the house—I couldn't go back there—and went to a friend's place not far away. An hour later, Judy and I left for the Pink House. Fleeing upstate was about more than leaving Quogue; it would have made more sense to return to the city. For once in my life, I wasn't thinking practically. In this moment of unbelievable desperation, I wanted to go to what I realized was my spiritual home. Not to recover or make plans. Both impossibilities. Rather, just to be.

We had just arrived at the house, when the phone rang. It was John Reynolds. I don't know quite how he heard the news, but he had heard and driven out to my house in Long Island only to find that I had come here.

"Do you want me to burn the house down?" John asked. "Because that's what I would do."

Remarkably, John found a way to break through and connect with a man in the depths of the most terrible pain. I appreciated it, but burning down the house wasn't going to do much for me. Nothing was. I didn't sleep or eat for several days.

Despite my grief, things had to get done. Calls needed to be made, and then there was the question of what to do with his body. That little body. I struggled with even contemplating such an awful reality. Unable to face the idea of this incredibly beautiful child decaying, Judy and I decided to cremate him. Almost immediately, though, I had feelings of guilt. Was I intimidated by the logistical problems of bringing his body upstate and where to bury him? Had we chosen the coward's path? Didn't Alexander deserve better? I couldn't protect him in life and didn't know how to honor him in death.

We put aside our conflicted emotions and moved ahead—because what other choice was there? The memorial service for Alexander was held on a piece of property I owned that has one of the most amazing views I have ever seen. Years earlier, a man who worked for me buying buildings in New York called to say he was up near our house in Chatham and that somebody showed him a "piece of land that is breathtaking beyond words." It took me all of a second to buy it after I visited: You could see forever as the Hudson Valley stretched out 360 degrees.

I watched as hundreds of people from all parts of my life slowly walked up the hillside where at the very top I had placed a small, classical sculpture of a boy in stone that reminded me of my beautiful son. I remember thinking at the time I bought the land that I had no idea what I would do with it.

I had wanted to sprinkle Alexander's ashes on that mountaintop, but we didn't because Judy couldn't come to a decision. I resented her for that and so much more. I held her accountable for our son's drowning.

"I blame you," I told Judy, "but I forgive you."

Judy was untidy and always late. What I had dismissed as distraction now that our son was gone reappeared as self-involved. How many times had I waited for her while she futzed with this or that aspect of her appearance? Being dressed perfectly was always a priority for her. I darkly imagined that if Judy hadn't taken so long getting ready in the morning, she would have caught him. It wasn't fair of me to think that. Accidents, by definition, are accidental. And I knew the judgment I leveled at her was very harsh. But I spoke from the heart.

Atop the mountainside, Judy's father led prayers and I read something I had written about Alexander. But I was nowhere near ready to memorialize my son. I wasn't even able to contemplate the enormity of my loss.

I didn't know how to live after Alexander's death. I took some time off work, but I don't remember how much because even when I got back, I wasn't really there. By four o'clock on most days at the office, I'd had it with banks, creditors, and disasters. My patience and tolerance, two traits I had prized in myself, were gone. I left early and headed straight out to Queens to play tennis.

Tennis was my only escape. Still, when I raced out of the office to play at Tennisport, it was for far more than just the game. The level of play and quality of pros were extremely high at the Queens club, with a reputation for being a real tennis players' club. (The sixteen red-clay indoor courts and eight Har-Tru outdoor ones built on the site of a junkyard in an industrial section of waterfront attracted movie stars, politicians, and business bigwigs. John McEnroe had his own court constructed there.) However, what made Tennisport a very special place was its warm environment. During winter, there was always a crackling fire in a fireplace. In the summer, the club offered barbecues on a wonderful terrace overlooking the East River with a spectacular view of Manhattan. Owner Freddie Botur, a native of the Czech Republic and self-proclaimed "tennis gypsy," took his food seriously. Among other things, Freddie owned a ranch in Wyoming, so the steaks from his ranch were fabulous (as were the crisp salads, steaming corn on the cob, and fresh swordfish).

Dinner tastes better after a hard game of tennis, and the best when shared with wonderful people. A whole family came out of Tennisport—including Javier Lattanzio, a ranked tennis player from Argentina, who was married at the club. The most amazing tennis player with whom I have ever shared the court, Javier has tremendous energy that he applied to real estate when he became a fantastic broker for me.

I love the basic tenets of the sport that I began playing at the advanced age of twenty-two—its subtleties, psychology, and endorphin highs. Beyond the physicality, the connections across various networks that it creates are equally rewarding. I have many close friends and colleagues—like Jeff Forster, Scott Kaufman, Jeff Ravetz, Ami Ziff,

Hollis Wharton, and Harry Newton—where tennis was the common denominator that led us to lives intertwined in many more ways.

Tennis also proved a crucial coping tool, not for the death of my son—I will never fully recover from that—but for getting through the time; I cried every day for a year. At least three or four days a week, I took my rage out on the ball and then was diverted for an hour or so by good food and people, even if I didn't feel like contributing much. It was a welcome respite from pressures at work, private grief—and my failing marriage.

The stress of the loss of a young child on any couple is certainly enough to split it up, but I was determined to avoid that for Judy and me. Even though I still harbored resentment toward my wife for the lackadaisical style I held partially liable for our tragedy, I couldn't resist the instinct to make things better. Francis the Fixer to the rescue, as usual.

My solution to repairing our lives was to have another child, and we started trying not long after Alexander's death. Judy was in her late thirties during her first pregnancy, so getting pregnant again was far from a sure thing. Every month that we discovered she wasn't pregnant, disappointment heaped itself upon a foundation of anger. I became almost dysfunctional with sadness.

Judy, who was also very affected by what had occurred but carried it far better than I, began talking about adopting. A child was a child whether it was biologically ours or not. One evening, while she soaked in the tub (Judy loved to take long baths), I voiced my concerns. I wasn't sure that adopting a child was going to repair the damage to our marriage or satisfy my parenting instincts.

"If you want to adopt a child, I'll go along with it," I said from the other side of the bathroom. "But if our relationship doesn't work out, we will have to share responsibility for the child."

She accepted my condition, and we began the complicated process of adoption. Organization and paperwork were not Judy's strong suits, so I spearheaded the filing of dossiers of information on our viability as parents with adoption agencies and lawyers. Then in the winter of 1993 while traveling in Russia with friends, I received a call from Judy, who had remained in New York; there was a child we might be able to adopt—but we had to be in Florida in three days!

So from the tundra of St. Petersburg to the wetlands of Orlando, I arrived with Judy to meet the birth mother, who was due any day. The woman agreed to let us adopt her unborn child, and a few days later, on February 21, Judy was in the delivery room while the young mother gave birth to Morgan. Three days after leaving Russia, I swore an oath in front of a Florida judge to take care of this child for the next twenty-one years and be his father.

It was a little disorienting bringing Morgan home. We soon settled into a new life with a child, but Judy and I continued to grow more and more distant from each other. The adoption didn't solve our problems, and not because I didn't love Morgan. I did. It was Judy and the way she lived that I could no longer relate to, and the addition of a child only highlighted the point. Our apartment was always a mess, even though she had all the resources in the world. I wasn't sure what she was attending to, because it certainly wasn't Morgan, who was primarily cared for by our housekeeper, a wonderful Thai woman named Wandee. From my perspective it seemed that Wandee was doing 70 percent of the mothering job while Judy came and went as she pleased.

Even so, when Judy told me about a year after Morgan's adoption the news that she was pregnant, I was ecstatic. I had come to realize that I loved children, and despite the state of my marriage, another was an unequivocal blessing.

Our second son, Noah, was born in dramatic fashion on November 17, 1995—too dramatic for my taste. Judy, perpetually late to all events, felt there was no need to rush to the hospital when her contractions began. Around five o'clock in the morning, however, her labor rapidly picked up and all of a sudden we were diving into a cab with her screaming, "Oh, my God! The child's coming!"

We pulled up in front of St. Vincent's—now Judy, the cab driver, and I are all hysterical—where some guy on the street opened the door of the cab and said, "Can I help you?"

"Well . . . thank you," I replied.

The Good Samaritan maneuvered Judy out and impressed me by being unfazed by her screaming, "The baby's coming! The baby's coming!" We made it into the middle of the double doors on the 11th Street entrance to the hospital when our helper took a look at Judy and announced, "I'm going to deliver the baby here."

"You're going to do what?" I asked.

"Don't worry; I'm head of Obstetrics," the doctor revealed. "Lie down here . . . The nurses are going to hate me for this."

Judy got down on the rubber entry mat, and that was where she gave birth with hospital employees arriving, stepping beside her like it was any other day at work.

Noah, a very good baby, was an unexpected miracle because after Alexander died, we didn't think Judy was going to be able to get pregnant. His addition did not change the dynamic in our family, or rather Judy's participation in it; but her new restaurant did. Nobody loved her kids more than Judy; however, once she opened the restaurant in a space in one of my buildings at 344 West 11th Street, she was around even less. Mono (a combination of the first two letters of each of our sons' names), a dream come true for her, became the center of her life. Seven days a week she was at the cozy brick-walled French bistro and didn't return home until one or two in the morning. I was up at six in the morning and took the boys to school before she woke up, so unless I ate dinner at Mono, I wouldn't see her.

My frustration grew until I finally confronted Judy.

"What do you consider your responsibilities in our marriage?" I demanded to know.

"Responsibilities? I have no responsibilities," she said. "I only do the things I want to do."

"You have no responsibilities? You really don't feel you have any at all?"

"No."

"I feel like I have responsibilities. Like, I have to make sure we have a place to live. I have to make sure, you know, that you, Morgan, and Noah are okay."

"Well, that's your choice."

Partnership has always been one of my core values—good partnerships are a huge part of my success in business—and here I was in the most important partnership of my life with someone who had no concept of the definition.

It wasn't that I didn't like Judy, but I was trying to work out in my mind why I was so unhappy. Perhaps, if I were truly honest with myself, my unmet expectations of her were a rationalization for my own less-than-perfect behavior—namely the romance I had rekindled with Isabelle.

I picked up with my former girlfriend, who'd broken off contact years before when she married another man, after I received a Christmas card from her out of the blue. We hadn't spoken or seen each other in eight years, but I responded immediately.

The connection between us was evident from the moment we saw each other. After all those years, there was so much to tell. Isabelle's marriage to the chain-smoking loner my pal Izzy Abrahami had introduced her to was terrible. They had grown so far apart, but she had been reluctant to leave her husband because she felt like she needed to take care of him.

Isabelle had evolved from a fresh-off-the-boat ingenue to a woman with opinions and experiences to back them up. Although one thing was the same since I had last seen her: She still had the piano I had given her for her birthday while we were dating. I'd bought the upright piano for her because she loved to play and played beautifully, but I had one stipulation: She would keep it, even if we split up. "I want you to use it,"

I said. Every time she played it, however, her husband seemed to resent it and would say, "If you're not happy, why don't you go back to your millionaire boyfriend?"

Talk about a self-fulfilling prophecy. About a year after Isabelle and I reunited, she left her husband, although it wasn't to start a life with me. She never pressured me to leave Judy, and I didn't give her any reason to think I would. We explicitly discussed how our relationship was based upon the mutual comfort we had sought from each other in the beginning and not about building a new future together. Isabelle remembered a fortune-teller at a fair we went to when she accompanied me on that business trip to Texas: When the twenty-four-year-old Isabelle asked if we were going to get married, the fortune-teller said, "No. Oh, no. He's too old for you.

"But you're soon going to meet a man in white."

Even when Isabelle got pregnant, she didn't ask that I leave Judy and the boys. Her reasoning for keeping the child was that she was thirty-five and always wanted kids—not the assumption that it would make us a family. She was ready to be a single mom, she said. I responded evenhandedly that it was her decision. However, I felt anything but sanguine. My already problematic life had just become *a lot* more complicated.

Judy was on vacation with a friend in the south of India where I agreed to meet her. They were in Kerala, a beautiful agricultural region with extraordinary beaches a couple hours south of Bombay. And the hotel they stayed in was equally magnificent. A German man had collected beautiful nineteenth-century wooden teahouses that the area was known for and moved them to the seacoast, where they became rooms of his hotel. On a bluff, high above the water, I looked out of the teahouse Judy and I shared and saw incredible beaches to the right and left, and carved into a rock formation below, a natural swimming pool for guests. The paradise before me couldn't have stood in starker contrast to the trouble ahead for Judy and me.

By this time Judy knew about my relationship with Isabelle. We had been living separate lives for a while now. Judy had become very wrapped up in her own world, and for an extended period of time, I spent half my life playing tennis. We were kind of like housemates. Judy wasn't thrilled about the presence of another woman, but the issue remained in the background. Until that moment. In the quiet of the wooden teahouse, I told Judy that Isabelle was pregnant and keeping the baby. Bloodcurdling screams pierced the sparkling blue sky and water all around us.

I kept my two lives together, but just barely. I visited Isabelle in her little studio apartment every day after she began bleeding in the fifth month and was put on bed rest for the remainder of her pregnancy because of preterm labor. The night of our daughter Julia's birth on May 7, 1997, however, nearly broke me. Isabelle began having contractions a few hours before a dinner and theater benefit I was hosting for 400 people. In my suit, I raced over to the hospital, where the doctor and I battled over her opinion that the contractions weren't frequent enough and she should return home.

The doctor won, and with Isabelle ensconced in her studio with a friend, I raced back over to the damned benefit, where I tried to do my best imitation of acting normal. After the dinner, I walked over to the theater to meet and greet guests but then slipped out as the lights went down for the play. Then I ran back downtown to be with Isabelle for a little while. I didn't have long because I had invited the guests to my house for dessert after the show. I did the dessert thing, feeling insane but again trying not to show it, and then raced back to be with Isabelle, now in the hospital, just in time to witness our daughter's birth.

From then until Christmas, I went back and forth between the apartment I lived in with Judy and the one Isabelle and Julia shared. Saddled with a lot of guilt, I shuttled back and forth between 10th Street off Fifth Avenue and 16th and Seventh at least twice a day. I had an obligation to Judy and the boys to be there for them. It was not in my DNA to leave two young children behind. Not that I didn't feel a deep sense of loyalty to Isabelle and Julia, both of whom I loved deeply. But I couldn't toss out my old family because a new one had come along. In my screwed-up ethical system, as long as I kept everyone else's life intact, nothing I did was truly wrong. Ping-ponging between my two families was not only absurd but exhausting.

Judy was the one who finally got fed up and called an end to the game. The straw that broke the camel's back came on Christmas of 1998. When I told Judy of my plan to spend Christmas Eve and morning with her and Christmas Day dinner with Isabelle, she said, "I just can't do this anymore."

The defeat I had been dreading ever since Alexander's death came as a relief, like finally calling uncle after a particularly punishing beating. I had to accept there were some things I just couldn't fix.

I moved in with my adorable seven-month-old baby girl and Isabelle, who, although she hadn't pressured me to, was in bliss now that we were together. It had been a long time coming for her—and for me. For the first time, in a long while, I was happy.

·  ·  ·  ·  ·

"Look. You've got to go see the doctor," I told Judy.

After her fiftieth birthday party on January 14, two weeks after I had moved out, she threw up all night. I had been at the big event she'd hosted at a SoHo club because even though we were officially separated and I was living with another woman, Judy and I remained close. We had agreed that I was to be a part of the everyday fabric of my boys' lives. My routine was to arrive at Judy's apartment by 6:30 AM and spend the next two hours taking care of the kids before dropping them off at school. After work I usually had an early or late dinner with Isabelle before or after stopping by Judy's to put the boys to bed. Reading them a story was one of the best parts of my day, and I tried never to miss it.

I wasn't alarmed that Judy had been sick the night of her birthday. She was a great party person, and her fiftieth was no exception. Filled with food, drink, and friends, everyone had a wonderful time—me included. We both figured she had probably drunk too much or eaten something that didn't agree with her.

But when she still wasn't well two days later, I insisted she see our doctor, who sent her from his office to a gastroenterologist. She had a blockage, and surgery was ordered immediately.

I accompanied her to Weill Cornell hospital at five in the morning for the surgery, which the doctor estimated would take two or three hours. So when I still hadn't heard anything after four hours, I began to feel uneasy. An hour after that, I started to ask the nurses what was going on.

"The doctor is still in surgery," they said.

By twelve o'clock I was panicked. I didn't know what to think.

When the doctor finally appeared at 2:30 PM, his first words to me were, "I'm sorry."

He hadn't expected to find what he found in her stomach.

"What is it?" I asked.

"Cancer. All over."

He had removed as much of it as he could.

"What happens now?"

"She has six to twelve months."

"What?"

Two weeks ago we were living together, three days earlier it was her fiftieth birthday party, and now she was terminally ill. I, who prided myself on managing great stresses and complicated scenarios, was not, could not be prepared for this.

The next morning I was by her bedside when our internist and friend came to tell her calmly, gently, and clearly of her incurable cancer. Even chemo, it seemed, was no match for this. Judy, however, would have none of it. She decided that she was going to beat it. Her enthusiasm—for food, friends, travel, and parties—had always been infectious, and this was no different. Great! I vowed to do whatever was in my power to help her as she—no, we—pursued any possible cure, Eastern, Western, orthodox, unorthodox, or other.

I threw myself into the task by setting aside two to three hours a day solely to track down every applicable treatment around the globe. I read endless papers related to cancer of the appendix, talked to countless experts and medical professionals, and hired research specialists when I found myself out of my depth. Making the arrangements for and managing her medical treatment became part of my every day.

Over the next two years, while Isabelle and Julia again had to take a backseat, Judy and I went to the Dominican Republic, Mexico, Switzerland, and all over the United States in search for her cure. It was an endless process during which treatments caused their own set of complications. In Mexico, she had her blood circulated out of her body, heated to some very high temperature, and pumped back into her. According to their instructions, radiation was required after this process. But since this was not an approved protocol in the States, when we returned home to New York, all her doctors refused to have anything to do with it and would not prescribe the radiation. I desperately sought a solution; the treatment had put Judy through so much physically that the idea it would be all for naught was intolerable to me. I finally was able to use a connection with a hospital upstate in Hudson for which I had raised funds and found a local radiologist who was amenable. In the end, though, her cancer was no better than when we started.

Through every overseas trip, injection, and piece of bad news, Judy didn't budge from her decision that she was not dying. Not even two more abdominal surgeries, which were hell on her body, could convince her otherwise. She was so adamant that when I approached her about making a will, she didn't want anything to do with it. As if the stress of the mother of my two sons dying wasn't enough, her refusal to work out a financial framework for after her death compounded it. I had given her many assets to hold for us on the order of the Sun TV stock investment. If she died without a will, I wasn't sure what would happen to all of it. It was a mess.

"Judy, you know, we have to deal with this stuff," I said to her gently from time to time.

"Not right now."

I was scared but I didn't fight her. We didn't fight at all—about anything. Does one fight with a dying woman no matter how infuriating she is? My top priority was for her to be as comfortable as possible and continue to live what remained of her life as well as she always had. That included not only in Manhattan, but also in Quogue and upstate in the Pink House where we had met. I didn't want to do anything that would interfere with her enjoyment of any of those places whenever and however she chose, which meant keeping Isabelle, Julia, and me out of them. But they were equally important to me and I didn't want to be in the philosophical position of waiting for her to die to use them again. Plus, looking for new homes gave me a project I could control, which has always been a great coping mechanism of mine. So in 1999, Isabelle and I bought all new homes in close proximity to my old ones.

Having two sets of homes also meant that Judy and Isabelle, neither of whom was particularly interested in the other, never had to interact. That is, until I planned a fiftieth birthday trip to Cuba. When I decided, a year and a half after Judy turned fifty, to celebrate my milestone by taking fifty friends to Havana, of course I included Judy. Not only were we still technically married and she the mother of my two sons, but she was also a friend. Whether or not she chose to come was her decision, but I knew Judy and I can't remember her ever missing a party.

True to form she said yes right away, and even though I'm sure people thought it was a little weird having my wife and lover on the same trip, everyone had a spectacular time from the moment we stepped off our chartered plane in Havana and were greeted by a band and fruity cocktails arranged by a Cuban general who was friendly with a Canadian real estate developer I knew.

All the kids came, including Julia, who was eighteen months old, and many friends with whom I had important experiences, including Jeff Forster, Bruce Forer, Bob Kantor, Carol Fredericks (my former assistant who has played many important roles in my life as a publishing and real estate colleague, fellow traveler, friend, and eventually family member after she married Judy's brother Ross), and Viktor Niemann (the intern at Rowohlt assigned to look after me on my first trip to Germany when I was still a teenager). There were moonlight skinny dips, dancing on the decks of boats, drinks at a bar that Hemingway frequented, fragrant cigar plantations, and a birthday dinner for fifty at one table that was a mile long in the ballroom of a grand hotel from the thirties that overlooked crashing waves. The magic of the place bound everyone on the trip together, even in a small way Isabelle and Judy.

The trip was a wonderful and short escape from the sad reality closing in on Judy and me. She felt reasonably and thankfully good while we were in Cuba, but not long after we returned, we had a consultation with our one hope left—a Washington, DC–based surgeon renowned for the radical, surgical measures he was willing and able to take.

The day of our appointment, there was a hurricane sweeping through the Eastern Seaboard that deterred most travelers. Not us, though. We didn't have the two or three months it would take to get another appointment with the highly sought-after physician. We drove beneath skies as dark as night, pounding rain, and howling wind so that he could examine Judy.

We made it, and after he was done and the three of us were sitting in his office, the doctor explained that he would dictate his findings into a tape recorder in the form of a letter to our primary doctor while we listened rather than tell us his conclusions separately.

With David Lebenstein (left) and Scott Kaufman (right)

Celebrating my fiftieth birthday in Cuba

"Judy Willows. White female. Fifty-two years old," he began. "Diagnosed with terminal cancer of the appendix, which has infiltrated her bowel . . .

"And who has a life expectancy of six months."

Judy went pale, and after he was finished with his letter she said to him, "What are you talking about?"

"What do you mean?" he asked.

"I'm not terminally ill."

"Hasn't anybody explained this to you?"

Three abdominal surgeries, myriad treatments that had been followed by bad news, and eighteen months since her first diagnosis when our internist first explained in plain language that she was dying, Judy had remained in denial, until now. When the doctor, who basically took whole insides out of people riddled with cancer, said, "I can't do anything for you," she finally accepted her fate.

After we returned to New York, she started to decline. For the last three months of her life, when she was mostly bedridden, there was always somebody—if not two or three people—sitting on her bed or sleeping by her side. Judy's hostess-with-the-mostest spirit drew a large group of devoted friends to her always, even at the end.

She remained at home, with the boys and her devoted brother Ross, even when things got really bad. Judy had never wanted them to stay with Isabelle, Julia, and me. I understood her need to control whatever she could while facing the ultimate loss of control in her own mortality. I made sure I was there every night and morning, mostly to be with my sons. While I offered Judy any support I could, she had her brother and so many friends. As their mother slipped away, my boys only had Wandee and me. In the last week of her life, however, I convinced her, "Let the boys stay with me, just until you get better." And she agreed.

I got the call from Ross in the morning at around 6 AM: Judy had died.

When I arrived at the apartment, the sight of her was frightful to the point of ghoulish. Judy had become the un-Judy. Her once-round face was hollowed out, her hands crypt-like in their boniness, and her lips, possibly the worst aspect, tinged green from a medication she had been drinking. Her aspect, as cold as she had been warm in life, sent me struggling with whether or not I should bring the boys back to say goodbye to their mother. It reminded me of the struggle over what to do with Alexander's remains. In both, there was no good solution.

The idea that she would just disappear into thin air didn't seem right to me. But what lay here, ravaged by illness, wasn't truly their mother. I worried that the last image of her would be the indelible one. I chose to return to ask Morgan, six, and Noah, four, if they wanted to see their mother one last time. They said yes, and we went back to the house together.

Years later, when Noah was a teenager, I asked him, in retrospect, whether he thought I had made a mistake in having them come back. He didn't speak to whether or not I had made the right decision but only

Morgan, Noah, Judy, and I in happier times

to what he remembered from that awful morning. It wasn't the image of his mother on her deathbed but rather the funeral home people taking her away. That, he said, he would never forget.

Noah and Morgan were so small—what did they know of death? They didn't understand their mother was gone (Morgan told me not to touch any of her things because "she'll want them when she returns"), even as I eulogized her at the Cathedral of St. John, where hundreds of mourners filled the pews of the massive nave. I walked up to the altar with a boy in each hand, seated them, and approached the pulpit to give the most important speech I could ever imagine making.

"Judy and I loved each other from the day we met to the day she died," I said that day in the cathedral. "Our love changed from romantic, live-together love to the love of two people who shared children together, who shared a world of friends and common interests together, who learned not to judge each other, and who faced tragedy together. Our bonds remained deep and uncompromised. She shall remain in my heart and my mind for the rest of my days.

"I want Noah and Morgan to remember three of her qualities: The first two are courage and grace. Judy consistently displayed unflappable, almost invisible, courage. Not the grit-your-teeth kind of courage, but the absolute grace kind of courage. Courage and grace when Alexander died, courage and grace when I faced overwhelming business difficulties, courage and grace when our relationship evolved, courage and grace when she became sick with cancer.

"The third quality was her willingness to accept and try new ideas, new people, and new situations. Judy did not fear the new or the different. Rather, she sought it out. Not as a thrill seeker, but as someone who was mesmerized by life's possibilities and anxious to explore them all . . ."

But while I paid tribute to their mother by remembering the best parts of her, the two boys weren't listening. They were playing behind me, rolling around on the altar like two little cubs.

## Chapter 10

# ART AS A WAY OF LIFE

. . . . .

When one enters the heart-shaped stone—outside rough; inside, smooth and shiny—it fulfills the cocooning promise of an egg or crypt. There are words on the interior that read:

*Alexander Jerome Willows Greenburger: May 27, 1988 to August 19, 1990*

Alexander, Allie Boy's birth was our birth. Each step of his growth was our growth. Before he died he had learned to say, "I love you"; "please"; "thank you"; and "I'm sorry." We believe he understood what these words meant. We remember his constant urgings that we read books and his snuggling in bed with us, and his knowing all the lines of his favorite stories: *Go Away, Wolf; Goodnight Moon.* He touched all who saw or knew him. He was a magic, perfect boy. He died in the water, a place he loved. We remain on Earth in awe of his brief presence here, graced by the aura of his short life. Our thoughts of him bring our greatest joys and deepest sorrows.

Then, the other side:

*Judith Elaine Willows: January 14, 1948 to December 2, 1999*
The Earth is dimmer, Heaven brighter. Her sparkling light is far
away. But in our hearts and in our minds her light burns bright
as ever.

Before Judy died, it was her wish that her ashes be mixed with
Alexander's, but she never resolved where they should be scattered.
After she passed away, I commissioned the stone-hewn memorial from
the sculptor Jon Isherwood and had it installed in the most beautiful,
meaningful, life-affirming place I know: Omi.

The circuitous journey that eventually led to these sprawling fields
in Ghent, New York, and an arts center known throughout the world
as a hub of creative exploration and exchange began in the mideighties
when I joined the board of the National Arts Club, whose mission is
to promote interest and education in the arts. I had been placed on a
literary committee because as the owner of a literary agency naturally
everybody assumed I knew a lot about literature, which, of course, I
didn't. Lack of qualifications had never stopped me from jumping into
an experience in the past, but my heart wasn't in it. I heard enough about
books around the office. All work and no play make Francis a dull boy.
I was looking to diversify my interests.

Although I had never considered myself an art collector, I had been
buying art ever since I was fifteen when I purchased my first work—a
round painting of an elevated subway that captured my attention when I
saw it hanging in a gallery where my girlfriend worked at the time. Her
boss, who saw me looking at the painting, asked if I liked it.

"It's kind of nice," I answered. "But I don't have any money."

"We're having a going-out-of-business sale," he said. "Make me an
offer."

My girlfriend whispered, "It's a terrible painting. Don't buy it."

I disagreed with her verdict and responded: "Fifty bucks."

"Sold."

Ted Xaras's painting of an elevated subway station

The realistic painting of an elevated subway station reminded me of the daily trip from Queens to the literary agency I took on the elevated IRT with my father as a kid. (I never knew much about the work by artist Ted Xaras—a portrait painter from Pennsylvania who oddly enough is also respected for historic railway scenes he creates for porcelain plate collections—until forty years after I bought it, when my curator decided to do some research on it. To my disappointment, she discovered that it was set in Philadelphia not Queens. Still, I have never tired of the painting even though it has hung in my personal office, across from the chair that I sit in during meetings so I'm looking straight at it, for over twenty-five years.)

Inspired by my experience giving a prize at the National Arts Club, I decided to indulge my interest in art by establishing my own prize. Without much experience in the genre, my biggest challenge was how to make the prize credible. I approached Clement Greenberg—a critic who for thirty years ruled art in America by making celebrities out of the artists he approved of (like Jackson Pollock) and destroying those he didn't—to ask if he would be a juror for my prize. Clem, a renowned curmudgeon, said he couldn't possibly do that.

"Why not?" I asked.

"I could never be on a jury with people I don't respect," he said.

"What if you picked the other people on the jury?"

"That's the problem. I don't know anybody I respect enough to invite to be on a jury with me."

"Okay, what if the jury was just you deciding?"

"I don't have time to look at a lot of art."

If this man thought he was going to wear me down in a negotiation, he had no idea who he was dealing with.

"What if you didn't have to look at art but instead chose someone you already knew to be worthy from your own experience?"

Clem had run out of excuses when I was just getting warmed up.

"Well, I guess maybe I could do that."

Clem wasn't the only important figure I roped into giving a prize. In 1986, the first year of the prize's founding, I had five jurors each giving a separate lifetime achievement award. There was Tom Messer, the director of the Guggenheim; André Emmerich, a prominent gallerist; Robert Motherwell, a major American Abstract Expressionist painter; and Eloise Spaeth, an important art collector and advocate. I decided to award each prize of $5,000 not to a famous artist but to an underrecognized one. When I asked André what he thought of the idea, he made an interesting comment: "The best and brightest of each generation are known but not to everyone. Ask the inner circle and they can tell you."

André, an extraordinary man who set the gold standard for art dealers worldwide, started inviting me to lunch at his gallery, which I felt privileged to attend. In addition to his legendary taste in art, he had a very special personal style that combined qualities one didn't typically experience in the same person. He was elegant but didn't suffer fools, an open and curious sophisticate. By the third lunch, however, I started to worry. "André, I enjoy being here, but I have a limited budget for art," I said to him. "Wouldn't it be better for you to spend time with clients who are more important?"

"The problem with more established collectors is that they have no room," he said. "When you try to sell them something, they want to trade back another painting. A younger collector might not have as much money, but at least he has room."

I wound up buying a few pieces from André, including a Ken Noland painting, a large Alexander Liberman sculpture that I keep in the country, an urn that dates back to 2000 BC, and one of Helen Frankenthaler's best paintings that I believe is the most valuable artwork in my collection.

André Emmerich seated with Clement Greenberg on Greenberg's eighty-fifth birthday on January 16, 1994

In retrospect, I wish I had bought more from André, but the real gift of my relationship with him was the impact of the time we spent together on my entire life. As with all my mentors—Ledig, Milton, Charlie Benenson, and, though on less intimate terms, Hillary Clinton—he provided me with an education in valuable subjects and experiences that defined me, which I couldn't have gotten in any school.

I have always valued the importance of mentorship and credit a large part of my success to it. Yet at the start of each one of these relationships, I never thought of any of them as mentors. They were all just people who, at the time that I met them, I liked. And in turn, I don't think any of them thought of me as their mentee—I was just someone they were willing to spend time with. Mentorship is like any other human relationship in that it involves respect, exchange, and chemistry. It is about friendship. Some of my mentors were famous in their respective worlds and others were not, but all of them gave me a wholly different perspective on their areas of expertise. As I evolved, I benefitted from their advice, encouragement, and introductions—like the one André made to one of his artists, Anthony Caro.

Anthony, or Tony, was famous for his large abstract sculptures, radical in their placement directly on the ground. Taking the welded-together metal—often found in industrial objects such as steel beams—off a pedestal invited the viewer to participate with the sculpture from all sides and on equal footing. Part of the 1960s movement known as Minimalism, Tony created livelier, brighter, and more playful sculptures than any of his counterparts, who worked hard to avoid any overt symbolism.

I knew of his work but nothing of the man until one afternoon while upstate a friend of mine invited me to check out Tony's artist colony. He and another Brit, the literary agent and art lover Robert Loder, had started the Triangle Artists Workshop near Tony's summer home in Pine Plains, New York, in 1982 as a way to "alleviate the loneliness of the studio." Well, I certainly found it fun. The environment in which twenty-five artists from Canada, England, and the States worked was very free. Although we had just stopped by uninvited, they asked us to stay for dinner and I naturally gravitated to the stimulating yet informal experience.

Hearing through the art-world grapevine that I had a good time at Triangle, André broached the idea of my becoming a board member of the organization, which needed an American partner. I was happy to join such an interesting endeavor, and Tony was equally happy to have me. It seemed that in its four years, the residency had "gone a little stale," according to Tony, who didn't know the source of the problem but was fine with me fixing it in whatever way I saw fit. Charged with giving the place a new face and new direction, I became the board chairman.

One of the big issues, if not the biggest issue, facing Triangle was that all its artists were culled from the same source—namely the American formalist critics led by their headstrong general and my former juror Clem Greenberg. In his austere definition of modernism, the emphasis of the abstract form meant the complete loss of any content or context, be it narrative, political, biographical, or historical. The lines and shapes should speak for themselves and that was that.

But the art world was moving on. Indeed, opinion had turned against formalism, and by the 1980s, Clem, who belittled pop art just as he had surrealism as nothing more than kitsch, was, to put it mildly, out of favor. Tony, however, had been a formalist darling, and around Pine Plains, hinting that Clem's taste wasn't the end-all, be-all was like saying the pope was fallible: that is to say, a little complicated.

For the next several years, as I tried to widen the envelope of Triangle, a pattern began to emerge. Basically anytime I tried to do anything different than what they were already doing, Tony would say fine to the idea, only to arrive in the States and then blow his top.

Like Clem, Tony believed in confrontation as communication. Although I rarely have a temper, working in real estate I have seen huge egos under heavy duress boil over into massive meltdowns. So I had a pretty thick skin when it came to Tony's outbursts. However, the young people who arrived for the Triangle residency and looked up to him were much more affected. I witnessed him and Clem crush a young German artist firsthand during a studio visit. Before the critique, I sensed the fear and excitement in the German artist, who had arrived only the night before, as the intimidating entourage of famous names peered at the painting he brought with him. Finally, Clem spoke up: "What's that?"

The young man began to explain, but Clem cut him off. His question was painfully rhetorical. "I don't know what that is," he said cruelly. "But it's not art."

The young artist's response was to take the painting off the wall, pack his stuff, and leave.

The prevailing spirit at Triangle was not what I was about and I, like the German fellow, decided to pull out of the whole experience. The truth was my presence wasn't doing much for the organization. Even in the area of real estate, where I certainly knew a lot more than Tony and his gang, they thwarted my initiative.

Shortly before I resigned from the board, I found a property for a permanent place to house Triangle, which rented its location in a situation that, much like other aspects of the residency, was operated in an irregular and irrational manner. Without fail, every year, days before the artists were set to arrive, the property owners called to cancel the lease. Tony, friendly with the eccentric owner, intervened and in the eleventh hour made some deal that invariably involved a rent increase. That incensed me as much as performance art did Clem Greenberg. The board was encouraging about the economical and large barn complex for sale I found in Ghent, New York, but in his typical fashion, Tony came to town and put a stop to the whole thing. "Oh, it's too far from my house," he said, and Triangle didn't buy it.

The owner of the property kept calling me up even after I left Triangle, because he had to sell the barn complex on forty acres. And every time he called, he dropped the price. "Nobody else is interested," he said. When the price went down to $60,000 and a fellow across the road offered to buy part of the acreage for $45,000, I found myself faced with the proposition of paying $15,000 for an enormous barn and fifteen acres. "I don't know what I'm going to do with it," I said after agreeing to the deal. "I guess I'll have the largest walk-in closet in Columbia County."

Six months later, summer loomed as empty as the barn I had bought. While I didn't miss the headaches of Triangle, I certainly missed the energy of its artists. I was lamenting as much on the phone with Sandi Slone, an artist who had been on Triangle's board, when the thought occurred to me: Why not hold our own workshop? We had the barns. Sandi agreed it was at least worth a try.

I sought out the advice of my great friend, the renowned French sculptor Alain Kirili. Although he lived in both Paris and New York, I called him the Mayor of SoHo since he seemed to know every important artist and collector of his generation. Alain was equally supportive and encouraged me to move forward with the idea.

With little time to organize it, I set to work right away, which meant calling Charlie Benenson. Ever since our meeting seven years before, when he and Harry Helmsley resolved their disagreement over the management of 25 West 43rd Street by giving me a forty-nine-year lease on the building, Charlie had taken me under his wing.

Second generation in a real estate family (his father was a developer of tenements in the Bronx), Charlie befriended all the industry's major players of his time. He was pals with fellow Yale alum Fred Rose, who for half a century headed one of New York City's largest construction, management, and development firms. Charlie was a bridge partner of Larry Tisch, the self-effacing billionaire who created the Loews Corporation, a powerful conglomeration of hotels, movie theaters, cigarette manufacturing, oil tankers, and more.

Whenever Charlie thought one of his powerful connections might be helpful in a transaction of mine, he didn't hesitate to make a personal introduction. I had access to the best minds in the real estate business because Charlie was always willing to put me forward. "Let's go talk to Larry," he said when I told him about the terms of the largest deal in my career up until that point: a portfolio of 11,000 apartments in Toronto worth $400 million. Just like that, the two of us went over to Larry Tisch's office.

In his office, the self-made billionaire looked at the screen of his computer while I presented my particular deal. According to Charlie, Larry was always looking at the screen. The legendary investor, along with his brother Bob, built one of the great New York family fortunes. He was not an easily distracted man. The *New York Times Magazine* described him in a 1986 profile as a "brilliant financial analyst who doesn't let himself get misled by current fads, or, indeed by the crisis of the moment."

I was grateful for 50 percent of his attention. Not only was he incredibly smart, so he could dual-task pretty easily, but this was an illustrious financier who was one of the key people responsible for the growth of NYU and at a certain point purchased CBS. It was like sitting in Warren Buffett's office.

What I remember most wasn't Larry's advice (something to do with watching out for the unions in Canada—the location of this particular deal) but the intimate way Charlie handled the whole meeting. Whenever I had a deal I wanted to discuss with Charlie, he would never say, "Send me the information and I'll have someone analyze it." With Charlie it was always personal. "Why don't you come up, and we'll talk about it," he'd say. His approach with Larry was the same. The discussion among the three of us was more relationship than numbers driven.

Even more significant than Charlie's network or his enormous personal holdings, however, was his high level of integrity. With his ethical view of real estate, which generally has a less-than-stellar reputation in that area, we bonded over a shared sense of fairness. For me to find someone who had achieved great success and yet done so within a moral context affirmed my own goals of wanting to work the same way.

Part of Charlie's moral compass included being an active philanthropist, something I didn't know too much about. Growing up, my parents didn't have enough money to pay their own bills, let alone give any away. When anyone came to our apartment soliciting donations, my mother and father's standard response was literally, "We gave at the office." Charlie introduced me to the wealthy's responsibility of charitable giving by inviting me to a dinner he and Helmsley created to benefit Lincoln Center and then to join the cultural center's advisory board. I was happy to do it because Charlie had asked. After that, he was forever calling to ask if I would join this or that, and I always followed his lead.

Charlie Benenson

Courtesy of Lawrence Benenson

It didn't take long for me to begin my own philanthropic endeavors. After Alexander died, I was approached by Chatham's Little League about creating a complex with new facilities and multiple fields. I provided the land to create the park and helped them in its construction. While I contributed a little bit of money and sourced an architect to design the complex, it was a big community effort and ultimately dedicated to Alexander's memory.

My philanthropic work has generally been divided between art and education (and later, criminal justice reform). There are exceptions—such as my position on the board for the Alliance for Downtown, the quasi-government organization for business improvement in Lower Manhattan—but for the most part I sit on the boards of museums, art councils, and schools. One organization that I am deeply involved in—Sports & Arts in Schools Foundation (SASF)—combines both of my areas of interest. I was initially brought into the SASF through its founder, Skip Hartman, who ran tennis clubs in New York. He was inspired by the New York Junior Tennis League, which taught tennis to inner-city children, to create an organization that helped struggling students in low-income neighborhoods achieve academically, athletically, and emotionally through afterschool and weekend activities. Although Skip is no longer involved, I continue to work with the inspiring nonprofit that serves more than 27,000 students in over 150 public schools. In all five boroughs, kids participate in everything from capoeira to basketball to comic book design in addition to receiving necessary academic tutoring. SASF not only provides a crucial alternative to hanging out on street corners or alone at home, it turns failing students into academic superstars. Teens who might normally have flunked out of high school wind up getting scholarships to college.

Charlie supported me as ardently in all my altruistic efforts as he did my real estate deals. He was also a big enough art collector to have a wing of African art dedicated to him at the Metropolitan Museum of

Art, as well as one at the Yale University Art Gallery of his collection not only of African art but also contemporary and modern paintings, sculpture, prints, drawings, and photographs, including works by Jean-Michel Basquiat, Fernand Léger, and Joan Miró. So I wasn't surprised that when I told him about the idea to start an artist's colony upstate, he sent me a check for $5,000 without blinking.

The donation was just the start of a lot of pitching in of all kinds from family, friends, and neighbors. By the summer of 1991, we somehow pulled together a group of twenty-one deserving American and international artists to spend three weeks working in the barns. In conceiving of a place for artists to commune, it was second nature to me that the participants should come from all over the globe. Having grown up in the world of international publishing, the importance of importing and exporting culture was part of my DNA. I wanted to re-create for the visiting artists the experience of my father's clients, who had friends in every port from trading in all those places.

With a lot of effort on behalf of a lot of people, everything was falling into place. The day before their arrival, I went to a house long uninhabited that I had purchased near the barns to lodge the artists. To my horror, the guy I hired to fix it up was such a procrastinator and over-promiser that nothing was ready. He hadn't painted, put lights in, or done anything else I could see. Everyone responded by pulling an all-nighter to get the place in order. The result wasn't the Ritz, but at least everyone had a bed.

Omi—named after the local village where the barns are located—was off and running.

I already considered the experiment an unmitigated success by the last day of the residency, when we had invited the public to tour studios and view the work the artists had made over their three-week stay. We didn't know what to expect in terms of a turnout (would ten people come, or twenty?) but it mattered little. I already had improvements in mind for next year.

Cutting the ribbon at the opening ceremony with Lawrence Benenson

Celebrating twenty years of Omi at the barns

A drizzle fell outside the barn where I stood that day waiting to see what would happen. Feeling the light rain peck at my skin, I turned to John, who had just come up from the road below.

"What do you think?" I asked.

Upstate, rain is a real event killer.

"What do I think?" he said incredulously. "The police just came. The cars are lined up so far down the road, they're annoyed at us for not having a parking attendant!"

Hundreds of people showed up that day to view our artists' work. I couldn't have been happier. That was just the start of Omi's success, which grew quickly and naturally the way good ideas often seem to do.

During the fall, at a dinner party in the area, one of the guests turned to me after learning I owned "those barns with that art thing" to explain how he had made an offer on the house adjacent to Omi but couldn't come to an agreement with the owner on the price. He and his wife had since bought another home, but "we got a call yesterday that the owner dropped her price in half. It's a fabulous property. Maybe you'd be interested." Famous last words.

The magnificent Italianate Period farmhouse, located atop a bluff with a front porch overlooking the rolling hills of the Hudson Valley and the craggy outline of the Catskill Range, came with 160 acres. Yes, I was interested.

The backstory on the property was that a woman and her husband had bought it about two years earlier and fought terribly over the renovation. When the house was all done, they got divorced. The woman now wanted to sell. The problem, however, was that she apparently drank a lot. When she was drunk, she said or agreed to one thing, but the next morning, she either no longer remembered the deal or completely changed her mind.

Nonetheless, my friend and real estate broker Frances Schools reached out to the owner, who agreed to sell me the house and land for the unbelievably low price the dinner guest had quoted—on one condition: The check must be at her house in half an hour. I didn't give her time to sober up or change her mind and ran the check over myself. Just like that, Omi blossomed into 185 acres and a new house that offered way more than just beautiful vistas.

On February 27, 1992, my great friend and mentor Ledig-Rowohlt died of pneumonia in New Delhi, where he had traveled for the International Publishers Association Congress. I was sitting around my kitchen table with a couple of other close friends of the eighty-three-year-old publisher after his memorial service in New York City when one of them suggested we start a residency for writers at Omi in his memory. "We have the house," I said, thinking of the farmhouse. "Let's do it."

That was the beginning of the writers' program, which since its inception in the summer of 1992 has hosted hundreds of authors and translators representing every type of literature from more than fifty countries.

Whether it was visual arts or writing, the free spirit I hoped for when I started this grand experiment ran through all of Omi. The residencies were about far more than just work. Omi chose talented artists from Botswana, Bangladesh, or Dubuque to come to Columbia County for an unbelievable opportunity to meet a host of top gallerists, dealers, critics, editors, and publishers. One could struggle in New York for a decade, or a lifetime, and never meet the people who came to Omi.

Yet what makes the experience life changing for many of the artists at Omi is the bonding that occurs among themselves over their stay. It's not too often in an adult life that one gets to spend three weeks with like-minded individuals. Over communal dinners at the outdoor tables set off the kitchen; at the Turnpike Inn, a local 1950s-era roadhouse bar complete with jukebox; or at late-night dance parties in the barns when more work is just not possible, indelible relationships are forged.

Freedom was also the hallmark of the founding of the various residencies themselves. In a complete reversal of the top-down process of doing things at the Triangle Artists' Workshop, at Omi if someone had

© Ross Willows

Residents and directors gather for a group photo in 1993—I'm seated in the front
row with Sandi Slone and Linda Cross

an idea, that person was encouraged to make it happen. There was never
a master plan for Omi, just different enthusiastic, interesting, committed folks who meandered into its midst and planted their inspiration in
its setting for so many others to enjoy.

Before her death, Judy, who loved music, suggested a music residency. "If you want to take charge of it, fine," I said. And she did by
finding the talented Jeff Lependorf to run it. With his eclectic abilities
and international bent, Jeff is a perfect fit for Omi. The composer of
operas and chamber music is also a certified master of the shakuha-
chi, a traditional Japanese bamboo flute for which he has created new
music, including a piece called *Night Pond*, a recording of which rode
into space with the shuttle *Atlantis* and remained for a year aboard the
Russian space station *Mir*. With that kind of experimental spirit, it's not
surprising that he conceptualized a program around improvisational,

new music. The need for a space for this kind of cutting-edge, often atonal composition and performance is big, he explained, because many traditional classic music-goers find the music too difficult. I'll admit I was in that camp when he began in 2000, but after all these years I have developed an ear for the music and an appreciation that it's what a lot of great musicians want to be doing.

My friend and fitness trainer Nicole Smith suggested we add a dance residency. By now the routine was set. "We have a rule at Omi," I told her. "We welcome all ideas as long as they come with the people to implement them." After giving me a much-needed education on improvisational dance, past, present, and future, Nicole energetically ran the Dance Omi International Dance Collective for a year before handing it over to the accomplished Christopher Morgan.

Over the years Omi continued to evolve with the spirit and energy of newcomers like Ruth Adams, a pivotal figure in its development as Linda Cross's successor as director of the art program and then overall director of the institution. Omi also continued to be fueled by ideas from its original supporters like André Emmerich, who by the time we shared a drink on the porch of Ledig House in 1996 had become a good friend. While I talked to the gallerist, the 160 acres below us transformed from unspoiled to unused. In light of all the creativity on the hilltop, the rolling fields below felt empty. I brought up the possibility of installing sculpture at Omi with André, who had created back in 1982 what he called "a sculpture farm" on 150 acres in Pawling, New York. The park, known as Top Gallant, boasted large-scale works by artists such as Alexander Calder, Keith Haring, and Tony Caro. David Hockney painted the inside of André's swimming pool with white wave caps. I asked André if he thought anyone would lend sculptures to Omi.

"Small sculptural objects are like jewelry, easily portable, easily accommodated, and so easily salable," he said. "However, large works, even if they're done by extraordinarily well-known artists, sometimes

The music residency at Omi

2008 Dance Omi International Dance Collective

can't find a home. People or galleries with them in storage might be willing to lend them to someone with the space to display them."

With no shortage of space at Omi, I asked Director of Facilities Kathleen Triem to look into the possibility of starting our own sculpture farm. Not a week after Kathleen and her partner, Peter Franck, an architect, began considering the monumental task of bringing large-scale sculptures to Omi, I heard from André, who had just sold his gallery to Sotheby's, which decided they didn't want to maintain his sculpture farm. "All that work is looking for a home," he said. What an opportunity to inherit a lifetime of work from a master collector. Omi was indeed blessed. Peter and Kathleen chose nearly forty sculptures from the collection for the Fields, where they were later married.

I had a vision that the sculpture park would also be a good way for us to engage the larger population of the area. I didn't want Omi to be some effete oasis but a vital part of the community, a completely

Etienne Cakpo, Benin (2006)

Joey Chua Poh Yi, Singapore, and Melissa Riker, USA (2008)

democratic oasis of creativity in which anyone was invited to partake. To that end, I tried to connect with the local schools for some time to have students visit our sculpture park. The bureaucracy involved, however, made something so seemingly simple very hard to organize—just getting permission for a bus was a major issue.

This seemed to be the one part of Omi that wasn't working, and I didn't have a clue how we could make an experimental art center accessible to the young people within our rural population until I found the answer in—of all places—the extremely wealthy beach community of Southampton, Long Island.

I had arrived on a Friday afternoon at our house in Quogue where Isabelle was spending the month of August with the kids, who now included our youngest, Claire, born on April 23, 2001. Like everything about Claire, her birth was well organized. A cesarean section had been scheduled for 11 AM. I went to a finance committee meeting for Hillary Clinton at 8 AM and made sure I was on time to meet Isabelle at the hospital for check-in by 10 AM. The check-in went quickly, and before I knew it there was a screen between Isabelle's belly and head. I sat in the operating room holding her hand while the doctor delivered Claire. When the nurse brought her to Isabelle and me, our daughter was perfect and beautiful.

Claire, now four years old, needed something to do, like the rest of our children, during those long August days in Quogue. So Isabelle had enrolled them at an arts camp at the Parrish Museum in nearby Southampton where she asked me to pick up them up that Friday afternoon. Well, when camp turned out to be a tent with some art supplies, a teacher or two, and a whole bunch of kids having a ball making art, a light went off in my head: All we needed was a tent? We could do this at Omi.

Of course, we also needed a teacher—and a good one is infinitely harder to find than a tent. However, I had the immense fortune to find a fabulously gifted art teacher, Sasha Sicurella. Our first session in 2005,

With my family in 2002 and 2003

we had twelve kids—half of whom were related to me and the Omi staff. But Sasha, a Canadian-born arts education specialist, is the pied piper of art. As director of Camp Omi, she gets kids to explore artistic techniques and ideas while at play. Because camp is stimulating, confidence building, and most of all fun, each year we doubled the number of children who attended. In 2015 over 350 participated in our camp and education programs. The impact of the camp is enormous. It has connected us with the community in a way that nothing else—not world-renowned artists nor big parties—can. We changed the minds of a lot of people for whom we were just "that art place" by showing their kids a great time.

I derive great pleasure from art, but not the object-in-a-vacuum art as Clem Greenberg's formalism might dictate. I love the way the pieces in Art-in-Buildings—my program to bring art to nontraditional exhibition spaces such as lobbies of buildings—spark dialogue between random passersby and interrupt everyday routines. The first lobby we transformed into an exhibition space was in 125 Maiden Lane, an office building in Lower Manhattan that I purchased in 1999. Suddenly, people who wouldn't go to a museum were encountering art. I watched office workers stopping to examine and discuss how an eight-foot-tall marble cone by Nick Hornby seemed to stand on a single, tiny point. The work was building connections between people who would normally never exchange so much as a hello. The experiment was so successful that, a few years later, I employed a full-time curator, Elisabeth Akkerman, who sadly passed away in 2013 but whose work has been taken up by the talented Jennie Lamensdorf.

I love the beauty and inspiration the color of a painting or texture of a sculpture can evoke. Still, I love the people and stories around the art almost as much as the pieces themselves—the humanity of the work. While I'm extremely proud that Omi's visual arts program is regarded internationally as one of a kind (every year, we get over 1,000 applicants for about thirty spaces, and in our twenty-year span, there is a whole cadre of artists who have come out of the program to become world famous with paintings that sell for a million dollars and more), I'm equally proud that in the proximate context of Omi, important relationships between like-minded people from vastly different places have been forged. We've had not only friendships form but also marriages and children (there are upward of twenty Omi kids—products of couples who met at the art center—running around).

One of my favorite stories to come out of Omi is Lexy Funk and Vahap Avsar. When they arrived in Ghent in 1995, Lexy was a polished young woman raised in England by her American mother and father, a successful businessman and friend of Linda and John Cross. And Vahap, a teacher in Ankara, was a Turkish artist. If you had asked me what the odds of them getting together would have been, I would have given you one in a trillion. But I was wrong. They emerged as partners not only in love but eventually in business as well. The married couple, who have two sons, founded Brooklyn Industries, a multimillion-dollar chain of clothing stores famous for its messenger bags made out of recycled materials and iconic logo of the view from a Williamsburg rooftop looking west toward Manhattan.

I have remained close friends with many Omi alums like Kinga Czerska, Joanna Pzrybyla, Graciela Hasper, and others. Through Omi I have found a whole new world.

It is immensely moving to think of Omi's alumni going out in the world, better for the experience of just being here. Take another example of an alum particularly near to my heart: Milton Newmark's grandson Seth Chwast. Milton was always concerned for the well-being of his grandson, whose autism kept his interaction with the outside world abbreviated and possibly perilous. Seth is extraordinary in his thinking, but his outward expression and relationship to the world isn't normal. He will latch on to an idea that he repeats over and over as if each time it has new meaning, like "Francis owns Manhattan!" or "Francis is building buildings!"

© Ross Willows

Artist Kinga Czerska at Omi (1996)

His grandson's future understandably worried Milton, but early investments that Milton, Abbott, and Art made with me became the source of Seth's security. Milton's daughter and Seth's mother, Debra, started the joke that it was called the Widow and Orphan's Fund after Milton insisted we include a woman named Ida Page because "she's a widow." As the fund grew and grew, we took care of Ida and many others until it even included some of Seth's doctors. More importantly, the income from Milton's original investments is part of what allows Debra to devote herself to helping Seth find a life—a heroic process that took a dramatic turn when in 2003, at the age of twenty, he enrolled in an oil painting class.

The result of Seth's experience in the class was astonishing. Not only did he become a remarkable painter, producing an amazing and huge body of work, but he also found something about which he could communicate. The process of creating art was the one thing he could talk about with others. With Debra as his tireless champion, he had solo exhibits at the University Hospitals of Case Western Reserve University, the Cleveland Clinic, the National Gallery of the Cayman Islands—as well as segments on *The Today Show*. In 2008, he came to Omi as part of the group of artists selected by more than a thousand applicants worldwide for the summer visual arts residency.

I'm a true fan of Seth's work and have purchased and exhibited several pieces, including the monumental *Manhattan Floating*. The mural, made up of 104 individual 16" × 24" panels brightly depicting the city surrounded by roller coasters, sea animals, and mythical beasts, was displayed in the lobby of my office building for more than a year before moving to its permanent home in the reception area of Columbia Memorial Hospital. When Debra decided to write about their remarkable journey, my literary agency sold the book of her words and Seth's images, published under the title *An Unexpected Life: A Mother and Son's Story of Love, Determination, Autism, and Art*.

With Seth Chwast in 2010

That my love of art, which helped to create a place like Omi, supported a miracle like Seth is way beyond what I could have ever imagined when I first began to follow my interest at the National Arts Club more than twenty years earlier. The miracle for me wasn't so much that an autistic young man gained public recognition or success. Instead, it was that, through painting, Seth went from an isolated human being to one with a greater sense of self and purpose.

If only I had been able to do the same for my son Morgan in his own impenetrable suffering.

# Chapter 11
# THE BOOK OF MORGAN

. . . . . .

Prepare now, because it's not going to be an easy road for Morgan. And there's nothing you can do about it."

My therapist's verdict came as a shock, although it shouldn't have. For years, one crisis followed another in my son's life, each worse than the last. Still, I couldn't believe that although I had thrown the full weight of my vast resources at his problems, this is where we ended up—with Morgan, now eighteen, on his way to a maximum-security prison.

I knew my therapist, Don Kaplan, was right. A businessman who had previously owned a successful shoe-importing business before waking up one day at forty and deciding to become a psychologist, Don had been a wonderful influence in my life ever since I began seeing him after Alexander's death. I trusted him implicitly and valued his combination of practical and sensitive advice.

"There's nothing anybody can do it about it," Don said. "There's nothing *he* can do about it."

Morgan's troubles began early. He was uncontrollable beyond the normal tantrums of a toddler. No matter the question, his answer was always a defiant "No." A game with his brother: no. A trip to the park: no. A lollipop: no. He even refused to go to the bathroom, which continued to be a problem long after it should have been.

His behavior was so difficult to cope with that by nursery school, he required an assistant teacher to "shadow" him so that his outbursts didn't distract the regular teacher from the rest of the class. Despite my hiring a dedicated person to do just that for preschool and kindergarten, the school decided in the middle of first grade that it could no longer support him.

While sadly this was to be only the first of many times an institution failed to be able to cope with Morgan, my son's rejection from school felt like a personal one. My emotional reaction aside, the school did Morgan and me a great disservice in the way it asked us to leave. Other than the fact that Morgan wasn't welcome back, the school gave me very limited information on what I should do next. My child was clearly *my* problem, and the school that I had previously considered a partner in my son's development became a disinterested party. I thought the school was failing along with us, but that was not how they saw it. We were on our own.

This experience wasn't unique to our family. In general, schools don't do enough to help parents transition to special education schools when it becomes necessary. They should offer counseling and a list of schools and placement experts so that parents can navigate with confidence and knowledge whatever new world they are entering, whether it is special education or psychiatric care. This is a common enough occurrence that the investment in creating a list of resources to assist those finding a better place for their child would have a big payoff. Some parting guidance would certainly help parents understand that if a school believes its environment is not working well for a child (through poor grades, behavioral problems, or any other clear evidence), *the child* will be better off at the right school. The move could be understood as a way to improve a child's learning and life instead of a totally negative and isolating event.

Alas, Isabelle and I were left to our own devices as we ventured down the road of Morgan's care, which became more uncertain and difficult with each step we took.

Firstly, Morgan's diagnosis was extremely broad and diffuse. It wasn't just an oppositional defiant or attention deficit disorder; it was an "everything" diagnosis. There was frightening talk about problems with his frontal lobe and pervasive developmental disorder (PDD). Whatever it was, something was wrong with Morgan's behavior; he started going to a psychiatrist and taking medicine.

Finding a school for Morgan turned out to be just as complex and frustrating as his diagnosis. After kindergarten, he attended Mary McDowell, a new special education school in Brooklyn where we were lucky to get a spot. Specializing in learning-disabled children, they did their best with him for three years. But by fifth grade, Morgan's behavioral outbursts went beyond the scope of what they were able to treat. He needed to be someplace where psychological development, not the treatment of learning disorders, was the priority. From there Morgan attended just such a school in Westchester, called the Andrus School, which he burned through as well after a few years.

Morgan's disruptive ways continued to escalate not only at school but also at home. The two-year-old, so wrapped up in his anger that it was impossible to calm him as he screamed for an entire hour, had grown into a complicated boy. On one hand, it was hard to get through to Morgan (I figured out later he had often only understood a fraction of a discussion or set of instructions). Yet he also knew how to press people's buttons with precision—particularly those of Noah. He seemed to get a kick out of taunting his highly reactive younger brother. He left Noah's favorite toy outside overnight so that it was ruined or gave him a funny look, and the two would be attacking each other with a ferociousness that surpassed fraternal competition.

When it became painfully clear that Morgan could not be treated like any one of our other children, we hired a caregiver specifically for Morgan. Five days a week, Troy, a young man Morgan had related well to at a summer camp, was at the house from the time Morgan woke up until he went to bed. That worked for a period, but then even weekends became unmanageable without Troy, so by eighth grade, we enrolled Morgan in Devereux Glenholme, a Connecticut boarding school for students with a wide range of issues from anxiety to Asperger's to bipolar disorder. Even at an institution with a stellar reputation for dealing with complicated and impulsive children, Morgan found a way to get in trouble—*big* trouble.

I was on a trip with Isabelle and the rest of the children when I received a message from the school to "call as soon as possible." The only problem was that we were in Africa's Okavango Delta, one of the most remote places on earth, with very limited phone communication. The message had come to our camp via walkie-talkie from the nearest town. Luckily I did have a satellite phone with me, but in order to use it I had to place the call from a clearing in a field, which presented its own issues. The tents we camped in were actually built on a platform fifteen feet off the ground so that none of the many wild animals roaming the land could attack us. To make matters worse, I received the message in the afternoon, which was feeding time for the animals. So a man carrying a shotgun came with me into the field to guard against any charging rhinos or hungry lions while I called Morgan's school.

I was more frightened by what I heard on the phone than by the African wildlife. Morgan, fourteen, had not only stolen a car (left at the town garage, unlocked and with the keys in it), but he drove it on the winding and dangerous Taconic Parkway toward home with two younger children he made sit in the backseat for their safety! So while twenty Glenholme faculty and administrators combed the area woods and roads, a dozen officers and a few German shepherds went on the hunt for the boys. Thank God, they were found several hours later by a New York state trooper who stopped the 1990 Dodge Shadow in Putnam County for driving without headlights. They were dubbed the "Teddy Bear Gang" in the *New York Post* because one of the younger boys in the backseat brought along a teddy bear. The story, picked up by the Associated Press and run in over sixty publications, was even mentioned by Oprah on her show.

Morgan walked away from the incident with the judge issuing a slap on the wrist that would be expunged from his record if he didn't get in any more trouble (thanks to my good friend and Morgan's lawyer, John Iannuzzi), and remained at Devereux for another year until he was finally kicked out for stealing another car that he drove all the way to New York City. I couldn't understand why he had stolen a car and driven it home on a Thursday when he was scheduled to come home for the weekend the next day. Morgan didn't have an explanation. It was as if he didn't know why he had done it either.

I had no idea what to do next. Barely sixteen, Morgan had already been kicked out of four schools and had stolen two cars. The chilling prediction of a psychiatrist we consulted some years earlier, who proclaimed, "This child will be in jail by the time he is fourteen," plagued me. At the time I dismissed it as a rash and shocking calculation from someone who had only talked to my son for a half hour. Despite the evidence in front of me, I still refused to accept its inevitability.

I took up somebody's recommendation for a residential treatment center for "troubled teens" called Turn-About Ranch in Utah. That I would choose a very structured and strict Christian-based program for my child, when I am none of those things, proved my level of desperation and quickly diminishing lack of options. Hoping for the "real change" promised by the facility, Morgan and I flew to Salt Lake City and then took a chartered plane to a remote part of Utah where teens suffering with a wide range of disorders from depression to Tourette's to substance addiction rose at sunrise to cut wood, feed the animals, ride horses, study, and go to therapy. "I take a lot of parents here," the pilot of the chartered plane told me. "When the kids go down, it's all 'Fuck you, man.' When we pick them up four months later, it's all 'Yes, sir,' 'No, sir,' 'Thank you, sir.'"

The man from Turn-About who met us at the plane was out of central casting in his reflective sunglasses, erect marine posture, and unsmiling face. As I left Morgan in his care, I hoped this was the cure that would help my son.

During Morgan's time at the ranch, I received ongoing updates that he was having a lot of trouble complying with the rules—often winding up in detention. But true to the pilot's word, when Morgan got through the program, he was a changed kid. Morgan acted in a respectful and controlled manner. He even reconciled with Isabelle.

He and Isabelle hadn't been on speaking terms for a long, long time. The end of their relationship years earlier happened after a day like any other in our family. We were out at our beach house, and Morgan had one of his usual meltdowns. This time, however, Isabelle, who had dealt with countless outbursts since becoming a stepmother to my boys, had her own meltdown.

Morgan was a constant disruption not just with the children but also between Isabelle and me. The extreme parenting situation highlighted the differences in our philosophies. As parents we had different points of view about setting limits. I questioned all forms of authority—even my own. Isabelle, raised in France where children are reared with a caring but firm hand, was all about setting limits. She wanted to help by bringing stability and order, which she did, but the disparity between our viewpoints and the stress of Morgan's behavior became too much to bear.

"I can't take this anymore," she said that day at the beach. "I've got to take some time off."

Isabelle returned to New York and shut a part of herself off. She was so desperate; it was too hard to be a mother to Morgan.

So when Isabelle attended family therapy sessions at Turn-About with Morgan and attended his graduation from the program in Utah, I was overjoyed. (The girls also joined us. Noah was the only one who didn't travel to the ranch. He didn't want anything to do with the brother he felt was only a burden.)

After Turn-About and his rapprochement with Isabelle, Morgan's fervent wish was to return home to New York, which we welcomed. The conditions were that he had to follow the carefully detailed points-based program laid out for him by the staff at the ranch, as well as attend a school for autistic and mentally retarded children I had found nearby—and one of the only schools that would accept him.

It only took three days for the whole plan to deteriorate. Rather than follow the regimen of respect he had been taught at Turn-About, he quickly slipped back into his old patterns. By the week's end, he had racked up so many "negative points" it seemed pointless to keep count. The "Yes, sirs" were already replaced by much less gracious terms.

When Morgan broke into Isabelle's study and stole a couple thousand dollars, I accepted Turn-About's guarantee that if a graduate acted out, it would take him or her back for at least thirty days and again shipped him out to Utah. In a restrictive environment in the middle of nowhere, Morgan still proved unmanageable. He ran away from the ranch on foot after attempting to steal one of the staff's cars. However, in this town of 700 people, he didn't get very far.

I would have paid any amount and sought any counsel to help my son. But there wasn't a program in the country able to cope with him. At a place in New Hampshire that offered therapeutic and psychological counseling, Morgan fought with one of their teachers. That was when they called the police, and Morgan, who by now had reached his full height and weight of 6'2" and 320 pounds, was arrested for aggressive behavior. Later, when a program on a working farm in Vermont threw him out for buying a BB gun during a mall trip, I asked him if he did that because he didn't like being there. "No," he said, "I love being there."

I got him an apartment next door to Stephanie, a woman who seemed able to control him whom I had hired to keep an eye on him. Three hours a day, he had a job cleaning the sidewalks outside one of my buildings and attending weekly therapy sessions. The next crisis,

however, escalated my son's already troubled situation. Shortly after
Morgan refused to work, he started bringing homeless people back to
the apartment. Even Stephanie, who began to fear for her own safety,
couldn't stop him. Then Morgan and one of his new friends decided to
rob a cab driver and were almost instantly arrested.

As I posted his $75,000 bail, my son suddenly went from a mentally
ill child to an eighteen-year-old criminal. In paranoid fits, he described
people "out to get" him. His terror was infectious. When he rang the
bell of our house at 2 AM, Noah, at home alone, looked out the window and refused to let in his brother accompanied by a strange man.
Morgan responded by calling the house phone over and over throughout
the early morning.

I had weathered economic problems that almost brought me to the
edge of bankruptcy, the drowning of my first son, Judy's cancer and
eventual death. And yes, I was banged up from all of it. But I was also
stronger in my ability to temper my hope and my disappointments to
maintain a clear vision of what I wanted to do—which was basically the
best I could for him.

I often replayed the moment, days after Morgan's birth and adoption, when I stood before a Florida judge and swore to be a faithful
father to Morgan for better or worse. I would always do my very best to
be true to that vow. Morgan had no other champion apart from me, but
that wasn't the only reason for my vigilance.

I could do no right when it came to my own mother—either as a
little boy or a grown man. She knew better, in everything from what I
should eat, to the apartment I should live in, to the fastest route downtown. "Ach," she said while I fumed behind the wheel, "you should have
gone *this* way."

George Bach, the German psychiatrist and early client of mine at
the literary agency, said my mother's opinionated manner was textbook
"Berliner." All I know is that it drove me nuts, and not just because

of the irritation of her constant contrarianism. It wounded me that she never acknowledged my achievements in any real way.

After spending ten years writing, rewriting, and failing to sell her second novel, she went back to her first passion: painting, which she had done in France during the war. My mother spent the next twenty-five years deeply invested in her art, creating an entire body of work. She painted realistic images of friends and a variety of scenes, but curiously, unlike with her writing, she never wanted to sell anything. Once I got a gallery to agree to give her a show, but a few days before the opening she called me to say she couldn't go through with it because she didn't want to sell any of her paintings. "My paintings are personal," she said.

My mother had always been subsumed by her work, but in the last years before her death in 2001, she wasn't well and for the first time needed me, which I was ambivalent about. On one side, I wanted to be a good son; on the other, I resented it. She was not an extravagant person, so it was very easy for me to support my mother financially. My success in business, which meant she no longer had any of the financial worries that plagued my childhood, wasn't mentioned. Instead, it was vaguely taken for granted. Even when I actively sought out her praise, it was all about her.

In the last few years of her life, she was lonely. So in addition to taking care of her financially, I tried to support her emotionally by doing things like taking her to dinner every Sunday evening. When Isabelle and I got married in the country on Christmas Eve of 2000, my mother was there but was immobile from a fall. We got married by a judge in our upstairs hallway so she could see us from her bed. That night, my mother, who couldn't get to the bathroom herself, rang a little bell every hour or so for me to accompany her.

Playing the dutiful son came more from my compulsion to be a caretaker than any filial desire. The hard truth was I had to take care of somebody for whom I didn't feel perfect sympathy. My mother did the best

Exchanging rings with Isabelle on Christmas Eve, 2000

she could in raising my brother, and she dealt with my father even when
their relationship was strained and he was difficult. We never talked
about how I saved the literary agency that provided her a social nexus
and reason to get up every day. (She continued to keep her meticulous
handwritten records of contracts and royalty collections on index cards
long after we changed over to a computerized system. Nobody could
convince her to stop, so she spent her time creating duplicate records just
in case the computer records proved inadequate—and, of course, it was
the most important thing in the world.) I could have bought the Empire
State Building, and after giving a bland response, she would return to the
subject of a painting she was struggling with or an urgent improvement
needed at the agency. Everyone needs appreciation whether for buying a
skyscraper, sweeping up a street, or simply being a son.

I had decided long ago that my job was not to be Morgan's judge and jury but his advocate. Still, for the sake of my own mental health, I tried to follow Don's advice and distance myself from the role of Morgan's savior. He was no longer a little boy that I could watch while he rode out a tantrum. So when I received a call from the facility in Houston where I had sent Morgan (and one of the few in the country willing to take him after the taxicab robbery) that he had gone missing, I told Isabelle I wasn't worried. "I'm done with that," I said.

It seemed another patient, a thirty-three-year-old billionairess from Houston, had befriended Morgan—and although he hadn't finished high school and she spoke five languages and had earned her doctorate, she and Morgan hatched up a scheme to elope. After leaving the facility together, which because it wasn't a locked-down facility, they had the right to do, she bought him a ticket to Hawaii, gave him her credit card, and said she'd meet him there in two days. The next day, however, she realized she was unstable and returned to the center. Meanwhile, my son was lost in Maui.

Despite my tough talk, by the third day of his disappearance, I was distraught. Eventually Morgan called ("I'm sitting on a bench in Maui"), and I got him back to Houston, where soon enough he did something else to get thrown out.

I was unable to solve the problem of Morgan and yet I didn't know what else to do other than to keep trying. Even after he described fantasies of hurting me and other family members to his caregiver, I was locked in an endless syndrome of hope. Even after his psychiatrist told him directly and forcefully in a session we had together, "You need to be confined and should return to jail. *Immediately*," I still imagined there was an undiscovered solution. I wanted to prove this psychiatrist and the one who had predicted my son would be in jail long ago wrong.

Then Morgan begged to go to jail.

"Revoke my bail right away," he said on the phone.

"What are you scared of?" I asked, trying to piece together reality from delusion from the most unreliable of sources. He had just called the police because he imagined that someone with a gun was after him. The police had come to the apartment but found nothing and left.

"I want to go to jail," he pleaded.

I could hear the fear in his voice. His psychiatrist said he should go to jail; the experts in the programs thought he belonged in jail; now Morgan believed he belonged there as well. Trying to think of what to do, I told him to call his lawyer. Meanwhile, I would talk to Stephanie and get back to him.

Ten minutes later, Morgan started a fire atop his stove, called the fire department, and was arrested.

As I sat in my therapist's office after Morgan's second arrest and incarceration in Rikers, Don explained, "Morgan was born essentially without a super-ego, so he has virtually no impulse control. He is like a car without brakes."

After Morgan was arrested for setting the fire in his apartment, the authorities took him to Bellevue for a psychiatric evaluation. That night I couldn't sleep; images of him in a straitjacket being given heavy drugs or subdued by burly bodyguards raced through my mind. As a parent, I couldn't imagine enduring anything harder.

The images, however, only worsened. The next morning, Morgan was transferred from the mental hospital to the jail at 100 Centre Street. The judge decided that because Morgan had already failed in so many other mental health programs, his case should not be heard in Mental Health Court where the result would be to offer him another program. Morgan was charged with arson and remanded to Rikers to await trial in criminal court.

I reacted unemotionally to the news, because that is the best state to handle any crisis. I called his lawyer and anyone else familiar with the criminal justice system. I acted practically, efficiently, and effectively. But none of that represented my true feelings. Inside, a chaotic mix of responsibility, anger, and confusion raged. Mostly, though, I carried a very deep sadness about Morgan. He was not motivated in his criminal activity by greed or malice but by an inability to relate to societal norms. I couldn't believe there wasn't a better answer than prison, especially with the means I had to provide. But if there was one out there, neither I nor all the professionals I consulted could find it.

After fighting for such a long time and in every way possible to help Morgan, it made me sad that I hadn't been more successful. In the end, I couldn't feel sorry for myself, but I could feel sorry for *him*. Because, really, what could be more challenging than being him?

## Chapter 12

# PURSUING SOCIAL JUSTICE

· · · · ·

A t 3:30 PM, Pierre, my driver, picked me up at the office, and within half an hour, we arrived at my destination: just past the corner of Hazen Street and 19th Avenue in Queens. Pierre dropped me off at the urban wasteland punctuated only by a check-cashing place and a store for police and corrections officer equipment. A half block away, the Q100 bus left for Rikers Island. I had no idea what to expect, as was quickly evidenced by the fact that my MetroCard didn't have enough money on it for a single ride (luckily, my assistant Elizabeth had anticipated this kind of thing and packed me a few rolls of quarters).

We drove along a bridge that crossed over the East River and onto the island whose only inhabitants are local offenders who can't afford or haven't been given bail, those with sentences of less than a year, and others convicted and waiting for transfer to prison. From the window, one building followed another, nondescript industrial and temporary complexes, everything surrounded by endless amounts of razor wire. Arriving at the intake center, we got off the bus to the roar of planes taking flight from nearby LaGuardia. The irony was not lost on me.

I had tried to dress down in an attempt not to stick out. But the color of my skin and my sex made blending in impossible. I was almost entirely surrounded by women of color, many of them accompanied by small children. Yet I joined the rest of the visitors in feeling helpless and unsure as we confronted the corrections officers, an endless number of giant men and women barking instructions about how to behave on their island.

No cell phones. All possessions were to be put in one of two sets of lockers. Only three books per person allowed. No clothes with any kind of logos can be given to inmates. Whether because we were nervous or the logic of this place was flawed, things weren't clear. Could I keep my money? I made an executive decision not to ask any questions of the edgy officers and kept a little money. The rest I put in a locker. After passing through security as I might at the airport, I gave the guard Morgan's prisoner number.

"He's not back yet from the city. You can just wait here. We don't know when he'll be back."

Morgan had a court appearance early that morning. It seemed inconceivable that he wouldn't have returned already.

Just then I was startled by another corrections officer screaming at the young woman next to me.

"You're not supposed to be here today. How old are you? How old! You're not sixteen. You can't be here by yourself."

The girl looked like she was going to be sick as she quietly said, "I didn't know that."

"Yes, you did!" the enraged guard screamed. "You're banned for 150 days!"

I believed the girl didn't know she had broken the rules, but what could I do for her? Intimidated, I stayed quiet and returned to my seat.

With no cell phone or reading for distraction, the wait was brutal. Unaccustomed to idle time, I found each passing hour longer and longer.

Five o'clock turned into six, and then it was seven. Every time I checked Morgan's prison number I got the same reply: not back. Stuck in this gray place, unable to access my cell phone to tell Isabelle I was going to be late for dinner or the office that I had to miss a board meeting, I got a small taste of what it means to be a prisoner. When they closed the desk at 8 PM, he still wasn't back, and I was forced to return home, like so many around me, defeated. I hadn't seen Morgan since his arrest and had promised I would visit today. I worried that he would think I didn't try.

When I returned two days later (prisoners can only receive visitors on specified days), I had the confidence of experience as I made my way through the crowds of mothers, wives, and children in the intake center. Morgan was there, so I got on another bus that took me out to his assigned cellblock, where a long line of visitors snaked under the mid-day heat. Over sun-soaked asphalt, wailing babies and fatigued mothers worked their way through slowly to another security checkpoint and the second set of lockers. Inside provided little relief, just more waiting with no information about how long the wait might be.

At some point (an hour? Two? Time had lost all relevance) a corrections officer announced, "None of you may get to see your inmate today because we had a lockdown last night. We're not sure whether there will be any visits. You can wait or go home; whatever you want to do." The crowd visibly deflated but no one moved. We had spent more than three hours (or something like that—my watch and cell were in lockers) to get to this point. We wouldn't give up until the guards made us.

An hour or so later, another officer began calling off names and people started to line up. When I heard Morgan's name, I joined the line. When I was asked to take my socks and belt off, I knew I was closer to seeing my son. A guard said something to me, but when I asked him to repeat it because I couldn't hear him, he began shouting. So when I got through to the next room, I waited silently. I would have remained like that if a more seasoned visitor hadn't taken pity on me twenty minutes later and said, "You can go in." I had no idea.

I searched among dozens of inmates and their visitors until I found Morgan sitting at a small table; I took the chair opposite my son. They got up in the morning by the ringing of a bell, he said, and then could either have breakfast or not. After that, he continued, they went into a big room where they remained for the rest of the day, eating lunch or dinner, watching TV, playing cards. Then they returned to their cells and went to sleep. He insisted he was okay.

How could I be sure? I, who knew better than anyone else how unreliable a narrator Morgan was, feared for his well-being. Morgan's mental

Morgan at Fishkill Correctional Facility

disabilities and illness made him low-hanging fruit for police officers eliciting confessions or the district attorney building a case. I wondered how many others like him were in this room with us right now.

Visiting my son in Rikers opened my eyes to a world that most people like me never see. Indeed, I could stop cocktail party chatter dead in its tracks by truthfully answering the classic small talk question, "And which college is your oldest son at?" All it took was one trip to Rikers to understand the inherent racial bias and detrimental effect on families of our criminal justice system. As I continued to navigate the system by visiting Morgan, working on his case, and researching alternatives for mentally ill people who have broken the law, I was so deeply disturbed by my discoveries I was compelled to do something about it.

Although I came of age in the 1960s when civil unrest was springing up everywhere, social action was not a focus of mine. As a young person, I was so busy running my various businesses that I didn't have time for hippies (unless they were girls) or political movements. Amid upheaval of all kinds, I leased office space and sold books. Working during the day and attending college at night, I missed almost every movement. One of the few times I attended an antiwar protest was also work-related. When an editor from Rowohlt and two of his authors came to New York and wanted to see a real live American demonstration, I gladly found some public foment to enjoy. As it turned out, the writers were none other than Rolf Hochhuth, the author of *The Deputy* and client of my father's, as well as the playwright (and future president of the Czech Republic) Václav Havel.

At that time, I was in a peculiar position: I sympathized with agitators and counterculture types, but they weren't that important in my world. Then I met Esther.

In 1967 when Esther, a blonde from upstate New York, applied for a job at my boating books business, which I ran out of the front of my offices on Lexington Avenue, I hired her on the spot. We started dating soon after, and I got my first taste of New England WASP culture. There was her father, the brilliant young man who had been a professor at Harvard but could never quite finish his book and publish so eventually had to leave the university. Uncle Tommy lived at the Cedar Tavern on University Place long after the Abstract Expressionist painters and beat writers who made it famous had dispersed (his actual residence was the Fifth Avenue Hotel, which sounded nice but wasn't). The family congregated for summers at their home in Blue Hill, Maine.

A strong feminist, early ecologist, and anti-elitist, Esther lived her beliefs. She didn't tolerate wasting water by flushing the toilet when it contained only urine or wasting money by dining at expensive restaurants. (For a period she worked on an organic farm in Columbia County owned by Chris and Rande Loken, whom I have remained friends with for forty years, eventually buying Love Apple Farm when Chris decided he wanted to retire.)

But perhaps the greatest tribute to her dedication was the job she took at the Eugene McCarthy for President office in Hudson, New York. Without a Democrat within a hundred miles, it was a lonely post, but that didn't bother Esther. A true iconoclast, she started talking about impeaching Richard Nixon on the very day of his inauguration, far before it became a national rallying cry.

In the three years we were together, Esther made raising my consciousness another one of her causes. She connected me with the events and issues of my time, about which I was neither sophisticated nor educated before meeting her. In doing so, she set me on a course of progressive politics and social reform that was far more enduring than our romance.

While Esther inspired and nurtured those interests early on, it wasn't until I achieved my success in real estate that I was afforded a position in which to do something significant about them. The first politician to knock on my door personally was Chuck Schumer, then a congressman who sought me out during his 1998 run for Senate. That resulting meeting in my office, where we talked at length about a wide array of issues from tax reform to foreign policy and ended up with my contributing to his race, was just the first of many. Chuck continued to stop by my office after the campaign to discuss a variety of issues.

That relationship organically led to more interactions with like-minded politicians, including one that I had admired long before I met her during her run for office. My respect for Hillary Clinton started with her political activist streak during her husband's presidency (I guess I saw a little of the Esther in her). It was during the Monica Lewinsky scandal, however, that I first became aware of her unusual combination of strength and subtlety. While I know some felt Hillary's support of Bill through his infidelity with a White House intern was condoning the behavior, I saw it as the courage to maneuver through a personal process while deftly confronting political realities. The way she managed to maintain her dignity during an unbelievably thorny situation was nothing short of heroic.

Because of that, when I learned that Hillary's campaign was looking for a local venue near the Pink House to hold a reception for her 2000 run to become the US senator for New York, I immediately volunteered to host it. While the event turned into an absolutely magical day for me, it did get off to a rocky start with a group of demonstrators who had gathered on the side of my rural road that steamy August afternoon with a fifty-foot sign pointing to my house with the word "Socialist" painted across. While the description made no sense (unless it was a humorous play on the color of my house), the protest, organized by an aggressive and complicated far-right Republican man from the area, only heightened the tension created by the Secret Service, who had spent days scoping out the place for security reasons.

Columbia County had changed a lot from the days of Esther's solitary office for Eugene McCarthy. We had a gigantic turnout with more than 300 people who came to meet the First Lady. What made the event special to me, however, was the chance to meet Hillary personally. Although I respected her, I didn't expect her to be so warm and

With Hillary Clinton at a 2003 senate fund-raiser

My family and I with Hillary in 2003

gracious; those important aspects of her personality did not come across in her television persona.

Her generosity started with our children. Politicians are supposed to kiss babies, but she was truly kind, particularly to Morgan. When it was time for her to move from the VIP reception at the house to the main event in a big tent set up by our pond, she walked hand in hand with Morgan, who had shown his particular brand of curiosity in this important visitor to our home. I marveled at how in this hectic, pressured environment of raising money, she was able to recognize and acknowledge his interest.

Her welcoming manner didn't end with our family. Hillary talked to each guest as if there weren't 299 other people waiting to do the exact same thing. With a natural and unhurried manner, she insisted on connecting with each and every person who had come to see her. Although the event was supposed to run from 5 to 7 PM, at a quarter to nine she was still out there shaking the hand of anybody who wanted to shake hers. She could not have been more courteous. For us, that was a big event, but for her it was probably number 39 of the day, let alone the campaign. Still, she took the time to call the morning after and thank us.

She continued to show her appreciation with a present she sent to the house—and then a call out of the blue to my office the December after she was elected to the Senate.

"Mr. Greenburger, we haven't heard from you," a White House staff member said. "Are you coming for dinner tonight?"

"Dinner?"

"Yes. For the White House Christmas Dinner."

Would I? Who wouldn't? I got off the phone with the staffer, then on with Isabelle to relay the news, and a few hours and a new dress later, we were on the train down to Washington for a festive evening among a diverse group of supporters only Bill and Hillary Clinton could assemble.

Ever since her first race, I have always backed Hillary—including her bid for the 2008 Democratic presidential nomination against Barack Obama. I wanted her to win so much that I flew out to Iowa to do grassroots campaign work. For two days, I was just another volunteer working the phones—a disconcerting experience as I heard more and more people expressing their support for her opponent.

That race didn't go as I hoped, but for the most part being part of Hillary's broad circle has been an overwhelmingly positive experience, not least of all because she has never lost the hospitable side I witnessed at our first event together. Even with all the pressures that went along with her being Secretary of State, she still remained an exceptional hostess. I had the privilege of visiting the State Department for an affair in honor of her initiative to refurbish a series of its historic rooms. Although the main event—her interviewing former Secretary of State Henry Kissinger—was at 5 PM followed by a reception, Hillary invited us for a more intimate gathering two hours earlier. When we arrived to the suite of rooms, it looked like someone had set down a feast for Thanksgiving Dinner. There were baked hams and roast turkey, mashed potatoes, and biscuits. Nobody goes hungry on Hillary's watch. With her one is always well looked after, in every possible way. Hillary's influence on me has been tremendous in so many ways, and her graciousness is no exception. That through all her trials and political positions she never lost her power to engage and relate to people is an example to anybody in a leadership role.

Through my support of Hillary, an even wider array of people became aware of my interest in politics and started to reach out to me during their campaigns. As early as that first reception for Hillary, I met Eliot Spitzer when he came bouncing across the lawn with his wife and children. Although I knew the attorney general's office well because it regulates the co-op and condo industry, I didn't know the attorney general himself. I had *a lot* of dealings with his office, including a frustrating one in process at the time of the event.

It involved a technical change in condominium developments that the AG's office was in the process of formulating. The frustrating part was that while they mulled over policy, they weren't approving the issuance of new plans. So I had a $50 million building standing there, with a correspondingly large mortgage, and no one could sell a single unit because the government refused to process the paperwork. After we had talked for a while, I decided to broach the issue with Eliot: "I know this is the weekend, and it's not why we're here. But I have a problem with your office . . ."

"No problem," he said. "Call me Monday at 9 AM."

I didn't know whether his answer was just lip service to appease a real estate entrepreneur at his own party. When I called him at nine o'clock, just as he said to do, Eliot answered the phone himself. I described the issue, to which he asked if I could come to his office the next morning.

"Can I come to your office? I'll go to sleep at your office."

In the meeting the next morning, he had the appropriate staff members on hand and we resolved the issue right there and then.

My role as a full-blown active Democrat continued to evolve. Former governor David Paterson always talks about the fact that on the day that Eliot Spitzer asked him to be his lieutenant governor, he attended an event I hosted at my house, where he was dying to tell someone the news but couldn't because Eliot had sworn him to secrecy. I have spent a lot of time with Senator Kirsten Gillibrand, including on the tennis court. And I sweated over a July fund-raiser for Christine Quinn, because who was I going to get to come to a party in July?

I have certainly used my relationships with politicians to highlight fiscal and social issues I think are of importance. For example, I was flabbergasted when I discovered that to be in compliance with the Financial Industry Regulatory Authority, Inc. (FINRA), the largest independent regulator for all securities firms doing business in the United States, after Time Equities became owner of a broker-dealer company, we had to install software to monitor the emails and text messages of our staff to ensure no one committed a securities breach. The government was mandating we spy on our employees. As an ardent believer in civil liberties, I was deeply disturbed. Wasn't this crossing a line if one believed in a constitutional right to privacy? I brought up this issue with Chuck Schumer, who was shocked that a regulatory agency was requiring private people to do this.

Likewise, when a federal judge ruled against the leading book publishers who may have acted too collaboratively in their attempt to raise the price of e-books, I immediately protested. The decision was a disaster for the publishing industry under the grip of Amazon's undercutting business strategy. One of my literary agents drafted an amicus brief that represented our view that the decision was contrary to the interests of intellectual property holders and violated the basic concept of copyright. The government rested its case on the argument that its decision minimizes costs to the consumer, which is true. But the whole point of copyright is that the owner of it, the creator of the intellectual property, can determine the price at which he or she wants the work sold. Nobody has to buy it. On the flip side, if anybody can use the work and pay whatever he chooses, that defeats the entire purpose. To deprive the author the right to determine pricing is to undermine the whole concept of copyright.

Ever since Morgan's incarceration, however, the issue at the forefront of my attention became the perversion of our country's criminal justice system. My journey into this dark world naturally started with my trying to find an alternative to my mentally handicapped son's incarceration. While I accepted that he and many others believed he should be locked up, I didn't think it should be in prison.

Although Morgan appeared to understand conversations or instructions, if anyone dug a little deeper it would become immediately clear he only really got about 50 percent of what was said. He was charged with arson in the second degree because of the answers he offered guilelessly to the police's seemingly innocuous questions right after the fire.

"Was there anybody else in the building?"

"Yes."

"Did you know that at the time?"

"Yes."

And like that, Morgan confessed to reckless intent with endangerment, or five years in prison. He put some garbage on his stove, lit it on fire, called the fire department to report it, and waited inside the apartment for them to arrive. Paranoid that a drug dealer was coming to get him, he wanted the firemen to come and protect him. To me, a layman, that was not reckless intent. Distorted and wrong, yes, but Morgan did not start a fire to burn down a building and collect insurance or hurt anyone. Of course, he didn't know the subtleties of the law. He didn't even have enough understanding to call his lawyer, even though his lawyer and I had tried to drill that into his head.

I wanted to get my son out of jail, but how? The system of state mental hospitals for the criminally insane was not an option. Firstly, the criteria to get into them are the most extreme one can imagine. However, the bigger issue was that they are really terrible places to go—so much so that inmates are afraid of them. Morgan relayed the jailhouse banter about them, which was something along the lines of: "At least in jail, if you get stabbed you know why you were stabbed. But in the mental hospitals, they stab you for no reason."

In my search for a substitute to jail that might be acceptable to the courts, the district attorney offered the possibility of a lockdown mental health program. So I looked far and wide for just such a program, and, to my surprise, I couldn't find a single one. The reason I couldn't find it was because it didn't exist. Doing anything other than throwing people who have committed crimes in jail or prison makes for tricky public policy.

The bureaucratic absurdity of the judicial system sending people out looking for programs that didn't exist infuriated me—and yet also compelled me to take a more active role in this issue. With a large percentage of the prison population suffering from mental illness or personality disorders, I couldn't simply walk away from the problem, even if I recognized that any solution I might be able to come up with would not come about in time to serve my own son. In this way, I started to imagine creating a lockdown mental health alternative to incarceration—at least, on a pilot basis. Although it would only be a drop in the bucket of a problem the size of an ocean, it would be a step in the right direction. But what did I know of the criminal justice system? Practically nothing. So I embarked on a Hillary-style listening tour.

Cheryl Roberts—an attorney and former local judge from Columbia County, New York, who early in her career served as a counsel to committees in both the US House of Representatives and the US Senate and more recently served as counsel for the City of Hudson—joined me in my effort. We pooled our various resources to find a wide variety of voices involved in criminal justice from the leading voices in the reform movement to those incarcerated themselves. In the extensive tour Cheryl and I embarked upon together, we met with many people, including Judith Kaye, who served as chief judge of the State of New York for fifteen years until her retirement in 2008; Jeremy Travis, the president of John Jay College, a leader in criminal justice higher education; JoAnne Page, president and CEO of the Fortune Society, a groundbreaking organization that supports prisoners returning to life through a wide array of services from housing to drug treatment to cooking classes; and Cory Booker, then newly elected senator from New Jersey, who instead of trying to avoid the issue of criminal justice like most politicians, considers it one of his signature issues.

One of the most unique perspectives we heard from was that of a man who had seen the system from both sides. Sol Wachtler was chief judge of New York's highest court before he landed in federal prison after stalking and harassing a former lover. Suffering from bipolar disorder, Sol experienced terrible delusions after he was placed in solitary confinement for his own protection. When he finished his sentence, he left prison with a newfound compassion for its incarcerated people, particularly those navigating the punishing environment with mental illness. He decided to devote his life to legal reform, such as expanding specialized courts so that people with psychological conditions can be treated instead of penalized.

The crux of the problem, as Sol has described it, is that "we just want to lock people up. It makes us feel . . . better." Yet our country's method of feeling better is destroying whole swaths of society.

Prison populations have exploded despite the fact that over the last two decades the national crime rate has dropped by more than 40 percent. Through mandatory sentencing and drug laws, our country incarcerates a greater percentage of the population than any other country on earth. There are nearly 2.2 million Americans incarcerated, which means that almost one out of every 150 American adults is behind bars. That number has quadrupled since 1980.

The depressing numbers continue to pile up. At the federal level, half the people are in jail on drug charges, most of whom have no prior criminal record for violent offenses. And although whites use drugs at a slightly higher rate than blacks, three out of four inmates imprisoned on drug charges are black. Instead of segregating black people, we're putting them in jail. One-third of all black males will find themselves in jail during their lifetime.

I can't imagine who this would make feel better. Certainly not the professionals Cheryl and I listened to, all of whom reinforced what I had come to on my own: Our system is extremely broken in a multifaceted way. It isn't a matter of one aspect or another. It is a confluence of problems—mandatory drug sentencing, the closing down of state mental hospitals, a system that's punitive as opposed to rehabilitative, racial prejudice—that has created the condition of mass incarceration, which in my view is the most important social justice issue of our time.

While I continued on my listening tour, Morgan's own situation within the system became increasingly complex. After he landed in Rikers on the arson charge, he remained there for six months, the last three months of which he spent in solitary confinement, or "the box" as it's often called. Although he had wanted to go to prison to escape his paranoid fears, in the end he didn't want to stay there, and I posted his bail. From there I sent him to the program on a working farm where he was thrown out—at midnight—for buying a BB gun on a mall trip. In Colorado, when I received the call that he was in rural Vermont with nowhere to go in the middle of the night, I didn't know what to do with him other than have the police take him to a motel—even though the police were the last people I wanted to call when it came to my son.

That morning, I still had the same problem of where to keep Morgan when he told me that he could stay with his friend Sarah in New York City for a couple of days. Sarah was one of two people he had befriended during a brief period at Columbia Presbyterian where he had undergone yet another mental health evaluation. The other person was Jerry, who like Sarah was in a drug rehab program. Jerry, whom Morgan quickly adopted as a second dad, started life as a combat trainer for the marines, but after murdering a man who sexually abused his young daughter, served a twenty-year prison sentence and wound up addicted to heroin. While running a highly regarded afterschool program she founded, Sarah was hit by a truck that crushed her back, and she became addicted to prescription painkillers.

I consented to Morgan staying with Sarah in her Upper East Side high-rise for a few days while I figured out another solution. But I didn't get that much time; Morgan took an overdose of drugs at Sarah's and was rushed to the hospital. I hopped on the next plane back east to pick up Morgan, whom the hospital refused to keep. "We don't think he tried to commit suicide," the doctor informed me. "He says he couldn't sleep, so that's why he took the pills." He had taken sixty pills. It was absurd, but the hospital was sticking to its story because they didn't want to deal with people like him. The upshot was again I had no place to house my son.

Jerry, who along with Sarah had been concerned for my son's well-being through the entire situation, offered to look after Morgan.

I put them up in an apartment in one of my complexes in New Jersey. The plan was for them to live there until Morgan came up for trial, both for arson and the taxi robbery, but one day my son left the apartment armed with a knife and corkscrew. Afraid that Morgan was going to hurt someone, Jerry went after him, but not before calling Sarah to apprise her of the situation. In Manhattan, Sarah flipped out and called 911, so that after Jerry got Morgan to give him the knife and corkscrew, and they returned to the apartment, the police showed up and arrested Morgan for making terrorist threats despite Jerry's pleas. With his bail remanded, Morgan was forced to remain in Rikers to await trial.

I have been to Rikers numerous times (as has a core group who visited my son, including Jay Acton, the editor-turned-agent who came on to Sanford Greenburger Associates right after my father's death and helped make it a success). But all it took was one visit to the island—where people spend five to six hours for a forty-five-minute visit and are treated like inmates themselves for the duration—to understand that when we imprison someone, we also imprison their family. We are training children who grow up with a parent in jail in the culture of incarceration. So it's not really 2.4 million incarcerated people; it's really multiples of that number. I estimate that at least 65 million Americans are in some way caught up in the criminal justice system, either directly or as the parent, spouse, or child of someone who is incarcerated or on parole—although the number is most likely much higher.

Then came a much-needed beacon of hope. It was during an international program on criminal justice and incarceration in Colorado Springs that Cheryl and I attended as part of our listening tour. There were a dozen or so panels every day, and I happened to wander into one being given by David Booth that would guide my efforts from that point forward.

In 1994, David was a counselor in a one-of-a-kind program that placed sex offenders and alcohol abusers in a separate therapeutic community within the Arrowhead Correctional Center east of Cañon City, Colorado. Therapeutic communities, or TCs, first gained prominence in the sixties as a group-based approach to dealing with substance abuse and certain forms of mental illness. People who know best because they share the same issues call each other out on their problems. At Arrowhead, therapy was the main aspect of the program, but the incarcerated men gained important new insights into themselves by policing, socializing, and working with each other. Roles were reversed with aggressive men given jobs that required them to take direction from passive ones. While in the program, they learned how to problem solve. The result was that many took responsibility for their actions for the first time in their lives.

Colorado deemed the program enough of a success that David has expanded the program to include seven therapeutic communities in the state prison system. I was intrigued enough by his presentation that I spent part of my Christmas holiday visiting him and his program to see his treatment modality in action. Watching these incarcerated men help each other confront painful realities that really only they could understand, correct mistakes that were bringing them down, and truly support one another through difficulties was a revelation.

When trying to conceive of an alternative to incarcerating mentally ill people like Morgan, I kept thinking that traditional psychiatric hospitals and psychiatrists, who are unaffordable and unavailable to most of those facing prison time, could not be the solution. Using David's program that employed many elements of true self-help as a model, we had a viable direction in which to work.

The Greenburger Center for Social and Criminal Justice, the organization I founded to advocate for reforms in the criminal justice system, is currently at work on just such an alternative to traditional incarceration for the mentally ill. Having assembled an astonishing group of board members with years of experience in criminal justice reform, security, and treatment, we have garnered support for the model from district attorneys, judges, New York State and City legislators, victims' rights groups, and others.

If we are able to achieve this, it will mean we have changed public policy to something that is totally out of the box in terms of the current system. Convincing the bureaucracy to take a chance will not be easy, and there will be those who argue against the idea, but I am not daunted by any of that.

Over the years, I have gathered some wisdom about what it takes to launch a new idea. When I was younger, I was still an innovator but I stumbled through the process. I didn't fully appreciate the need to get buy-in from a spectrum of opinion makers and leaders in the field. Co-oping the complex in Clinton Hill, an extremely innovative and out-of-the-box concept at the time, taught me the value of gathering consensus. While I met with all the political leaders and the borough president because I worried they would misunderstand my intention to let the existing residents stay in their apartments, it turned out to be a critical piece in my getting a mortgage since the Citibank lending officer called the borough president to vet the project. And I wouldn't have had the idea of a listening tour if it had not been for Hillary coining the phrase.

This collective experience has given me—and everyone from our tour—a sense of optimism and confidence. I have been extremely surprised how willing the experts in criminal justice and others involved in the lives of the incarcerated have welcomed help—even from a newcomer like me. When I spoke to the thought leaders, I fully expected them to protect their work and institutions, but almost without exception they said, "What we have doesn't work and what we are doing is wrong." People in the system feel like this is the moment for change. It is wrong to incarcerate the mentally ill, but no one has an alternative. I hope the Greenburger Center can provide that alternative.

I'm humbled by how many efforts have failed in the past. But Herb Sturz, a key social innovator and the grandfather of criminal justice reform, put it best when he said, "At the end of the day, you just have to do it. You just have to engage and go."

A proud moment—receiving an award from the Fortune Society on October 29, 2015, for my work with the Greenburger Center

Never in a thousand years would I have anticipated being involved in criminal or judicial reform. But because of Morgan, these are issues that I have come up against and can't ignore. In the spring of 2014, he was sentenced to five years for both charges. After repeated efforts by the best lawyers I could find, this was the best sentence the lawyers and I could negotiate for him, so we decided to take it.

My son's experience in Rikers has corroborated all the problems detailed by the experts of putting people with mental illnesses in prison. He has had constant infractions, some of which have landed him in solitary. The first time, he was put in "the box" for more than two months. The second time, a month. Morgan claims he doesn't mind solitary, and I believe him. Because of his mental limitations, it is hard for him to interact with others. If he struggles with relationships in normal life, I can't imagine what it's like in jail where the social signals are even harder to read. He has been beaten up by correction officers a couple of times. Once he got a black eye; another time he was maced. It is a very rough environment and the prisoners don't win.

Having experienced great success, I feel it is my responsibility to give back, not only in the broader ways of charitable giving and supporting institutions like Omi or the Sports & Arts in Schools Foundation, but also by taking on the challenges for others who can't. So I imbued the Greenburger Center for Social and Criminal Justice with a dual mission—to create a lockdown alternative for offenders with mental illness *and* to serve as an advocacy group for criminal justice reform. I'm amazed at the amount of credibility the Greenburger Center has established in the short time since its inception. The New York City Council awarded us $150,000 to develop our plan, which they rarely do. (They give money for concrete projects all the time, but not to ideas.)

I'm not claiming I'm going to change the world, only that I will make a little difference. I don't have any special knowledge or ability that makes me better suited than anyone else to this kind of effort, except perhaps for my doggedness.

When it comes to indefatigable determination, I take another page from Hillary Clinton. In describing her frustration that Al Gore hadn't fought harder against losing the 2000 presidential election to George W. Bush, she said if there was one thing she had learned from her husband, Bill, "It is to never, ever give up."

*Chapter 13*

# INTELLIGENT RISK: AN INVESTMENT STRATEGY

· · · · ·

Standing outside the two-story villa apartments that led directly onto a perfect horseshoe beach of white sand, crystal-clear Caribbean waters, and a cloudless sky, I was reminded why I call this area of Anguilla the island's best-kept secret.

In the spring of 2008, I was on my yearly tennis trip, an annual tradition that began in the late nineties when I first gathered a group of tennis players, all men and all good friends, for some informal male-bonding time. We played tennis every morning from nine thirty to noon, stopped for a big lunch at one of Anguilla's many wonderful restaurants, hung out on the beach or went swimming, played tennis again from 4 to 6 PM, then cleaned up for dinner. It was heaven never to get out of your bathing suit or tennis shorts and not to have to worry about anyone else's needs. This year, however, I didn't have that last luxury.

We had just finished up lunch at the little restaurant down the beach from our villa that served fried conch sandwiches at rustic picnic tables. The guys were either napping or swimming in the water that was the same mild temperature as the air. I looked out on the blissful scene feeling anything but serene.

How could I relax while everything I had worked for so hard for the last forty years was threatened by a global financial crisis, the likes of which no one had ever experienced, let alone understood? What had started with a French bank freezing three investment funds after it couldn't value their holdings due to massive losses in the US subprime mortgage sector then unraveled into such a steep downturn in stock markets around the world that the future of many of Wall Street's most venerable institutions was in question. People were calling this the worst collapse since the Great Depression.

And housing was at the center of the crisis. We had come to this point because of a confluence of factors. Banks gave loans to Americans who couldn't afford them and whose terms they didn't understand. Investment firms bundled these loans into new and complex financial instruments that not even their own investment bankers always understood and were based on the absurd assumption that housing prices would continue to rise. Meanwhile, regulators and ratings agencies completely missed the warning signs of the disaster that usually arises when short-term profit takes precedence to lasting value creation. When the values of securities tied to US real estate prices fell, the entire system came down like a house of cards. The banks and insurance companies didn't have enough capital to back the financial deals they had made. As countless homeowners found themselves underwater with their mortgages, evictions and foreclosures swept the country.

Normally when I go to Anguilla, I don't take much more than a tennis racquet. But these were not normal times. I had toted all my files and worries along with me to paradise. I felt not only anxious but depressed. One of my really good buddies, a guy who had actually been a real estate partner of mine, sat down on the beach near me. Loren was going through the exact same stuff. Looking out at the still water, we shared our experiences and strategies to protect enough assets so that we wouldn't end up on the street, which was the ultimate fear.

To find support when it would have been so easy to sink into despair was incredibly meaningful. The source of my depression during that period wasn't simply the financial chaos happening all around me but the fact that I wasn't able to protect my company from it. After the S&L crisis of the eighties, I had vowed never to find myself so exposed to the economic forces over which I had no control. The only way to do that is, of course, diversification.

I have always sought diversified investments beyond real estate not just as a method of financial hedging but because my entrepreneurialism makes me naturally curious about the work others do. That's how I got started investing with Michel Zaleski during the early eighties—and using the money from that fund to save Time Equities during the fallout from the S&L crisis when lending completely dried up.

When Michel retired (at the ripe old age of forty-eight to pursue interests like windsurfing and international development policy—eventually becoming a member of the Council of Foreign Relations and the Soros Economic Development Fund), I wanted to continue the kind of investment I had done with him, so I tried to look for new "Michels." I speculated in a number of new companies on the advice of financial experts or friends, but they all turned out to be disasters. One of them, a new aerosol can company with environmentally friendly technology, was going to revolutionize the industry. It seemed legitimate—a French company had just invested $5 million and they were on the cusp of filling a series of factory orders from Gillette. So I invested half a million. Well, it turned out the shaving cream didn't come out of the can fast enough. When the dust settled, my investment was worthless.

I don't pick investments; I pick jockeys—not horses. It's less about the particular vehicles they have found and more whether their general approach makes sense to me. (I go with the jockey approach with real estate as well: Bill and Matt Felton are a great example of this. I met

Matt, the son in the father-son real estate team, while playing tennis. He overheard me talking about a property in Portland, Oregon, that I was thinking of making an offer on. As it turned out, Matt and his dad and I were bidding on the same property. He suggested we make an offer together. Although Matt was only in his twenties at the time, I quickly realized how smart and capable he was and so agreed to buy the building with them. We hit the jackpot and ended up making approximately ten times our original investment. We also went on to buy another fifteen or twenty properties together in the Portland and Seattle areas.)

Another crucial factor for anyone I invest with is that they have a substantial amount of their own money in the game, so that they aren't just losing *my* money. When Steve Clearman explained his philosophy—basically buy cheap, sell dear—I understood him perfectly. I first met Steve around 2000 because he was having bat problems at the Pink House, which he had bought.

In his experience as a venture capitalist, Steve explained that many people had good ideas for new companies, but they were all pricing them too high. Even if an entrepreneur had never sold a thing, he wanted 10 million dollars for his concept. But, Steve noticed, there were many small, existing public companies with similarly good ideas but also low valuations. What he was interested in doing was, rather than invest in new ventures, buy existing but undervalued public companies—or at least make long-term investments in them. It sounded very similar to how I approach real estate. So when he said he was looking for investors for what eventually became his investment advisor firm—Kinderhook Partners—I went for it. His eye for value turned out to be keen. He picked many winners, such as one of his early investments, a diet company that delivered food and whose stock went from $1 to $50 while it was part of his fund.

Steve is smart and disciplined, two qualities I consider essential in an investor. But there is no one more disciplined than Jim Melcher. In the twenty-five years I had known him, Jim, an immovable bear, was always waiting for the sky to fall. During most of that time, it didn't.

So while everyone else on Wall Street was riding high, he had small returns on his $30 million Balestra Capital. A passionate fly fisher and fencer, Jim wouldn't alter his thinking for anyone or anything. (His conviction that the world was going to collapse was so strong that he sold his apartment in the Century on Central Park West and put all the money in his own fund.)

Not long after I began investing with Steve, I decided to invest with Jim as an insurance policy. It occurred to me that if things did an about-face from the good times we were in during the early 2000s, Jim might not lose money. And that was exactly what happened. In 2008, when everyone else lost 50 percent, he *made* 30 percent. In 2009, he made 100 percent and became one of the top two funds in the country. It took thirty years of waiting, but the day came when Jim was absolutely right.

When I believe in a fund manager, it's not because of how widespread their popularity is. I have to be personally convinced of their intelligence and integrity. When I met a parent at my children's school, all I knew of him was that he had made quite a bit of money investing in tech but had sold his company. Fred struck me as a super-smart guy, but for the first three years I knew him he was retired and spending all his time renovating an expensive town house on 10th Street. Around 2003, however, Fred mentioned that it was a good time to get back into tech. When I heard his ideas on the subject, I said if he needed an investor that I would be interested and wound up committing several million dollars.

In the year that it took for him to start up his new fund, *New York* magazine ran a cover story that Fred Wilson, everyone's favorite tech venture capitalist, was back. Only then did I realize that he was well known to everyone but me. He lived up to his reputation as a phenom with Union Square Ventures, which he founded in 2004. As part of that group, we have invested in numerous tech companies such as Zynga, Foursquare, and Tumblr. As second-round investors in Twitter, we bought into the social networking site at ten cents a share, which at its peak went up to $70.

Since then, I have added about ten other hedge funds to my investment portfolio. No matter the fund, however, the formula is always the same. It begins with how I feel about the fund manager; he or she must be able to convince me of the strategy and, again, have a significant amount of personal money invested. I don't invest in funds run by large investment companies. I also don't invest in any big funds, anything more than $200–$300 million, because after that I find the investments are no longer targeted. I always start small with my investments to test the water, and if a fund proves successful I invest more. A pretty obvious strategy.

All investing, however, involves some level of risk. Still, the risk can be intelligent if any deal includes strategies to mitigate it. The level of risk must be proportionate to the reward. If you know your overall business, then you will do well even if you incur losses.

From a first glance, a shopping center Time Equities considered acquiring in Washington State seemed like a risk because all four of its main anchor tenants had leases expiring within two years. The fear of acquiring a retail property with a short-term roll is that the current tenants won't renew and the assumptions about the income will be off. That risk becomes greater the fewer tenants a shopping center has.

I learned that lesson the hard way from a previous investment in a property that relied on the income from only one tenant. In 2005, we bought a building in Virginia that had been occupied by the same yarn company for fifty years, but at the time of the purchase, the company was experiencing severe financial problems. The proceeds from the sale of its 500,000-square-foot building that housed its manufacturing facility and several hundred employees was a way of recapitalizing. The yarn company's leadership convinced us of the business's future, and we decided to buy the building for $15 a foot. They signed a twenty-year lease that earned us 10 percent on the purchase price in rent alone. Add to the equation, bank financing at 5 percent, and the building was very profitable. That is until the yarn company went bankrupt several years later. Their going out of business resulted in a loss of the entire investment.

With the shopping center in Washington State I wanted to understand the risks in order to mitigate them. The annual income was $4 million with a purchase price of $36 million. If one of the anchor tenants didn't renew, the rent would go down by $600,000, bringing the total income down to $3.4 million. Whenever you take over a new property, you always have to consider additional reserves for leasing costs. Estimating for those costs, I took the income down to a true net of $2.8 million. Based on that, we offered $25 million for the shopping center. At that price, $2.8 million a year would mean an 11 percent return, high for that kind of property. Even if in addition to losing one of the anchor tenants, we lost a third of the small tenants, the return would only drop to 9 percent, which would still be strong. In the worst case we had a good deal—and possibly a phenomenal deal.

Risk is not scary when it's quantifiable. In part, that is what was so devastating about the financial crisis of 2008. I thought I had taken the kind of measures—in terms of diversification and other forms of insurance—so that I wouldn't find myself fighting for my life. But a crisis so large that it brought down the 158-year-old investment bank Lehman Brothers was obviously beyond any kind of cycle anyone could anticipate. (One rule I always apply in dealing with TEI's investors, partners, and banks is to under-promise and over-deliver. The world of all investments is filled with risk. It behooves all investment sponsors to present risk fairly and to provide conservative realistic outcomes of property income projections—in fact, investment law and regulations require it.)

It took several years to navigate the new world created in the wake of the crisis. From 2001 to 2007, Time Equities had been buying between $100 and $300 million in new properties every year. In 2009, we bought zero. Just like values that cycle relative to market conditions, so credit cycles dramatically as well. When credit is tight, many buyers are excluded—and that is when someone can get very good deals, provided they have the cash. When the banks go out, we go in. In 2010, we began to pursue assets across the country that were viewed as being unfinanceable, and closed entirely with our own equity (all cash). Assets with higher cap rates provided the same returns to our cash as we would have received from leveraged assets with lower cap rates. As operations improved, the returns became outsized and we could also pursue mortgages if we wanted to.

Perceiving risk differently than other people is another important way of creating value. In 2012, we looked at a condominium project that had only been able to sell ten of its fifty units. The remaining forty units were being rented by the bank, which wanted to sell them to satisfy the loan. A lot of buyers in the market weren't interested because they couldn't control the whole project. They weren't comfortable sharing ownership of the building with the other ten condo owners.

When we looked at the market, whole complex properties were trading on a 5 percent cap rate on rental income, but broken condo deals had a 7 percent return because of the perceived operational risk. Well, I didn't mind dealing with condo boards. I had spent decades doing just that. And the idea that at a later time we could sell the forty units at retail was really appealing to me. Where someone else saw operational risk, I saw market advantage. That deal worked out so well, we bought broken condo complexes in Tallahassee, Florida; Panama City, Florida; and Grand Rapids, Michigan.

Early on in my career, I decided it was better to buy other people's development mistakes at 25 or 50 cents on the dollar, as I did with the broken condo complexes, and make them worth 75 cents a dollar—rather than making those mistakes myself. Developing real estate is highly risky in that it's hard to predict all the variables involved. In order to be successful in any project, the developer must be correct with all of his assumptions, or at least more right than wrong. The market must cooperate over the duration of the project, which is as likely as getting hit by lightning.

I didn't turn to development until 2002, when there weren't any opportunities to buy income properties in New York that I thought were a good value. My first building, the Esko Royale, is located in the heart of Forest Hills, the Queens neighborhood where I grew up, coincidentally next door to a building I used to deliver newspapers to when I was twelve years old. Although it is a relatively small building with sixteen units over four stories, it was a struggle to get it done.

Developing is frighteningly sensitive to timing, which no one has any control over. When I bought four lots on which to build new town houses and a large old mansion to convert into several apartments in Cobble Hill in 2005, I didn't worry. The location in the hot Brooklyn neighborhood was so fabulous, what could go wrong? The recession—that's what. I carried them until 2010 when the market had recovered and I decided to sell. Although I more or less got back what I paid for the property, I had been carrying it for a couple of years, so in effect I lost a couple of million dollars.

I lost a lot more than that, however, in a Canadian deal that I went into a year earlier. Peter Freed, a development partner that I have worked with on a lot of Canadian projects, approached me about buying land in Muskoka, a vacation spot right outside of Toronto, where the price was cheap—$4 million for a thousand acres on which we would build houses. I had never done a massive land development of this type, but I always like a new challenge. The plan was to sell houses to buyers with the idea that when we sold enough of them, we would build a golf course.

When our model homes didn't fly off the shelf, Peter suggested we build the golf course in a build-it-they-will-come strategy. He proposed getting a high-interest non-recourse mortgage, where someone else would give us the money to make the golf course with no personal liability on our part—we just risked the land. I didn't think he could find anybody to do that, but he found a private company that agreed to lend us the money at 11 percent. Six months later, he had cut down 100,000 trees to build a very high-quality, and expensive, golf course in the middle of nowhere.

Of course they didn't come. We sold fifteen houses in one year, but we would have had to sell fifty houses that year to carry the golf course. In order to get out of the expensive mortgage we took to build the course, we had to put a regular mortgage on the property on which we continue to lose $2 or $3 million a year. My takeaway from that failure was never *ever* build a golf course (there are too many of them and they are very expensive to create and maintain), but especially not in the middle of cow country.

The Muskoka deal was an anomaly for the extraordinary investment opportunity that has been my experience in Canada, which began with a 320,000-foot office loft building in Quebec once owned by the Bronfman family that we bought for $6 a foot. That price wouldn't have paid for the marble in the lobby. Today, that building is worth at least twenty times the purchase price I paid for it. Once I got my feet wet, I realized that Montreal was one of the greatest bargains in North America and ended up buying about fifteen more buildings in the city as well as others throughout Quebec, Toronto, and eventually as far east as Newfoundland.

Time Equities also had tremendous successes with development projects in Canada. As fast as we lost money in Muskoka, Peter and I made it in Toronto, where we built a number of lucrative condo complexes in the city's Fashion District. We made $50 million on one project alone, 550 Wellington, which boasted 300 apartments and a 100-room hotel called the Thompson, which for a long time was the chicest place in town.

In development, there is potential for enormous losses and for equally big profits. It's high risk and high reward—not unlike the real estate industry in general. In this business, there are never any guarantees. Even with decades of experience and efforts to protect against the downside of a deal, some of them simply go bad.

That's what happened on September 25, 2007, when we bought fourteen flex buildings in Amherst near the Buffalo airport as part of a 1031 tax exchange. The property was leased up to 85 percent with many small tenants (per our experience with properties like the one in Virginia, it was better to have many smaller tenants than a few big ones). No one would have called the deal risky. A year later, after the financial collapse, our occupancy went down to 70 percent. In the post-recession economy, Buffalo hasn't fared well. We have been able to meet our mortgage payments, but we still aren't earning any money—plus we had to put some additional capital in for improvements.

Buying a building that is more or less fully occupied, a "sure bet" in good times, will in bad times lose tenants and income. The best time to buy a building, in my opinion, is with a low occupancy around 50 or 60 percent and at a price that reflects that percentage. In this scenario, there is an opportunity to create value by building up the occupancy. All real estate is about location, timing, and, frankly, luck. Whether you make your own luck or it's a gift of the gods, I can't say. But it's crucial to this business, and I've enjoyed more than my fair share of it.

In 2006, I partnered on a project to build a condo tower in Seattle that quickly went sour after the financial collapse. Having bought the property for $4.5 million without a mortgage and having spent $2 million developing plans for it, we just sat there watching the world collapse. When the situation got better in 2010, I wanted to sell, but nobody was willing to pay our low asking price of $2.5 million. After we got one offer for $1 million, I begrudgingly began considering a rental strategy. Suddenly, though, Amazon decided to build its new headquarters near the building. Overnight the property went from a good location to a phenomenal one, and an unsolicited offer came in for $16 million. In the end, the final deal was struck for $21 million.

If that wasn't pure luck, the flip of my contract for 230 West 41st Street in the early eighties undoubtedly was. One of my first big office building deals, I had done my due diligence and figured out that the insurance company that owned it wasn't charging the correct rents. So although I agreed to buy it for $6 million, a huge sum for me at the time, it was still a very good deal. I lined up a partner to put up the money because I didn't have the $2 million down payment in those days. But five days before we were supposed to close, the partner backed out. I was devastated. One of the biggest deals of my career thus far and many months of work was gone with nothing more than a phone call. Then one of my employees, Steve Renfroe, suggested we try to flip the contract.

"Come on, Steve," I said. "This deal has to close within a week. What are you going to do? Take an ad in the *Times* to sell a multimillion-dollar office building that has to close within a week?"

"Yes, a three-line ad," he said, adding, "it won't cost much."

It was the stupidest idea I've ever heard, but if he wanted to do it I wasn't going to stop him.

Monday morning at nine, a man who had seen the ad in the *New York Times* called the office to say he was interested. I still didn't hold out much hope, but the caller showed up an hour later to meet Steve. A Hasidic man from Brooklyn, he only had one condition for the deal: "I want to sign the contract right away." As it turned out, his rabbi had advised him to go into the real estate business, and Steve's ad presented him with his first opportunity. He wasn't personally wealthy but all the congregants of his synagogue had given him money to invest. We made a half-million dollars in profit, and the man closed five days later. If I were religious, I would have believed he was a miracle from God.

Most of my real estate deals, however, have been made through simple hard work. Extremely hard work. The deal to buy an office building, hotel, and parking complex in Pittsburgh, Pennsylvania, that was set to close two weeks after Black Monday of 1987 went through every real estate challenge known to man, but because my partner on the deal, Larry Georgiadis, overcame each and every one of those challenges, it wound up to become so phenomenally profitable that it could conceivably provide me and Larry with enough money to live on for the rest of our lives. Or there is the example of the property on the corner of Hoyt and Schermerhorn Streets that Abby Hamlin, one of my development partners, and I turned from a no-man's-land in downtown Brooklyn to twenty-one single-family town houses that won prizes for innovative design and included affordable housing units while making ten times the original purchase price of $5 million.

Still, more often than not, I feel like the fact that I have survived, let alone succeeded, in my business *is* a miracle—particularly when I've seen how hard other realtors I have admired have fallen. When a real estate investor who had been worth hundreds of millions of dollars reached out to me in his time of legal and financial troubles, I was more than empathetic. Here was a prominent philanthropist who had called me countless times before to raise money for various causes now trying to raise money on his own behalf.

"I'm desperate . . ." said the eighty-year-old man, who needed to settle with a bank to avoid being charged with fraud not because he was a crook but because of a sloppy business mistake. I sent him a check for $25,000 on the spot with the full understanding that there but for the grace of God go I.

Real estate is a tough business where you can lose money even when prices are going up. Like so much else in life, there are always unforeseen variables, and it is never as easy as it looks.

## Chapter 14

# MAKE HAY WHILE
# THE SUN SHINES . . .
# BUT CARRY A LARGE
# UMBRELLA

· · · · ·

Men in hard hats walk the grounds, testing the old caissons. An excavator dips into the earth for the very beginnings of the foundation. After five years of waiting, construction has restarted on 50 West.

As the construction site awakens, picking up right where we left off in 2008, I feel a combination of fear and pride. The amount of money involved is staggering. With Time Equities' typical developments, we can pay for our mistakes even if they make us very unhappy. But a major mistake on a $500 million project could deplete even the deepest pockets. But that is the responsibility of building a sixty-four-story tower, a privilege not afforded many.

When it is eventually completed, 783 feet of glass and steel will rise up just a few blocks from the Freedom Tower. The German-born architect Helmut Jahn—who has made his own mark on the tradition of European modernism through buildings such as Sony Center in Berlin,

One Liberty Place in Philadelphia, and O'Hare International Airport—put the latest technological advances in building to use in an iconic design that will grace the most important city skyline in the world.

When we made plans to break ground again on 50 West in the summer of 2013, it made the news since most thought it would never happen.

Back in 2008, Time Equities was once again fighting for its life. When things are good, it is easy to be the boss. But when things get really bad, as they did during the global financial crisis that froze capital around the world, that's when one's true character as a leader is tested. Instead of firing employees wholesale, I asked everyone in the company to take a pay cut so that we could retain talent and minimize individual losses (most adjusted; a few didn't). I tried as best I could to spread out the pain, communicate the plan, and lead. Everyone was scared. I was scared. But we had to stick together and stay tough.

It came as quite a blow when the director of acquisitions and development I hired in 2003, a highflier when the markets were good and who convinced me to pursue building the gigantic tower on 50 West before the market crash, quit in 2009, abandoning the project and leaving me with no building, only a pile of debt.

In the middle of what some were calling a depression, I decided to give one of the ex-director's analysts, Rob Singer, a shot at managing his old boss's substantial portfolio that included what could potentially be the biggest project in the history of Time Equities. A former driver for Governor Jim McGreevey, Rob was all of twenty-eight, but I believe in young people and take chances where they are warranted. Rob was super smart and extremely hardworking, so I said, "Let's try it."

Every year, I renewed the short-term line of credit on the land for 50 West that I had struck with the bank after the crash, but it required an enormous amount of patience, economic wherewithal, and faith in my own convictions. As financial predictions continued to forecast gloom, it became harder and harder to stomach that very expensive hole in the ground.

In real estate, sometimes new development happens quickly, but more often it takes forever. When in December of 2001, Douglas Durst, the third generation in his family to run the prominent New York real estate development firm Durst Organization, demolished the last standing building between 42nd and 43rd Streets, bound by Broadway and Sixth Avenues, it was supposed to be the beginning of the end of the project his father, Seymour, started when he bought the family's first parcel on the block in 1967. But the economy went south after September 11, and he wasn't able to build his office tower. So he actually erected a one-story retail building because he knew he would have to wait another ten years until the cycle came around, and the retail rents in that neighborhood are very lucrative. In 2010, he finally realized his father's dream with One Bryant Park, a stunning, spiraling fifty-one-story office tower at Sixth Avenue and 42nd Street.

Once in a while real estate dreams happen, but they often don't. Who knew how long it would take to build 50 West, or if we ever would?

In the fall of 2011, construction loans began to be available for small for-sale housing projects up to $10 million. Soon that number crept up to $50 million. Still, loans over $100 million weren't in anybody's vocabulary. Meanwhile, I kept renewing our loan on the land and paying the taxes, mortgage, and other costs to the tune of $350,000 a month, until finally in 2013, the bank's appraisers said the value was up. We had to figure out our development scenario or sell the land. I didn't want to sell, but finding someone to partner with us in developing 50 West wasn't going to be easy.

We were in talks with two different private developers from India, which was going through a big real estate boom at the time. Over several months—which included endless amounts of documentation, flights back and forth from India to New York almost every two weeks, and a number of vegan dinners prepared by Isabelle—they kept retrading the deal. What began as a $40 million investment turned into $10 million initially, plus $2 million a month over five months until the whole thing fell through. We spent months working with an American investment group, which was very enthusiastic about the project. But it turned out for tax reasons they could only be involved in a rental and not a for-sale housing project. We found another equity group, but the kind of loan they wanted to give us wasn't allowed under new lending guidelines, so that fell through. After more months negotiating with another group, they pulled out at the penultimate moment because they had spent too much money on other new deals.

The twists and turns that I went through with 50 West felt endless. Given the deal size and all its issues, just as soon as I thought I was at the top of the mountain, I realized there was another mountain ahead—and each one seemed insurmountable. But I kept persevering and not taking no for an answer, and in August 2013 we completed a construction loan for the entire project of nearly $300 million with $110 million in equity financing from a hedge-fund management firm and six banks, including a $288 million loan with PNC Bank as the lead.

("Carry a large umbrella" means be ready for bad times—with cash. I remember in 2008 all the major banks and investment banks were at risk and a friend from Goldman Sachs called to tell me that Goldman carried over $100 billion in cash and liquid assets on their balance sheets. I follow their example and maintain cash of over $100 million throughout our various entities, properties, and accounts.)

In the fullness of time, I was proven correct about the value of 50 West. The value of the property alone went up at least $100 million between 2008 and 2013. And that is just the land. When we released the first thirty-five apartments of the residential tower's 191 units in May of 2014, it was a blowout. With no advertising, we had offers on 50 percent of the first release in three days! Two months later, we had sold sixty-four apartments with gross sales of those contracts at $260 million. This is during the traditionally dead real estate months of summer, for a building that was still underground and three years away from delivery, which is a long time to tie up the kind of money needed for the down payments on these apartments.

Making progress at 50 West

Bob Kantor and I at the groundbreaking for 50 West

If we had sold thirty apartments in three months, I would have been beyond thrilled. Even though the least expensive unit is a one-bedroom $1.615 million (and the priciest, a 62nd-floor five-bedroom penthouse for over $80 million), I knew we offered a lot of value. Still, this was more of a response than I had bargained for. (Isabelle, Claire, and I rushed down to the sales office to reserve a couple of units for ourselves.)

With projected sales of over a billion dollars, I am deeply gratified by the outcome of 50 West. By spending $25 million to carry the land value during the economic downturn, I have already realized a gain of $90 million on the land and potentially two to three times that in development profits. I am gratified not just because I made a lot of money, but also because 50 West will be an iconic addition to downtown Manhattan's skyline.

I thought 50 West was going to be my swan song, but I was wrong. In 2015, I announced two new major development projects: 1000 S. Michigan Avenue, a new tower designed by 50 West's architect Helmut Jahn, which will stand at eighty-six stories in Chicago's South Loop; and a project for five eighteen-story towers in West Palm Beach that, although not as tall as 50 West, will have about double the square footage. I'm as surprised as anyone that I'm doing it, but here I am. As many developers will attest, building gets in your blood.

Part of the reason that Time Equities is in a position to do such projects stems from Bob Kantor's son David Becker, who, after returning to work for me a second time, set up a division to raise money in the public markets upon my request. It is a long, involved, and difficult process to set up a public market fund-raising department (which runs the gamut from meeting all the securities regulations to getting approval from independent rating agencies to finally convincing brokerage companies to sell us to their clients). But David is a great salesperson and businessman, and three years into the new department, it has given us

A rendering of 50 West as part of Manhattan's skyline

the ability to raise ten times the capital we had when it all came from private markets.

Embarking on development projects of any size is risky, but even more so when they are as large as 50 West or 1000 S. Michigan. But as my therapist said to me, "Your willingness to risk is completely different than most people and certainly from mine. You seem to enjoy risk and even thrive on it." I know a lot of people think I'm crazy living my life the way I do, but my therapist was right. I've had more fun embracing intelligent risk than I would ever have if I had proceeded cautiously.

During 1980s, I was one of the four or five companies riding the crest of the wave of conversions of hundreds of thousands of apartments from rentals to co-ops and condos. We were coming out of a desperate situation in New York in which politicians, as they often do, promised an unsustainable situation: rents so low they didn't cover the cost of maintaining the properties. The result was thousands of abandoned apartments that owners couldn't afford to maintain. Although the politicians didn't have the will to change the system, they did change the conversion laws so that the owner and tenant became one and the same.

Enormous wealth has been created in New York City by the concurrent rise in real estate values. When we started selling apartments in Clinton Hill, they were between $25,000 and $30,000 ($15,000 if you were a resident). Today they are selling for $500,000. With Maiden Lane as a rental, we returned the original $7 million we borrowed from our investors as well as $17 million in annual distributions—plus, after reinvesting the profits from the condo conversion, the partnership (one of hundreds of Time Equities partnerships) now has investments in twenty-six other properties valued at almost $75 million.

I have owned many buildings that are worth 300 to 500 times what I purchased them for. Not in a million years could I have ever imagined that would happen. It hasn't been a straight line. Each one represented a ton of work and titanic struggle. Still, there is no greater feeling than when I meet someone who has bought an apartment from me and says, "It was the best investment of my life." To run a business that rewarded not only me but also my customers, the people who believed in what I was creating, is of enormous personal satisfaction.

In converting over 100 New York City apartment buildings comprising over 10,000 units, with a retail value today of somewhere between 5 and 10 billion dollars, I transitioned them to another form of ownership in a way that I believe made them better. Co-oping didn't only create wealth, it also created responsibility and a sense of ownership in the community. That was the vision of home ownership, to change the city from the decay of the seventies to a place of pride where individuals of every type and description now own apartments.

Even though I co-oped a lot that I owned, I have still kept quite a few properties as rentals—particularly my early buildings, such as the seven-story walk-up on Sullivan Street that I bought for $35,000 or a wonderful building on the corner of Thompson and West 3rd. The seller was so tired of being a property owner that he created a deal where I didn't need to make a cash down payment, only personally guarantee the mortgage interest payments. So at the closing, he had to give *me* money because he had the rent securities from the tenants. Today, that building is probably worth $40 to $50 million (more than forty times what I paid).

I often wake up in the morning and say prices in New York are so insane, how can I not sell these buildings? But so many friends have lived in them—people who needed or offered a helping hand, sons and daughters spending their single years, those who made me who I am today—that I am just happy to have them.

*Epilogue*

# NEVER EVER GIVE UP

I hold on to people, just as I do with some buildings, because the relationships I have made over a lifetime are as crucial to me as wealth.

Despite our fraught relationship growing up, my reclusive brother, André, and I see each other three or four times a year—and his son, Michael, works for me. In my parents' country home, which hasn't changed much from when I was a boy, André lives in his own reality that's interesting but can also at times be hard to follow. He doesn't fly but travels all over the United States in his RV with his partner, Susan, and his beloved dogs. Although as a kid I resented him deeply for causing strife in our house and commanding my mother's affection, whenever we meet for lunch at a diner in between his house and mine in the country, I enjoy his company as we tread over the common ground of memories of our childhood and parents.

Heide Lange, my night school classmate whom my father hired to help out at the agency in 1964, not only still works at Sanford J. Greenburger Associates, she's the president. We've worked together going on forty-five years, our entire adult lives. In the elevator of my father's office building, Heide met her husband, with whom she has two phenomenal kids (I recently attended the wedding of her daughter, who was valedictorian of her high school). Heide, whom I would trust with anything, was very close to both my parents until their deaths, for which I'm eternally grateful.

I'm also grateful to her for signing up one of the highest-selling authors of all time to Sanford J. Greenburger Associates.

Before 2000 Heide represented mainly nonfiction writers, but she decided to represent Brad Thor, who not only became a hugely successful, best-selling thriller writer but also recommended her to his friend Dan Brown. At that point, Dan had published three books to modest success. However, when Heide read his latest manuscript, she thought it was the best thing she had ever read and believed with every fiber of her being that it was going to be a big, big best seller.

Simon & Schuster, with whom Brown had published his most recent two books, made an offer for his fourth novel. Heide, who decided to take him on as a client on the strength of his newest manuscript, played hardball and asked for many times more than what was being offered. After the editor not surprisingly balked, Heide called the publisher at Simon & Schuster to warn him that the editor was "making an incredible mistake."

"You should do something about it," she said. The publisher came down on the side of the editor and didn't increase the offer, so Heide went over to Doubleday, which didn't blink and paid seven figures for the book called *The Da Vinci Code*.

Brown is just one of the heavy hitters on the roster at the agency thanks to all the talented people who have come through its doors. One of those folks was Theresa Park, a Harvard Law grad and an associate at an entertainment firm in LA, who contacted us when she decided she wanted to change careers and become an author's agent. She left her job at the firm, where she probably earned three or four times the $20,000 she made at the agency, to learn the business with us. As an assistant, she did a lot of clerical work, but Theresa also read unsolicited manuscripts in an effort to develop some of her own clients.

She happened upon a first novel that needed work (so much so that sixteen other agents didn't think it was worth the postage to submit to a publisher and declined to represent it), but that she liked. After taking the initiative to help the author rewrite it, she sent the manuscript out and a day later was made an offer of half a million dollars by Warner Books. Without consulting or even cluing anyone into what was happening, Theresa refused the offer. "Absolutely not," she said. "It's worth double that." Apparently she was right, because the next day, Warner Books called back and offered a million, preempt, take it or leave it.

By now, word had gotten out around the agency about her manuscript and a bunch of agents were crowded around her desk. I went over to see what was going on and couldn't believe my ears. After hearing Theresa say, "Oh, I don't know whether it's enough" for a first novel, I said to her, "Theresa, look around you. There's a hundred years of agenting experience on the floor. Nobody has sold a first novel for a million bucks. I suggest you take it." She did, and the book became *The Notebook* by Nicholas Sparks.

Whenever I'm at the airport, I take a second to stop at the bookshop to see what they are selling—typically the major best-selling writers and books of the moment—and it's with a certain pride that I realize how big an impact our little agency has had on the industry as a whole, because between Brown, Sparks, DeMille, and others, a good part of those bookshelves belong to us or began as one of our discoveries.

I'm also thankful to have contributed in this way to my father's legacy. He was a terrible businessman, but he loved books, and he loved me. He thought I was capable of anything and that anything I did was wonderful. I attribute to him my self-confidence, the source of a lot of my success. Bill Goldstein, a friend of mine and promoter of the Virginia Slims tournament, once said while we were watching a match between Monica Seles and a lesser opponent, "You know what the difference of play between those two players is? It's not the level of their game; they are both equal. It's self-confidence. And the player who has the self-confidence, the winner mentality, is going to prevail."

To have my father's name on the top of letterhead in deal memos circulating throughout the office or in news articles on the latest release from one of the agency's authors is to have him around me. Not even death prevents me from letting go. I keep loved ones who are no longer living present not through ghostly memory but by attaching them to a literary agency, charities, and, of course, buildings.

For me, that is one of the great pleasures of walking around Omi. It is a visit with old friends whose complex histories are solidified into structures of concrete, brick, clapboard, and metal. It's all very friendly and in a way reassuring.

As I pass the Charles B. Benenson Visitors Center, a modern building of Albany bluestone, wood, and glass nestled in the green grass at the entrance of the sculpture fields, an image flashes before me of Charlie's smile. He had a way of smiling that was not overly expressive but definitely comforting.

The contemporary architecture, crafted from natural materials in a design by Kathleen and Peter, fits with Charlie's taste. An avid art collector, he had one of the best African art collections in the world, as well as major contemporary and modern collections. After he passed away in 2004, I approached his son Lawrence (himself an extraordinary collector, who put together a show for Omi titled "Vote for Me" that offered an eclectic and unique view on voting rights) about partnering on a capital campaign to build the visitor's center. "I would love to name it for Charlie if you thought that would be appropriate," I said. Lawrence, who often says generously that what he and I shared was a great love of his father, approved.

I wondered if Charlie would approve. In his lifetime, Charlie never promoted himself, despite his extraordinary success in real estate, art, and philanthropy. Being a public name in the way of Trump was his worst nightmare. When Forbes put him on the Forbes 200 list, he threatened to sue them if they didn't take him off.

Over our last lunch together, about ten days before he died, he told me a story about when Larry Tisch approached him about finding a piece of land in Manhattan for a big convention hotel. This was back in the 1950s when New York lacked anything of the kind. Charlie put together the site on Sixth Avenue for the Americana, the largest convention hotel in New York that subsequently became the Sheraton.

After assembling the land, Charlie went to Larry and said, "I think I did a good enough job of putting the land parcel together that I'm entitled to a bonus."

Larry agreed with him and offered a couple of hundred thousand dollars in Loews stock. "I'll lend you the money for you to buy the stock. Loews is a good investment," Larry said about his own company. "When the stock goes up over time, you'll have a great bonus."

Charlie thought about it but, uncomfortable with borrowing money from Larry, suggested instead that he give him a paid-up life insurance policy for him and his wife in the amount of $10,000. "I'll be happy with that."

Larry took out the life insurance, which, since Charlie lived to be ninety-three and $10,000 was pretty insignificant compared to his estate, turned out not to be much of a bonus.

"The other day, I looked up the price of Loews and calculated if I had bought that stock what it would be worth today," Charlie said to me over lunch. "Do you know how much it would be?"

I had no idea.

"Five hundred million dollars."

Then Charlie looked at me and said, "But what would I have done with another $500 million?"

That was classic Charlie Benenson. Funny, self-effacing, and fully aware of how much one really needs in life.

Back at Omi, the Milton Newmark Gallery is a reminder of another great man and mentor. I went to visit him whenever possible in Cleveland, where for the last five years before his death in 2005, he crammed his entire New York life into the third floor of his daughter's home. Surrounded by his walls of erudite books, his tasteful art, the furniture lovingly picked out by his wife, Sandra, I never ceased to value his insights. Sometimes I sent him to look at a shopping mall in Austin or office building in Topeka to see if I should buy it. I trusted his advice implicitly. Not only was he one of the most principled people I have ever known, we also had similar takes on real estate. A few years before he died, I told him to pick any car he wanted; Milton picked a Jaguar. Debra said he really loved that car because it tied us together.

It was the least I could do for a man who championed me my entire career. When Sandra was still alive, she hosted a kiddush at the apartment after synagogue services for her husband's birthday and invited all of his friends without telling him. I got up and gave a toast to Milton, who, I said, "keeps me honest and believes in me in a way that pushes me to be more than I ever imagined I could."

At Omi, I pull people back from the dead by invoking their memory in a place that is very much alive with young artists, writers, dancers, and musicians. The impetus behind the writers' colony at Omi began when Ledig's successor at Rowohlt, Michael Naumann, suggested the idea and vowed to support it after Ledig's New York memorial service in 1992. One of the residency buildings was named for John Reynolds when, after we refused to accept money from his widow that he owed from business investments, we settled on donating the amount toward the cost of the building. A plaque with a photomontage of John commemorates his life.

One of my favorite spots at Omi, however, is the Ingrid Café. If the writers are in residence, I like to come for special dinners, where it's always an amazing experience to talk with incredibly bright, sophisticated people from the remote corners of the world and find out that intellect is not an exclusive product of the West or developed countries. The pleasant space of the café, light and airy, is also a nice place to have lunch and watch visitors discuss the art they've seen and delight in the terrific food prepared with ingredients fresh from local farms.

In some ways naming the café after my mother was ironic, since she was neither light nor airy. Whatever I felt about my mother as, well, a mother, I respect what she herself considered the defining moment in her life—her actions during World War II. Leaving her native country because she couldn't reconcile her conscience with the terrible law of the land was important and brave, and I will always admire her for it.

That quality of hers, sticking firmly to one's perspective regardless of whether it runs contrary to Nazis, publishers, or family members, is something that, while at times was painful to experience as her son, I am also grateful for inheriting. Just as my father provided me with confidence, a necessary ingredient in believing in oneself, so my mother did the example of truly independent thinking.

The history of my business philosophy—to find different niches and pursue them as long as the market supports it, and then move on when I believe the market is going against them—is a direct descendent of my peculiar upbringing.

Although I made my fortune in New York, taking apartments no one ever thought anyone would want to own (walk-ups, studios, those in transitional neighborhoods) and turning them into coveted properties, I had no compunction about walking away from the city to which I owed everything as soon as I understood it was no longer a good investment.

And I remember exactly when that was. Around the time I did the deal with Helmsley for Tudor City in 1985, I partnered with a converter from Chicago to purchase four buildings in the West Village from the Bing & Bing estate. The properties at 59 West 12th, 299 West 12th, 302 West 12th, and 45 Christopher Street were among the best prewar apartment buildings in the Village, if not all of New York. They were selling for $20,000 per room, but we got a two-year stretch deal. We bought the four buildings for $50 million with $5 million down and two years to get our legal documents in order, present the plan to the tenants, and negotiate with them. By then we would have enough money coming in from the tenants to pay the balance of the $50 million, which is what we did. It was my standard formula.

After that, the estate decided to put up for sale the remaining twelve Bing & Bing buildings, located all over the Upper East Side, and one last building in the Village at 2 Horatio Street. We offered the same deal we had made three months earlier, but instead the estate put the buildings out to bid. Well, the remaining buildings wound up trading for $45,000 a room on a cash basis, which was the equivalent of $60,000 a room, or three times what we had bought the other buildings for three months earlier.

Fueled by money rolling at the banks, co-oping was just as hot as it could possibly be when the MacArthur Estate went on the market, causing every New York real estate person under the sun to start drooling. Naturally, we bid on it, but lost out to a partnership between Marty Raynes, a well-known converter and one of our competitors, and Bernie Mendik, a real estate entrepreneur who had previously worked exclusively in office buildings. When one of my employees heard of his involvement in the deal, he said, "What's Bernie Mendik doing in the condo business?" It was a harbinger of what was to come. They paid $90,000 a room, almost double what we bid, in a gigantic transaction that totaled $500 million.

All these people had overestimated the potential of the market . . . and paid for it. As history would have it, Raynes and Mendik ended up turning the project over to the banks. (In fact, I ended up buying all of the retail in their conversion buildings from the bank that took them back and still own them today.) I couldn't buy any buildings in New York to convert them to condos because leather started to cost more than shoes. Other real estate people in New York called them investments, but they were clearly using different math. Even though they controlled huge amounts of capital, these business folks weren't using the right pencil. New York is a graveyard of those decisions.

It was the same story about twenty years later when Stuyvesant Town and Peter Cooper Village were put up for sale.

We did the normal underwritings we would for any large conversion project in 2006 when Metropolitan Life Insurance Co. put on the market the 11,000-unit complex that it built in the 1940s on twelve acres in the Lower East Side. The solid, no-frills middle-class housing complex, which Mayor Fiorello La Guardia spurred into being by offering MetLife not only the land but also a twenty-five-year tax break, was much beloved by generations of residents, who handed down apartments as coveted inheritances.

After a comprehensive analysis that included comparable apartments, turnover rates, capital improvement costs, taxes, and much more, we estimated we could pay $3.2 billion in a plan of ultimately selling the entirety of Stuy Town for about $4.3 billion to individual apartment purchasers. The $900 million profit was a fair and normal margin on the purchase price.

During the process, BlackRock, the world's largest asset manager, approached us about joining forces in the purchase of Stuy Town, and we agreed on a meeting that they walked into with all the swagger one would expect of a financial services behemoth. "We've allocated a billion dollars cash for this transaction," a BlackRock director said. "We're ready to go."

We presented the information and numbers from our analysis: According to Met Life, the property made $100 million the year before, so, at my number the purchase price was a 3 percent return.

"You'll never be able to buy it for that," the director said matter-of-factly. "We are prepared to pay more."

This had been our business for years; we created an organization with our own in-house experts on co-op and condo sales, mortgages, taxes, construction, leasing, and other departments necessary to peel back the layers of the complex onion that is the real estate industry. I was confident in our assessment of what Stuy Town was worth and why.

But the BlackRock guys had already made up their mind. "We're interested in a rental strategy," the director explained.

I was totally confused by what they meant by a rental strategy. Rental income from the complex would never cover the interest payments on such a massive mortgage, not for years. But our discussions didn't go much further than that. BlackRock went from me to the New York real estate firm Tishman Speyer and paid a whopping $5.4 billion for the complex. Their purchase price was one billion dollars more than I thought would be realized from converting the properties (and in my mind we were being aggressive), so in effect they paid more than retail. They also put aside another $400 million to pay the difference between the rental income and interest payments on the mortgage until they were able to raise rents.

Their "strategy" was to bank on a halcyon estimate of increased income (after the politically unpopular move of getting rid of low-rent tenants) that would eventually make up the difference in their mortgage payments. There were banks taking first mortgages, and second mortgages, and a very aggressive capital stack that left me absolutely speechless.

When the whole thing imploded, that was the only time during the whole Stuy Town story that I *wasn't* surprised. How could it be any other way? They ran out of money in January 2009, missed $20 million in payments, and had to return Stuy Town to the bank. Shortly after, Fitch Ratings, a global ratings agency, valued the property at $1.8 billion. (Stuy Town was traded again for $5.45 billion in late 2015. The new owners, the Blackstone Group, received some special concessions from the city as part of the deal; still, I hope they have a better business plan than the last group.)

If I bought a New York City apartment house now, I would be lucky to get between a 2 and 3 percent return, which in my book is too low.

Even though I love New York and think that it will do well over time, that's a substandard return. If I were to go to the bank and borrow money at its cheapest, it would still cost 3 or 4 percent. So even if I agreed to take that kind of a low return, I wouldn't be able to pay the bank. I learned early in my career that one can't fall in love with the bricks, meaning one can't fall in love with the idea of a certain kind of real estate. What works at one price doesn't work at another, and returns must be at a sustainable rate, even when interest rates increase. If you accept a 4 percent return today because interest rates are at 3 percent, you will have a disaster on your hands if interest rates go to 6 percent.

All of that only means that I have to work harder in my search for value, push the boundaries of the status quo even further. You can still always make a good deal, even in New York City, if you are creative enough. Take 125 Maiden Lane, a 350,000-square-foot office building that we turned into office condominiums—an idea that was against the mainstream. When I considered the idea, there might have been fewer than ten commercial condominiums in New York City, and most of those were not traditional condos (for example, two office users sharing a building could technically make it an "office condo"). Conventional wisdom stated: Why would any business buy its office? But one of my employees had converted a commercial condo in the nineties that was successful, so he was one of the few people who understood the process and the market. I coined the phrase "Own your future," by which I meant if you own your office, your long costs are fixed. Independent thinking turned a building that was 70 percent vacant into one of the larger multi-unit office condos in Manhattan.

People hold on to the status quo because they feel more secure in the known than the unknown. But that's a false sense of security. According to my observations, the world is constantly changing, and static approaches or answers are not sustainable and therefore not secure. In the 1950s, if you were an investment advisor to a widow or orphans, you would have suggested buying thirty-year government bonds with their money. They were considered the safest investment option because they offered continuous income with a dividend of 2 percent. But during the sixties and seventies, when the rate of inflation was high, a 2 percent return meant those widows and orphans were actually losing money. What appeared like an ultraconservative approach—thirty years of fixed return payments—turned out to be a gigantic loser. It's a simplistic example but one that makes the point that what seems straightforward in one environment is not necessarily true in another.

Real security comes from adaptability. Change, with its unknowns and periods of turmoil, is hard for many. I find it exciting, even comfortable. Perhaps this is another gift from my parents, who raised me with a lot of financial and emotional insecurity. I was very much loved and supported, but there was a lot of *Sturm und Drang*. Upheaval is something with which I'm at ease. I'm not fearful of it but challenged by it.

Independent thinking in its simplest form means not assuming that the status quo is the best answer, the right answer, or the most effective answer. After a decades-long study of creativity, neuroscientist Nancy Andreasen defined it as "recognizing relationships, making associations and connections, and seeing things in an original way—seeing things that others cannot see." That holds true for creativity in business as well. Business and financial planning is based on models, which in turn are based on assumptions. A million complex calculations are made on those assumptions, which produce a result. It's easy to lose sight that the result is an artificially created reality that, depending on its assumptions, can and will vary. It is not gospel.

I question all gospel. I don't feel like I have all the answers, or even a small number of them. I'm not even sure I believe there are answers. There are just points of view at given moments in time, and I'm interested in as many of those as I can take in. Maybe I'm too open sometimes, but for me, it's not a choice.

I despise orthodoxy and the presumption of righteousness. The fixed principles of organized religion—celibacy, anti-intermarriage, sectarian

Looking out the window from my fifteenth-floor office in NYC

violence—create scenarios that are completely inconsistent with human instinct. Infallible truth is not the experience of life. Whether it's gay marriage or co-oping walk-ups in the West Village, society has been known to change its viewpoints radically with time and experience.

Not that dogma only exists in religion. Even in so-called progressive environments you find conservative decision making. Sometimes it is a fear of trying something new, like when I advocated for student evaluation of teachers at my children's ultraprogressive school (the idea went over like a lead balloon). Often, though, it's a fear of being criticized for having a dissenting view. The director of a museum whose board I sit on made a proposal on how to deal with a dispute involving an artist that I thought was completely the wrong approach. While I tried to express my opposition, the director called for a motion to ratify his plan, which everyone voted for except for me and one other director. The result was the massive litigation I had predicted but no one would listen to. People are reluctant to assert authority in the face of what they perceive as an important voice.

Alternative perspectives are crucial to being competitive in the marketplace (and they can come from anywhere, including seemingly insignificant voices). If you follow the mainstream, usually the margins are very small. You have to see things differently than the next person. If you discover something worthwhile, the market will reward you for your originality.

Since 1985, I have turned away from New York real estate when the margins in co-oping became practically nonexistent. And since the financial crisis of 2008, I have focused on office and retail properties in distress across the country. Recently we bought a 100,000-foot, attractive, modern office building in Cherry Hill, a formerly very strong suburban community outside Philadelphia. The last time it was traded, it sold for maybe $15 million; we bought it for $3.5 million.

We also just bought another wonderful building in a suburban New Jersey office market for which we paid around $60 a foot. The last time that building traded, the price was about $180 a foot.

In Gaithersburg outside of Washington, DC, it was the same story for another industrial building that last traded for $11 million but for which we paid $5.5 million. Then there's another large office complex we recently bought in the Detroit suburb of Southfield.

Going against the market doesn't ensure success. If you see things differently but wrongly, that doesn't work either. There are always two sides to the story. Today retail properties are in question. Many people believe that it's a doomed market, that there are just too many stores in the United States, that many retail chains go bankrupt, and that the growing percentage of retailing going through Internet sites will only make the scenario worse. Statistically, that is all true.

That's where the work and thought comes in. Vision without diligence is just an idea. We analyze every property from the numbers to the people behind it, until we feel we fully know its story. I challenge my staff to challenge the assumptions given to them by the sellers, and eventually we get a pretty clear picture.

In the retail scenario, we eschew the big-box chain stores that, part of large conglomerates, go boom and bust regardless of the community in which they are located. The kind of shopping centers Time Equities buys is more in the vein of a community center containing services vital to that place, which people won't necessarily buy over the Internet. That could be anything from a doctor's office to a hair salon to a dollar store. One of our recent purchases is a shopping center in Philadelphia that has a famous Russian grocery store where the city's sizeable Russian community comes from all over to shop.

Once we locate the property, our strategy is pretty uniform (just as it was during my heavy co-oping years). Buildings in financial trouble generally have low occupancy rates that can dip down to 25 percent or lower, so we offer the space cheaper than the going rate to get people back in. We can do this because we have negotiated an advantageous purchase price and our costs are so much cheaper than everybody else's.

Buying what we call cheap bricks will on average and over time do well. That's based on the idea that, eventually, the world usually heals itself. It's an assumption that I espouse. That fundamental optimism in people, places, institutions, and markets is what has kept me going not only through financial crises but also personal ones—and what hopefully will keep me going indefinitely.

Retirement is not in the makeup for a man who in sixth grade took over the school milk crew from drunk Mr. White. My plan is to continue to do what I'm doing until I'm at least seventy, and then maybe I will give up one of my titles and some of the activities associated with it. Instead of working fourteen hours a day, I'll work eight. I recognize that is not much of a plan, and my true choice would be to die in my chair.

But I also recognize that as the classic symptoms of "founder anxiety." The anxiety over one's succession and unwillingness to let go clearly stems from an uncomfortable confrontation with mortality. I've seen this played out too many times to recount—in a charitable group where a charismatic leader undermines any possible heir even if it means driving his organization into the ground—with my own mentors.

Ledig suffered terribly from this condition. He hired two different would-be successors for Rowohlt Verlag and then ended up eating them alive for different reasons. The first one was too intellectual and radical, the second too corporate. The end for both, however, was the same—they were fired. Ledig was one of the brightest men I knew with a business acumen that I admired, and yet, in this one, crucial area, he could not make a decision.

He wound up selling his publishing house to Holtzbrinck, another big German publishing company, for nearly a quarter of what it was worth because nobody was running it. In the end, the owner of Holtzbrinck, who did not have anywhere near the literary sensibility or sophistication that Ledig did, chose Michael Naumann with astonishing, heartbreaking, and effective ease. A former journalist and newspaper publisher who resurrected Rowohlt before entering politics, he was a very worthy successor. It wasn't rocket science, but Ledig couldn't do it himself. It was almost an unconscious death wish—as if he didn't want to find somebody who was as smart or capable as he, but in the end because of that he buried his legacy.

Even in his rare misstep, Ledig was my mentor, and I have realized that living forever isn't a viable plan to ensure the longevity of Time Equities. I am indebted to the group of senior managers who came in around 1985 and have been there ever since, seeing the business through the inevitable ups and downs of real estate. The members of this loyal and talented group, however, aren't viable successors for the simple fact that they are aging at the same time as me. It's been my great fortune to have a group of extraordinarily talented thirty- and forty-somethings, who could be the leadership of the future. When you have people who are that good, they will not wait around forever to get responsibility. I have a fairly deliberate plan for the future: By my seventies, I plan to give up my CEO title and its day-to-day duties and ease into the role of chairman. Transitioning the company for a vibrant future is my wish and my legacy. But that doesn't mean it will be easy for me.

Isabelle has said that with all my careers, enterprises, friends, lovers, and kids, I have lived the lives of several people. Certainly it has been an adventure. I've had a lot of accomplishments as well as defeats; known extraordinary people both professionally and personally; fostered the creation of many beautiful things from art to babies to a tower reaching the sky; experienced terrible tragedy and unparalleled happiness. Would I go back and do it again? Of course I would. Not to do it better or differently, but because I loved it all.

# ACKNOWLEDGMENTS

Each of my children—Claire, Julia, Noah, and Morgan—has a unique personality and set of talents. I expect that they will develop themselves in different ways, achieve great things, and each will find a meaningful life. I hope to live long enough to see their respective accomplishments flower, their lives unfold, and their personal stories be created and told. Perhaps one day they will write a book like this one to share their lives with their children and all who are interested.

Isabelle's parents welcomed me into their lives from the first moment we met, without judgment, even though I was still married. I think they could sense the love and respect I had for their daughter, and that I made her happy, which was the most important thing to them. They have been grandparents to all my children, who hold them in high regard. Everyone is happy when Mamie and Papi are around.

Finally, my life has been one of close and intense friendships with people I have loved, people with whom I have shared interests, business associates, political friends, and family. You are my world and mean everything to me.

Readers may contact me at fgreenburger@timeequities.com.

# ABOUT THE AUTHORS

**FRANCIS J. GREENBURGER** is the founder and CEO of Time Equities, Inc., a multibillion-dollar real estate investment and development company, as well as chairman of Sanford J. Greenburger Associates, a literary agency representing some of the most successful writers of our time. He is the founder of two important not-for-profit organizations, the Omi International Arts Center and the Greenburger Center for Social & Criminal Justice. He has served on the boards of over fifteen nonprofit organizations for the arts, education, and criminal justice reform. Greenburger is also an active tennis player and skier, political cheerleader, and loving father of four children, each taking their unique journeys through life.

**REBECCA PALEY** is the #1 *New York Times* bestselling author of more than a dozen memoirs and other books. She lives in Brooklyn with her husband and children.